SEMI-FAMOUS

SEMI-FAMOUS

A TRUE STORY OF NEAR CELEBRITY

JOSH SUNDQUIST

LITTLE, BROWN AND COMPANY
New York Boston

Little, Brown and Company
Hachette Book Group
1290 Avenue of the Americas, New York, NY 10104
Visit us at LBYR.com

First Edition: July 2022

Little, Brown and Company is a division of Hachette Book Group, Inc. The Little, Brown name and logo are trademarks of Hachette Book Group, Inc.

The publisher is not responsible for websites (or their content) that are not owned by the publisher.

Library of Congress Cataloging-in-Publication Data
Names: Sundquist, Josh, author.
Title: Semi-famous : a true story of near celebrity / Josh Sundquist.
Description: First edition. | New York : Little, Brown and Company, 2022. | Audience: Ages 14 & up | Summary: "Social media star and comedian Josh Sundquist takes readers on his hilarious journey to the fringes of viral stardom to discover if it's possible to be both very famous and very happy"— Provided by publisher.
Identifiers: LCCN 2022011550 | ISBN 9780316629799 (hardcover) | ISBN 9780316629744 (ebook)
Subjects: LCSH: Sundquist, Josh—Juvenile literature. | Tumors in children—Patients—United States—Biography—Juvenile literature. | Ewing's sarcoma—Patients—United States—Biography—Juvenile literature. | Skiers with disabilities—United States—Biography—Juvenile literature. | Motivational speakers—United States—Biography—Juvenile literature. | Internet personalities—United States—Biography—Juvenile literature. | Comedians—United States—Biography—Juvenile literature.
Classification: LCC RC281.C4 S8367 2022 | DDC 618.92/994—dc23
LC record available at https://lccn.loc.gov/2022011550

ISBNs: 978-0-316-62979-9 (hardcover), 978-0-316-62974-4 (ebook)

Printed in the United States of America

LSC-C

Printing 1, 2022

To Luke,
Sorry we didn't get to name a character after you,
but I hope you become turtle famous

INTRODUCTION

It recently came to my attention that I am semi-famous. I learned this from an Instagram story. I'd never met the girl who posted it, but it showed up in my alerts because she tagged me. Here's what she wrote:

I saw @JoshSundquist on the sidewalk today.

ME: omg! hey mom, look that's Josh Sundquist!

MOM: who's Josh Sundquist?

ME: he's like this semi famous internet comedian.

Okay, so I want to point out several things about this post.

First of all, no kid has ever said they want to be a "semi famous internet comedian" when they grow up. I'm not saying it's a bad gig exactly, just that it wasn't anyone's childhood dream. I myself wanted to be a computer programmer. Which is a strange aspiration for a six-year-old. Especially because this was before pop culture's appropriation of nerd culture—before fantasy novels and superhero fandom flipped from geeky to trendy. What I'm saying is, I was a nerd back when nerds were still just, you know, nerds. I like to think of myself as a hipster nerd.

Anyway, obviously it hadn't yet become clear that nerds could grow up to become tech billionaires. So when I taught myself a programming language called BASIC on this old-school computer that my grandfather had given me, most parents would've probably thought, *Oh no, our eldest offspring is a loser*. But not my parents. They went out and bought me a book about another, far more complex programming language called C++. Oh, you want to be a computer nerd? Fine. But you are not nearly there! You must nerd out, like, way harder!

The computer was wedged between my dresser and my gerbil cage. When you turned it on, you got that interface you see in hacker movies: blank screen, blinking neon-green cursor. I programmed a little game where you could move the X character around the screen to dodge asterisk*bombs. Over time, though, I got interested in writing prose (specifically, sci-fi novels—the narrative cousin of computer programming) instead of writing code, and I dropped the programming hobby. Sometimes I wish I'd stuck with it. Maybe I could have been a software engineer at Instagram by now, wearing Insta-logo branded hoodies and pounding free green juices from the stocked fridge down the hall. Surely it would be better to be working *at* Instagram today than to be reading ambiguously demeaning stories about my work *on* Instagram, right?

Seeing that story really made me pause. Sure, it's cool to be tagged in a post. But, like, what am I doing with my life? Is this who I want to be when I grow up? A micro-influencer who you tag in your story but probably don't follow? A person who is maybe just barely famous enough to be occasionally recognized from a distance and posted *about*, but not quite famous enough that you'd, like, want to get a selfie? Or say hi? Or even make awkward passing eye contact?

What I realized is, I'm not so much famous as I am *familiar*. I'm like one of your teachers from middle school.

Oh look, Mom, there's Mr. Turner.

Who's that?

My semi-dorky seventh-grade Gym teacher.

I'm someone you mention in passing to your mom— who definitely doesn't know who I am. Sort of a comedian but not quite, so when you describe me to her, you qualify it with the word *internet* before the word *comedian*—kind of like putting the word *junior* before *firefighter*. Or *Instagram* before *model*. Or *home* before *school record*.[1]

In fact, she used not one but two of these prefixes-that-make-the-otherwise-cool-thing-kind-of-sad.

Not famous. *Semi*-famous.

Not comedian. *Internet* comedian.

Look, I'm not trying to complain about her post. I think that's a spot-on characterization of my middle-class rung on the internet-influencer ladder. If anything, I think it's a wonderfully strange thing to be recognized at all. I'm delighted she tagged me. Really. If she hadn't, I would never have known someone recognized me in the first place. Once you become a semi-famous internet figure, your fragile ego can't help but wonder if anyone ever recognizes you. You hope so, if you're being honest.

Being recognized means you matter. You are *somebody*.

It makes you feel good about yourself. For a minute. Then human nature kicks in. You want more. You need more to feel better. But more is never enough, no matter how many people recognize you or how many zeros or *K*s or *M*s are on the end of the numbers on your profile.

A few months ago, YouTube sent me an email saying I

---

1   Sidenote: I was homeschooled. But you probably guessed that by, like, the third paragraph of this book.

was going to lose my blue verification badge because they'd raised some threshold for subscribers or views or something. I freaked the eff out. It was like I'd just been told I had cancer. (And I'm saying that as a person who *actually knows what that feels like.*[2]) A few hours of Xanax-mitigated panic later, I got a second email from YouTube full of vague corporate-speak about how they were mistaken, they apologized for any inconvenience, and I would keep my verification badge after all. Which felt like the doctor popping back into the exam room and saying, *Oh dear, so sorry, we confused your X-ray with some other unlucky chap's. You're perfectly healthy.*

But see, clearly I am not healthy. Mentally, I mean. That verification badge on my screen measures approximately the size of a housefly. Its presence or absence is nothing more than a 1 in a binary toggle between 1 and 0 in a computer program (which I know because childhood hobbies), meaning the blue check mark does not *exist* by any practical definition. If I get a cancerous-tumor-sized panic attack based on whether or not it happens to be displayed on a screen, that...Cannot. Be. Healthy.

What I'm saying is, clearly I care a lot about fame. Like some part of me really, really wants it. And I'm not the only one who feels this way. A recent survey of one

---

2   This is kind of a spoiler for one of my other books, but don't worry, I survived.

thousand people under age eighteen showed that 75 percent would like to have a career creating internet videos. Being a YouTuber, specifically, was the number one career choice of those surveyed. Twice as many would prefer being a YouTuber to being an actor or singer. Three times as many want to be a YouTuber than want to be a doctor. Or a professional athlete. This is all very interesting because, for one thing, three-quarters of the human population cannot be famous internet stars. There can't be more stars than fans, after all. I mean, somebody has to teach seventh-grade Gym and program Instagram app updates. So if the vast majority of the millions dreaming about fame will never achieve it, is the journey still worthwhile?

This seems like an important question given how many of us want it. I recently asked my Instagram followers if they hoped to be famous someday.

WOULD YOU LIKE TO BE FAMOUS SOMEDAY?

YES 47% 53% NO

I'm pretty sure that 47 percent figure would be higher if this survey wasn't *on Instagram*, where it feels like anything you say or do becomes public and will come back to haunt you when you're applying for college or whatever. Like if this survey question was asked in some private, encrypted corner of the dark web where everyone felt comfortable anonymously confessing their deepest secrets, I think more of my followers would have admitted to wanting to be famous. I believe that because other, more scientifically or privately administered surveys (like the one I mentioned above[3]) show that an overwhelming majority of teenagers and even children admit to wanting to be famous.

And I use that word *admit* deliberately. Because that's how it feels. Like a shameful confession. Like a substance addiction you need a support group for. Call it "fame-seekers anonymous." *Hi, I'm Josh. And I...ugh, it's so hard to admit aloud to you all....I uhh...well, I want to be famous. There, I said it. It's out there. Now you know my shame.*

Part of the reason we might not want to admit it is because it just sounds, well, shallow. Wanting fame goes on the

---

[3] By the way, surveys of my followers are not at all scientific and don't represent anything other than the opinions of those particular followers. But that data is still insightful here because I assume people who follow me online have some similarities to, and overlap with, people like you who read my books.

same shelf as wanting to be rich when you grow up or trying too hard to be popular at school. We associate people who openly want to be famous with those you might overhear saying into a bedazzled cell phone, *Daddy, my Tesla is like so old now, will you please buy me a new one, please, Daddy, please?*

I'm also conflicted about pursuing more fame because I have a sneaking suspicion being truly famous might kind of suck. On the one hand, I like being recognized... so maybe I'd like being recognized more often? Plus, if you get famous enough, there are serious perks: free swag, access to other famous people, brand deals, even more blue check marks—you know, everything you see scrolling through celebrity Instagram. On the other hand, it seems kind of stressful. In fact, the most interesting result of that Instagram survey was the DMs I got, an endless scroll of unsolicited comments on how terrible my followers think it would be to become famous: the lack of privacy, the internet haterz, the paparazzi. But most interesting of all, some people volunteered that even in spite of all this, they would still want to "try" fame someday.

Which made me curious about the relationship between fame and happiness. Like, if you happen to win the viral lottery and your dance blows up on TikTok or Katy Perry loves your *American Idol* audition or whatever, is that development likely to (A) make your life better and more happy or (B) make it worse and less happy?

A or B?

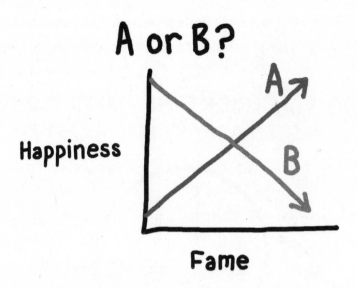

So I asked my audience a follow-up question: Do you think being famous tends to make people *more* happy or *less* happy?

Keeping in mind that 47 percent of this same group wants to be famous, guess what percent said fame would make them more happy? No, really. Take a guess. I'm going to drop a page break here so you don't cheat by reading ahead.

Okay, the answer: Only 16 percent said that fame makes you *more* happy. A whopping 84 percent said it makes you *less* happy.

DO YOU THINK FAME MAKES PEOPLE MORE HAPPY OR LESS HAPPY?

LESS HAPPY 84%

MORE HAPPY 16%

Wait, pause. Didn't 47 percent of this same group say they wanted to be famous?

Okay, I'm going to do some math gymnastics here. You can follow along or just skip the next paragraph and trust me on these calculations.

So let's assume that all 16 percent who think fame makes you more happy are *also* part of the 47 percent who want to be famous. Which makes sense, right? We'd assume people want things they think will make them happy. That means 16 percent of my followers want to be famous *and* think fame will make them happy. That leaves a 31 percent chunk of my followers who want fame but also think it makes people *less* happy.

<whew, end of math!>

Conclusion: Apparently 31 percent of my followers *would rather be famous than happy*. Like, they think fame will make them unhappy. Yet they still want it. One out of three of those surveyed, in other words, would trade happiness for fame. Now look, they might not realize this consciously, and they probably wouldn't acknowledge it if we asked them directly. No one wants to seem shallow. But the numbers don't lie. And if I force myself to be just as ruthlessly honest, I have to admit that most days I'm also part of that 31 percent. I might *claim* I'd rather be happy, but my actions often say something quite different. My actions online say I want to be famous, not because I think it will make me happy, but because...well...actually, I'm not sure. Why in the world wide web do I want a thing that would make me less happy?

It begs the question: Why would so many of us be ready to choose fame over our own happiness?

These questions about fame and happiness matter a lot to me because being a comedian and writer is the sort of career where success is literally measured by how famous you are. If you were to tell a friend about a comedian who was "so funny but never got famous," you would mean they were basically a talented failure. I'm on a career path whose ideal destination is, by definition, celebrity—or at least wide name recognition. Does this mean I'm also on the path to unhappiness?

I don't know because unfortunately, social media stardom wasn't a subject we covered in high school. Nor did my college offer a degree in semi-fame. So I've decided to do what any hipster nerd does when faced with a knowledge gap: Read books. Study history. Review case studies. Interview experts. Apply scientific method.

You hold in your hands the results of this investigation.

This book offers six classes (subdivided into snack-sized chapters!), each looking at a specific subject area. Basically our hangout within these pages is like a day at school, where period one is English, period two is History, and so on, except at this school you have the same teacher in every class; he entertains you with confessional stories about his awkward behavior as he recounts the beginning of his own interest in fame; and at the end of the day at *this* school maybe you'll actually have learned something useful.

We'll start by attempting to define the word *fame*—it's harder than you'd think. Then we'll turn back time and figure out who the first celebrity was. When did fame become a thing? Was there even such a thing as a recognizable face before modern technology? We'll dig into the numbers (yay, math!) and question the urban legends associated with stardom. Do stars really tend to die young or does it just seem that way?

I'll talk to people who are already semi-famous or even famous-famous. Creators and musicians and actors who are farther down this path than I am. I'll ask them, straight up: Is this fame thing making you happy? If not, why are you doing it? If so, what's your secret?

Question(s) for Famous People

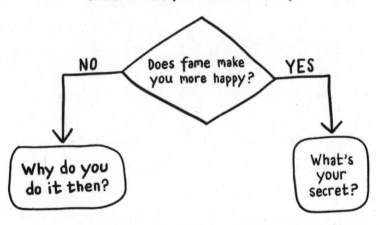

Because even if stardom makes *most* people less happy, maybe there are some celebrities out there who beat the system. Who figured out how to be happy and famous at the same time. If such stars exist, we'll find them and learn their secret.

Basically, we're going to hack fame. We're going to

hack happiness. And then we'll see if we've discovered any possible way to make them overlap. That's my main question in all this: Can I reconcile my urge to be known with my fear of what that might mean for my own well-being? In other words, can I (or you!) be *both* famous and happy?

Because if not, I should get off this path ASAP, right? If increased fame always leads to *decreased* happiness—if it's all mo' followers, mo' problems—then presumably I should deactivate my social accounts and/or join a fame-addiction recovery/support group.

But before we start answering all these questions, maybe pause to take a pic or screenshot of this page to post on your story? Oh, and don't forget to tag me because as you may have heard, I read all my mentions. And sometimes I write, like, entire books about them.

ENGLISH

Sometimes I'm in denial that I'm really famous. It's too much, I think, for someone to reach that kind of magnitude to really understand it. I feel like when you're younger, it's easier. But as you get older, it's one of those things that's just kind of like "Huh? What is this? This is kind of crazy."

—BRITNEY SPEARS

STUFF WE WILL LEARN IN CLASS TODAY:

- How do we define this word fame, anyway?
- What are the different kinds of fame?
- Which is the best kind of fame to have?

CHAPTER 1

Look at the time! The morning bell is about to sound for first period. Lockers are slamming. Phones are getting silenced after being refreshed once more in case he texted you back. Those who have boyfriends or girlfriends are lingering by their lockers to show off their romantic success with one last flourish of PDA while you frogger your way through the bodies and backpacks to make it to class before the bell rings.

In English class you learn about things like words, what they mean, and SparkNotes. As I've embarked on this research, I've been asking friends to define *fame*. Most say things like: paparazzi, being on TV, eye-popping follower counts. But those are *results* of fame, not a description of the thing itself.

I think we can boil down the definition to four words: *being known by strangers*. Fame is when humans you don't know recognize you. The more such strangers are familiar with your name or your image, the more famous you are.

Is there a difference, though, between fame and

celebrity? Absolutely. All celebrities are famous, but not all famous people are celebrities.

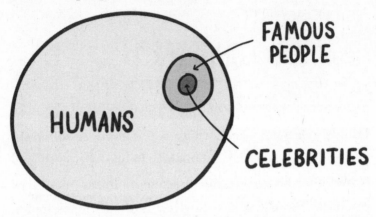

Celebrity is a certain flavor of famous. Like, historical figures can be famous, but unless they are resurrected by hologram or a hit Broadway musical, the dead aren't usually celebrities. A celebrity is generally a living person whose image gets replicated so many times on so many screens that whether we want to or not, most of us know about them—and whether we want to admit it or not, most of us are also curious about them. You probably have blood relatives whose personal lives you know less about than many tabloid regulars.

According to fame historian Antoine Lilti, another characteristic of celebrity is being known by people who don't pay attention to the thing that made you famous. The fame of, say, a singer who is familiar "to those who do not listen to his songs" or a soccer player "when he is recognized by those who never watch soccer games." Put another way: You might know about a particular social media star because they're famous, but that person hasn't become a *celebrity* until your mom knows about them, too.

Celebrities are famous people who outgrew their subgenre and made it to the mainstream. There are many paths to celebrity but only one destination, one big tent of glammed-up alt-reality. Watch a Hollywood awards show on TV and you'll see NBA players in the audience. Watch an NBA game and you'll spot movie stars sitting courtside. In that sense, there is only one kind of celebrity: the kind the camera zooms in on for a close-up if they're in the audience.

But even if there's a single type or definition of celebrity, there are many different types of fame that can lead to it. And in today's English class, we will be searching for vocabulary and definitions of each of them. To investigate the first of these categories, let's travel to South Korea to meet a girl named Euo. At age twelve, Euo had a shot at the job of her dreams—the job she'd do anything for, the job that could make her famous—when she auditioned to become a K-pop idol trainee.

Idol trainee auditions are like the open casting calls for talent shows you've seen on TV. More than two thousand children were in front of Euo in line, sitting in rows on the cold floor of a giant convention center waiting for hours for their moment in front of an entertainment company executive. Most got through only a few lines before he cut them off and motioned for the next person to step forward. That was it. That's how fast your dream got snuffed out.

Euo, obviously, was terrified. I mean, this was her big moment, and she'd wanted to become a K-pop idol since she was a little girl. It had always been her dream to be *that* famous. K-pop famous. Idol famous.

Idols aren't just members of a musical group, they're a genre of celebrity. They sing, dance, act in movies and television shows, and pose as models in product endorsements. Idols are selling an image. And that image is everywhere. In Japan—which has its own set of idols who perform a related genre, J-pop—more than half of all commercials feature an idol. In Korea, idols are so recognizable that one time when a popular K-pop act, Girls' Generation, disguised themselves in an effort to move freely in Seoul, fans still recognized them based on, wait for it, the shape of their exposed arms and legs. That's right: Even their limbs are famous. The *New Yorker* asked Girls' Generation how they felt about having such well-known appendages.

> "It is," Tiffany said, shooting an accusatory glance at her arm. "It's just so..." She paused, searching for the right thing to say. "Freakishly cool!"

That kind of freakishly cool fame was precisely what Euo was dreaming about while she waited for her audition. Even getting an audition is hard—Euo had recorded video submissions for the entertainment companies before (there are exactly three agencies that control the idol market in South Korea). Then on a trip to see her grandmother in Seoul, she finally got invited to perform in person at a giant audition.

Euo began by reciting a monologue, but the judge stopped her in the middle. Was she being dismissed? No, he wanted to hear her sing. She hadn't prepared a song, but on the spot she chose "A Whole New World" from *Aladdin*. Which, I mean, great choice. Who among us doesn't love a Disney sing-along?[4]

He stopped her in the middle of that, too. Not to dismiss her, *whew*. To ask her to dance. They played "Low" by Flo Rida and she made something up, feeling sure she looked silly. She was sure it was over. But no! She was ushered to another area where she was photographed from many different angles, like the cringey angles you only see in selfie outtakes when you're scrolling through your photo roll. A few days later, lo and behold, she was offered a trainee contract.

---

[4] Let the storm rage ONNNNNNN! The cold never bothered me anyway.

Trainee contracts are long-term binding agreements that mean moving away from home to train and attend school elsewhere, for the length of the contract. Depending on your view of home and parents, that might sound like a pretty great deal. But training is not an endless summer camp—unless when you think of summer camp you think of a high-stress lice-outbreak scenario. Basically, moving away to trainee school is less Hogwarts and more cupboard under the Dursleys' staircase. Even so, Euo begged and pleaded and finally persuaded her mom this was really, truly what she wanted.

She was swept away to live in a dorm with other trainees. There were a couple hundred aspiring idols already enrolled there. The buzz of potential fame hung in the air like that electric hum right before lightning strikes (or at least, that's how it sounds in movies, I've never actually been struck by lightning). Sometimes former trainees, those who had *made it*, would return after their debut to visit the trainees still living in their old dorm. *Yes, it's real. I got struck by that lightning. You could be next.*

The truth, though, was most of these girls, even after making it this far, would never become idols. There were monthly showcases where every trainee had to perform in front of her peers and instructors. If the instructors weren't impressed, she'd be sent home. A snap of the fingers, a wave of the hand. Gone. Just like that. And some other eager young thing, who'd made it through the video audition and then been plucked from the mass in-person audition, would show up, suitcase in hand, all fresh-faced and innocent, ready to fill the empty spot. The message was clear: You are replaceable. You have four weeks to prepare to prove yourself again. And again.

Trainees were required to stay below 104 pounds. There were weekly weigh-ins. Public affairs. If you were over 104 pounds, everyone saw. You ate your now-rationed food in shame until you returned to the *correct* weight. Sometimes your diet was limited to water for a time. Bulimia was common. Periods didn't come. Passing out was normal. Girls would collapse during training and their friends would carry them back to their beds to rest. Far from being horrified, though, her friends would be impressed.

"The attitude among the trainees after [someone passed out] was like, 'Good for her! She wants it so much!'" explains Euo. "Looking back on it now, I think it was really disgusting."

Competition was a way of life. Even where you slept said something about your standing. There was an A-group that got a bed in a smaller room with just a few bunks. The A-group was the top 10 percent of trainees. Euo was lucky enough to be one of them. But the bottom 90 percent, all 180 or so of them, slept on mats on the floor in one big room. See what I mean? This was no summer camp.

Trainees woke up before dawn for a training session. Then they'd attend school. Normal school with classmates who slept in actual beds at their parents' house. Then they'd return to the facility for more practice. Each girl was issued a stage name and a number. Instructors referred to them by their numbers. *Number twenty-two, again, please.* As you progressed in the program, your stage name was expanded into an assigned stage persona.

Euo's stage name was Dia.

"She was supposed to be very reserved, sweet, and innocent," says Euo. She was also told she'd be "the visual." The visual was the pretty girl, the lead face in the group photos. You know the one. "As the visual, I would be expected to personify those characteristics. But Dia just wasn't me. I'm opinionated and loud. I doubted I would be able to keep up this docile personality in public."

Not that her agency thought her face was pretty enough. Not yet, at least. The next step for trainees, inevitably, was plastic surgery. Euo was told her nose needed reshaping. And her jaw should be shaved down because her face was "too big." The cost of the surgery would be covered. But that expense, along with *everything* the agency invested in her during her training, was being added to a ledger somewhere. It was a debt she owed. If she quit before her contract expired, she would have to pay it all back. And if she eventually got selected for a group and became an idol, her earnings from touring, merchandise, album sales, and the like would count against that debt. In other words, she wouldn't get paid above a base salary, even if she was in a successful group, until the agency felt she'd earned enough to recoup the investment they'd made in training her. That could be a sizable number. The agency might decide your debt is a few hundred thousand dollars, maybe a million. According to the *Wall Street Journal*, talent agencies might invest as much as $3 million per trainee. So even if your group blows up, you don't necessarily walk away rich. The average successful K-pop idol group lasts about five years. During that time, you may get a base salary of around $30,000 until the group's profits pay the agency back for your training costs as well as your travel expenses when touring.

If you're thinking all this is sounding a little like a real-life *Hunger Games* or something, well, yes. In fact, after a recent investigation by the Korean Fair Trade Commission, restrictions were set on how much trainees can be "fined" for leaving early, violating a morality clause, or not renewing their contract after it had expired. That's right: Reportedly, if the agency wanted the trainee to renew after their contract expired, but the trainee didn't want to, the trainee might be fined double what they'd been paid while working under the previous contract. Like, what? Coriolanus Snow much?

Oh, and that morality clause: Trainees are not allowed to be out past curfew, take substances, or otherwise engage in behavior that could tarnish a precisely defined image of wholesomeness. Idols and trainees must also submit to limitations or outright bans on romantic relationships. Why? Idols are selling a fantasy. Idols, so the thinking goes, need to be unattached so fans can plausibly imagine dating them. They must be both impossibly beautiful and romantically attainable.

After a J-pop star named Minami Minegishi—member of supergroup AKB48[5]—was caught by paparazzi sneaking out to meet with her boyfriend, she shaved her head and posted a long, weepy apology video. Endless internet debates ask whether she was forced to do this or did it voluntarily. But does it matter? She apologized, interestingly, not so much for having a boyfriend as for disappointing you all, the fans. As if she let you down by dating someone who was, um, *not you*.

You've seen apology videos—for the problematic tweet that resurfaces, the joke that was taken too far. The celebrity apology video is an art form unto itself by now. No makeup, hair down, sitting on the floor in the living room, starting with a sigh and a gap of silence. "Hey guys...so..."

---

5   Idol groups tend to have names that look like the unbreakable password of random characters your browser likes to suggest.

But an apology to fans for *having a boyfriend* is another thing all together.

The lifestyle of an idol is astonishingly restricted. But remember, Euo *chose* this path. She talked her mom into signing that trainee contract. She wanted it. The agencies can get away with this slightly—okay, maybe very—disturbing business model precisely because so many thousands of other eager kids are currently sitting on a convention center floor somewhere, hoping to be the next top K-pop star.

Despite having declined the suggestion of having her face reshaped, Euo was eventually offered a part in a new K-pop group. Which was...the realization of her dream, right? The culmination of everything she'd worked so hard for? She could tour the world, gain a social media following, and sing and dance for shrieking fans who screamed her name (well, her stage name) and knew everything about her (well, about her assigned persona and approved social posts) at Madison Square Garden and music festivals. Like, say, Coachella, where Blackpink became planetwide-level stars in 2019, three years after being assembled by a guy in a suit at the corporate office of YG Entertainment.

Euo's original trainee contract lasted two years, but if she joined a group, she'd be locked in to a much longer agreement. She can't disclose the details of the offer, but these contracts typically last a long, long time. Sometimes more than a decade. Your career is forever tied to that agency. Former idols report years of working seven days a week, no days off. Seventeen-, eighteen-hour days—shooting endorsement commercials, appearing on television, interacting with fans online. Every hour of your day is scheduled but never provided to you in advance so forget about ever making plans to hang out with friends or just, like, chill.

And saying yes would be no guarantee of that kind of success. After Euo's hypothetical group was formed, they would "debut," which is when one of the talent agencies announces a new idol group and trots them out on one of those TV shows to perform a new single. About sixty groups are debuted per year—more than one per week—in South Korea. Probability of success is not high.

Deep down, though, Euo most wanted to be an actor. The group she was offered a part in seemed like it would be more focused on singing and dancing. Plus, there was that persona she had been assigned. That lack of control over her own, you know, personality.

In the end, Euo chose not to join the K-pop group. The one she was offered a part in, she says, is successful enough to tour now. She can't reveal which group it is, but safe to say (A) they're out there working long hours each day to keep their corporate overlords happy and (B) the group has a name that looks like the alphanumeric euphemism for a swear word in a cartoon. As for Euo, when her two-year trainee contract expired, she left that life to find her own path on YouTube and Instagram. Not as Dia, as herself.

I asked Euo in an email how it would be different if K-pop stars were allowed to use their own names and be "themselves" in public.

"That would definitely be very liberating and healthier for everyone," she replied. "But there's a reason why companies put up an image for idols...that 'image' of you is what sells. Honestly if everyone started showing their real personalities, I think some fans would be disappointed."

So if you're a K-pop idol, you gain fame by projecting an image of what fans happen to be buying. Project something else and you limit your appeal. Euo seems to be saying that while it may be possible to be both famous and happy, you can get a little more famous if you're willing to be a little less happy.

Which raises the question: Does that mean, at least for Euo, that happiness is maximized at the point of semi-fame? Like there's a certain vertex (that's math speak for the highest point of a curve) after which additional fame requires a sacrifice in well-being?

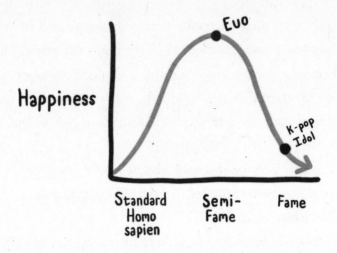

Maybe. But it could also be that maximum happiness is possible right at the start, when you're non-famous, and every unit of fame from the very beginning means giving up a unit of happiness.

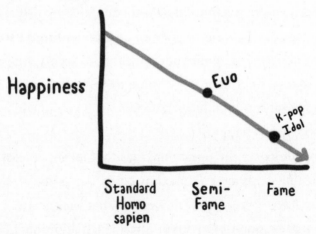

There's only one way to find out: more investigating.

CHAPTER 2

Euo's story isn't one of those strange foreign things that could only happen in some other country. Young people across the world (read: me) make eyebrow-raising, wtf-level choices in the pursuit of fame. So I'm not judging anyone who wants to be a K-pop star, nor am I criticizing K-pop music (I happen to currently be obsessed with Blackpink). If anything, I'm saying, *I get it*. When I was sixteen, I decided I wanted to become an Olympian. Not just wanted to, *had to*. It was my destiny. Like I was the Chosen One in a YA sci-fi novel. Or the protagonist in a feel-good sports movie. Matter of fact, later I would spend one miserable summer training on a high-altitude glacier, getting on the ski lift before dawn. Every afternoon I would watch an underdog sports movie (*Rudy*, *Rocky*, *Remember the Titans*, as well as others that didn't start with *R*). I had to convince myself I was living the first half of one of those stories. Sure, I was terrible at my sport when I began, I mean like *so* bad, but that's how these movies always start out. At first, the character sucks.

It seems impossible they could ever win. Cue a pep talk and a soundtrack-fueled training montage and blammo, they're in the championship.

I definitely checked the sucking-at-the-start box. My first race I literally fell five times. I got last place. Obviously. The winner went through the course in about thirty seconds. My time was two minutes and thirty seconds. A couple seasons later, when I finally started racing on the international World Cup circuit, in my first eight races my best finish was second.[6]

But all this failure, in my mind, was going to be helpful in the long run because it was the perfect foundation for making me famous. Would anyone chant for Rudy if he hadn't been cut from tryouts so many times? Would anyone remember the Titans if they hadn't started at the very bottom of their division? That I was clearly not suited to be a ski racer would make my slo-mo gold-medal moment all the more epic.

So yeah, I was basically delusional.

But there wasn't a monthly showcase where I could get cut (really, it would have been a mercy) from my training program. My coach did warn me that I didn't have much of a shot at making the Paralympics—specifically, he set

_____

6   To last.

the odds at one in a million; no joke: that was an actual statement from a guy I was paying to, you know, encourage me and stuff—but I kept showing up at the mountain every day. I stayed there, I trained, I toiled, living my own version of the K-pop trainee program.

In terms of body composition, I had the opposite challenge of aspiring idols: I was too skinny. It turns out that in ski racing, heavier means faster. Doesn't matter if it's muscle or fat—more pounds equals more momentum. So weight gain became my obsession. I figured I just needed to do the opposite of everything nutritionists recommend doing to *lose* weight. I never left home without snacks in my pockets. Instead of water, I drank sports bottles filled with a mixture of whole milk and a powdered weight-gain formula clocking a thousand calories per serving. I ate a pint of ice cream every night right before bed.

All those carbs might sound blissful, but here's the thing. The taste of food is a classic declining marginal utility curve. At first it's great. Like when you're hungry. But at some point your body is like, okay, enough for now, we're good in the eating department. I know, how could you ever get tired of ice cream? Trust me. This curve is real.

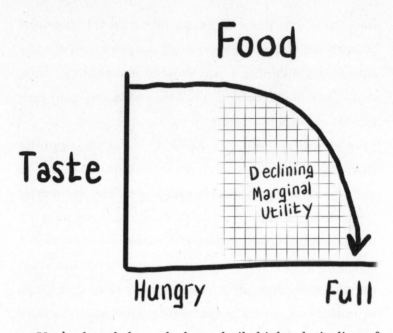

Food

Taste

Declining Marginal Utility

Hungry   Full

You've heard about the legendarily high-calorie diets of Michael Phelps and other elite athletes. I was training up to eight hours a day so I was burning a ton of calories. Despite how much I ate, my weight gain was slow. But it was also steady. Over my five years of training, I put on forty pounds. A lot of it was fat. Stretch marks developed on my hips. I wore them as a badge of pride, like cool scars I'd gotten in a morally justified knife fight. My appearance had changed so much, actually, that I occasionally ran into high school classmates who didn't recognize me. Like I'd literally have to tell them who I was. *Remember me? We sat at the same lunch table?*

Incidentally, I did make that Paralympic team. Which

was cool. I didn't win medals or anything.[7] But I've since realized how stupid that whole plan was because *winning a medal would not have made me famous*. I mean, of the hundreds (hundreds!) of athletes who won a gold medal at the last Olympics, how many can you name? How about the silver medalists? Bronze? What about the Olympics before that?

That's the thing about fame. If you want to be remembered for an achievement, it's not enough to just do something impressive. You have to do something *unprecedented*. Winning one medal isn't enough. You have to win more medals than anyone else in the history of the Olympics, or in addition to the medals be the first person to have diamond-studded braces and fake a robbery in a foreign country. It's not the winning, it's the winning in uncharted territory. That's how you become what I like to call *feat famous*:[8] being known for something you did. Write that definition on a flash card and put it in your SAT vocab file. Wait, was that just me? You don't have a flash-card box?

Like, I remember the name of the guy who won season one of *Survivor* back in the day, but now they're on season

---

[7] Come on. If I had, don't you think I'd be wearing them in that author photo?

[8] By the way, since this is English class, we should note that the phrase "feat famous" is a great example of alliteration.

eighty-six or something and I can't name any other winners or even contestants from the rest of the series. Reality
shows are like that, even the ones people actually watch.
Season-one winners can become celebrities. Subsequent
seasons only produce D-list horror movie actors and US
presidents. So if you want to be feat famous, you have to be
first at something. Not first as in winning a single race, first
as in inventing an entirely new category. Not just walking
on the moon, being the first to take that one small step or
giant leap for mankind. Not just sailing across the Atlan-
tic, but instead having a publicist who can convince the
world you were the first one to "discover" North America.

By the way, I classify K-pop stardom as feat fame. As
an idol, it's not really *you* who's famous. You're not going
by your real name or actual personality, after all. It's the
group that is famous, and you—or rather, your persona—
are famous for being a part of that group. For something
you did.

Anyway, as far as my personal feat fame journey, having
failed to achieve it by *gaining* weight, my next fame scheme
would take me in the exact opposite direction. About
six weeks after competing in the Paralympics, I took a
"before" photo to enter a fitness contest in which I'd be
judged on before-and-after pics taken twelve weeks apart.
I approached this with that same Olympic-sized determi-
nation, aiming for three hours of cardio per day, usually

biking or hiking. I was eating so little I was often dizzy or shaky. One afternoon I rode my bike out into the country-side, maybe twenty miles from home. I was so weak from not eating that it was like I was pedaling in slow motion. The sun began to set. I didn't have a cell phone with me. It seemed like I was going to end up stuck here on this quiet country road all night. That's when I spotted a Reese's Peanut Butter Cup wrapper, torn open and lying by the side of the road. Nearby were both of the actual peanut butter cups, lying facedown in the dirt.

Why had a passing motorist apparently ripped open the packaging, only to throw both cups out the window un-eaten? I have no idea. To be honest I'm normally pretty judgy when it comes to anyone who litters. I mean, every-one knows it's wrong. I'm convinced even serial killers, deep down, feel a little guilty if they don't put their candy wrappers in a trash can. But just this once, I was thankful for roadside litter. It saved me in my time of need.

I hopped off my bike and carefully lifted one of the upside-down peanut butter cups off the road. It was a humid summer evening, so the candy was soft and runny. Bits of sand and gravel coated the chocolate like a layer of frosting. I picked out the larger rocks with my fingers, but most of the dirt had sunk far into the chocolate. It was too melted to peel from the brown wax paper and take a bite with my teeth, so I just licked it all out with my tongue—peanut butter, melty chocolate, and road grit, together. It was the best thing I've ever tasted.[9]

Those two peanut butter cups revived me enough to pedal home. Just like Euo and her friends complimented fellow trainees who passed out from training and low blood sugar, I congratulated myself for having pushed myself right up to the line of what my body could endure. That's how you win a fitness contest, I told myself. That's how you become feat famous.

Oh, and if you're thinking all this—both my weight gain for the Paralympics and weight loss for this fitness contest—sounds *kind of like an eating disorder*, yeah, absolutely. The truth is, most residents at your average Olympic training facility would probably test positive if they did one of those internet checklists for warning signs of an unhealthy relationship with food.

Sometimes aspiring athletes ask me what it takes to make it to the Olympics. Is it discipline? Ambition? Talent? Those things help, sure. But primarily, I think it takes something close to a personality disorder. Delusions of grandeur and all that. You have to fool yourself into thinking the Olympics will bring you enough fame—or make you rich, or make you feel good enough, or make your

---

[9] Refer to the marginal utility curve illustration earlier in the chapter.

parents love you, or whatever else you should probably be talking to your therapist about instead—and then finally all that grit you displayed (or ate) will have been worth it. I imagine K-pop trainees make similar mental bargains with themselves: The fame will make it all worth it.

Anyway, that same summer I was training for the fitness contest, I was also planning to attend a student journalism conference. Looking back, that journalism conference changed my life.

You should know that my interest in journalism had begun at a young age. I started dabbling in news reporting at age six, in between those self-instructed lessons in computer programming. I know what you're thinking. Why didn't this poor kid have any normal, fun hobbies? Point taken. Regardless, all this productivity was made possible because I was homeschooled in elementary and middle school, meaning I had loads of free time that I filled with odd hobbies.

I had discovered that by speaking loudly into the air vent in the corner of my bedroom, the sound traveled through the ductwork and out all the other vents in the house. It was basically analog Twitch. Or ancient podcasting. At the time, I just called it my "radio station." I did a daily morning show with commentary on household events and family news. I soon expanded my growing journalism empire into print with "Kids' Newspaper," a hand-lettered, photocopied newsletter I composed each week.

In fact, a major reason I switched from homeschool to public school in high school was so I could write for a real newspaper. Okay, a "real" newspaper, quote, unquote. This was high school journalism, after all. But by my junior year I was writing a monthly column for an actual honest-to-God newspaper called the *Richmond Times-Dispatch*. Second-biggest paper in the whole state, in fact. In college, I started contributing to a news magazine that was published by *Newsweek* and distributed at universities nationwide.

The summer between my senior year and super-senior year—yep, I took a fifth year because I just can't quit you, school—I got the invitation to a one-day conference *Newsweek* was holding for its student writers in New York City. A few weeks before the conference, an email was sent to all the student attendees from a guy named Ocean MacAdams—the sort of name you never forget—who happened to be vice president of MTV News. He was going to be one of the speakers at the event. The message began:

> We are searching for new on-camera talent for MTV News.

That opening sentence seized my attention.
On-camera talent?
MTV?
OMG.

Here's the weird thing about this instant interest. Having grown up in a pretty conservative homeschool household that didn't get cable television, I had not actually watched much MTV in my life. But I was aware of it in a general sort of way, like how you might know about the teachers' lounge at your high school even though you've never been inside it. You've peered through that little window in the door, though, and you've seen what appears to be a vending machine—with real soda, the kind with actual high-fructose corn syrup in it! Basically, you don't know for sure what's behind the door but you sure wish you were inside.

This teachers'-lounge metaphor breaks down, obviously, on one point: the coolness spectrum. On the scale of things that were vaguely mysterious to me in high school, I knew enough to be aware MTV fell on the far opposite end from the teachers' lounge on any possible measurement of cool.

Uncool ← Teachers' Lounge — MTV → Cool

How you feel dancing   How others look dancing

I saw MTV as America's premiere fame factory, the country's leading celebrity-manufacturing plant. Like the Korean musical variety shows that make or break K-pop acts, artists went into an MTV appearance as raw human material and came out *stars*.

MTV News, as you may know, is the journalistic department of MTV. If MTV was the cool party everyone in the world wanted to be at, MTV News was the slightly more serious older brother with the bedroom over the garage who occasionally drops by the party to offer a hip take on world events or a sophisticated opinion about the music that's currently being played. MTV News correspondents appeared in brief segments on the hour in between MTV's regular programming, blending pop culture and celebrity updates with traditional news subjects—politics, climate change, the politics of climate change—packaged for young adult viewers.

Basically, being an MTV News correspondent was the dream job I never knew I had been dreaming about. I'd certainly been aware that very special young people of approximately my age did get to hold that MTV logo–wrapped microphone and interview celebrities on red carpets or whatever, but it had not occurred to me that this was a job you could just, like, *apply for*—specifically, by replying directly to an email from the vice president of MTV News. It would be like if the student secretary general of Model UN was told there was a slot open to be actual secretary-general of the actual UN and would she happen to be interested in applying? Um, duh.

Becoming an MTV News correspondent seemed like

the culmination of every weird hobby I'd ever had—talking into the vents, the "Kids' Newspaper," all that. It was the gig I was made for.

When you boil it down, the thing those weird childhood hobbies, student journalism, and being on MTV had in common was, well, they were all paths to becoming famous. Getting my name out there. Broadcasting myself. I don't know why, but clearly I've been drawn to activities that *make me known to strangers* since early childhood.

I proofread my cover letter dozens of times.

> Dear Mr. MacAdams,
>
> Thank you so much for this opportunity! Attached please find my:
>
> - Resume
> - Headshot
> - Writing sample
>
> Based on my writing sample I hope you can see that my interests (politics, music, celebrities) are a good fit for the job bla bla bla...

It was basically the sort of boring-ass corporate-speak form letter I'd learned how to write in, well, English class.

Fine for applying for the basic office internship, but not exactly the first impression I needed to fool Ocean MacAdams into thinking I was a very cool on-camera-type person rather than a very ex-homeschooler-type person who retained moderate knowledge of two computer programming languages.

I didn't hear back from him within a day, so just in case he hadn't seen my message—I mean, he probably had an assistant who screened his email, right?—I called a work number that I'd dug up by deep googling him, also known as spending many hours consuming every single page on the internet that mentioned his name.[10]

"Ocean MacAdams's office," said a female voice, which probably belonged to the same person who had deleted my email.

"Josh Sundquist calling for Ocean," I said crisply, like I was definitely the sort of VIP whose name Ocean would recognize and want to talk to.

"Sorry, who?" she said. It was a gut punch, like when your crush gets a new phone and replies to your text with those two devastating though not quite grammatically correct words "WHO DIS."

"Josh Sundquist," I said, the VIP in my voice now entirely deflated.

---

10 Did I tell you the one about what it takes to make it to the Olympics?

"Sorry, Ocean is not available right now," she said, apparently having concluded that my name was not the kind of name that would result in him being available. "Would you like to leave a message?"

I hung up.

Part of me was relieved, to be honest. Talking on the phone is literally the worst. Typing is more my native language. Much easier to fake a personality behind a keyboard.

Since the phone call and email had both failed to get a response, I drove to that same copy store I used to go to as a child to make "Kids' Newspaper" and printed off my cover letter and all the attachments, splurging on high-gloss paper for my headshot. I overnighted the documents to him in an envelope on which I wrote "IMPORTANT DO NOT BEND" in big Sharpie letters. I also paid extra for signature confirmation. With any luck, the delivery person would require a signature from Ocean himself, not his Josh-Sundquist-WHO-DAT assistant.

If I did land that job as an MTV News correspondent, I decided, I would immediately drop out of school and move to New York. I mean, I liked school as much as the next nerd. But I liked the idea of this job way, way more. Plus, after I was on TV a few years, I'd be set up for life in a way I could never be from a college degree. I might not be a household name or anything, but I would at least have the sort of face where people are like, "Hey, don't I recognize you from somewhere?"

I call this kind of fame, by the way, "face fame." Which, it turns out, is definitely the worst of the three types of fame. But similar to the specific snack options available in the teachers'-lounge vending machine, this was something I wasn't yet aware of.

CHAPTER 3

The best way I can define face fame is with one name: Pauley Perrette.

Being recognized in public is usually the first experience that comes to mind when we imagine being famous. But weirdly, it turns out you can be recognized without being identified. People know your face from...somewhere... *you look so familiar but I just can't place it.*

Well, that's face fame.

You may not recognize Pauley's name, but you'd probably recognize her face. She was that girl on *NCIS*. You know, black hair usually in pigtails, tattoos, kind of goth. Her character, Abby, was a scientist who ran all the DNA and stuff. Pauley appeared in an astounding 352 episodes of the show. *NCIS* might not be your top show to binge, but your mom and your aunt and maybe your grandparents probably love it. On for nineteen seasons, the show has consistently been the number one most viewed scripted series on television. It's consistently the most popular TV drama on the planet. Pauley has left the cast, but when you scroll through Netflix, her face is often still the thumbnail image for *NCIS*. At one point, her Q Score (a number Hollywood execs rely on to measure how positively the public views a celebrity) was tied with those of Tom Hanks and Morgan Freeman.

You can't undo that kind of fame.

"Such a familiar pose for me is sitting outside on my steps while my dogs are in my yard and thinking, *What have I done to my life? Like, what have I done?*" she tells me. "Because there's no going back now."

It's not like she could just leave Los Angeles and move to another part of the country. Based on the viewer demographics of *NCIS*, she'd probably be recognized far more *outside* Hollywood.

"There's nowhere I could go. There's nothing I could do. There's nothing that will ever, ever make me for the rest of my life not be Abby," she says.

It's not that she doesn't like the character Abby. She loves her. But Pauley never set out to become this famous. If anything, she always thought being famous looked terrible. She got into acting as a way to pay for school. The money was great. And she just...never stopped acting. At one point, years ago, she remembers thinking, *Crap, if it keeps going like this, I'm going to get famous.*

Sure enough, here she is today, hanging out inside her house in Hollywood because she can't really go out in public anymore.

"I just got too damn famous," she tells me one evening while we sit at her kitchen table.

Pauley doesn't like to venture out in public, but like anyone, she does appreciate a change of scenery now and then. So she's been slowly buying up houses in her neighborhood. Just so she can feel free to, like, leave the house—even if only to walk to another house next door. There's the house she sleeps in. Then there's another for, like, hanging out with friends. It has a backyard and a bunch of bedrooms. At any one time she might have friends or family members from back home in Alabama staying upstairs. Anyway, that's the house where I've sat many times with her at the kitchen table.

Fame, she says, is dehumanizing.

I ask her what she means by *dehumanizing*.

She gives this example: Say you're in the store, like the supermarket, and someone bumps your cart with theirs. They say, "Sorry about that," and you say it's no big deal. Forgettable encounter, right? Unless...that person happens to be famous, in which case you go home and tell everyone what happened.

Pauley extends this hypothetical story forward in time: "Everybody's sitting around the table at Thanksgiving and they're telling stories. 'Did you guys hear what happened to Bobby? Bobby was in the supermarket in the fruit section, and Pauley Perrette tapped—Abby! Yeah, yeah, girl with the pigtails—Her! Yeah! She tapped her cart into his.'" She changes her voice to portray another family member: "'No way! *No...way!*'"

That's what *dehumanized* means for Pauley.

But, I tell her, that's exactly what a lot of people—especially young people in general and maybe also including me—would say they want. They *want* to be the person who runs into a shopping cart and gets recognized and talked about next Thanksgiving. That was, like, *exactly* the experience I was dreaming about in my MTV fantasies.

So can Pauley explain why that experience actually sucks?

She describes more of what it's like to go out in public. She calls it "the Bees." If someone recognizes her, they freak out OMIGODOMIGODOMIGODOMIGOD and run over to her. As soon as that happens, everyone nearby takes notice. They swarm. The Bees.

To be clear, Pauley is always nice to fans. She never says no to a selfie. When she does leave the house, she carries a Sharpie and little postcards with her photo on them so when someone recognizes her, she can quickly give out an autograph before a swarm forms.

"All they want is proof. They want to prove to whoever they're going to run back to or whoever they're having Thanksgiving dinner with at the end of the year that they saw you, that they got a picture with you, or that they got an autograph. Once they have proof, you don't matter anymore," she explains. "There is no 'how is your day?' There is none. It does not matter. Like, the humanity part of me is irrelevant."

Which is all very ironic because, as Pauley points out, many people who long for fame want it in order to validate their existence. To literally verify themselves with a blue check mark. But ironically, if they *do* become famous, the very thing they wanted to validate their existence has made them cease to exist, at least in terms of other people seeing them as anything other than a famous shell. Pauley calls this problem "the Dichotomy." She has a name for the phenomena of fame.

She says she'd tell anyone who wants to become famous to figure out why they want it. If it's just for validation, well, "Is there another way to validate yourself? Other than fame?"

At her kitchen table, she offers to make me a cocktail. Before she was an actor, Pauley was paying for school as a bartender. She also did a stint in a band that played on the Vans Warped Tour. She has a lot of tattoos. Not, like, giant sleeves of ink, just little doodles here and there.

"Abby is the only character I've ever played who has more tattoos than I do," she says offhandedly.

Pauley wears her dark hair in a ponytail. I've never seen her in anything besides a T-shirt and jeans or sweatpants.

She talks very, very fast. Conversation veers from one

subject to the next. She has this new cookbook out—want to see a copy? Hey, wait, has she ever told you about her favorite cousin from Tennessee? Oh, check this out, she's been working on civil rights legislation for the LGBTQ+ community and also legislation to improve access for people with disabilities.

Honestly, it's hard to keep up.

She's mentoring a kid who recently played her son on another TV show she starred in. He's talented. She's sure he's going to be famous. Her advice to anyone like him, anyone so talented they can't stop fame from eventually happening, is to "know at your core who you are."

For her, that starts with her faith. Which is not so much a set of rules as a philosophy of why we should be good to each other.

I can confirm that she lives out these values because Pauley is a friend of mine. We met when she emailed me out of the blue, after she loved one of my viral videos. It was weird to get an email from someone saying they were a certain famous person. After all, anyone can send an email with this claim. How could I know if it was for real? So I DM'd her verified Twitter account just to make sure. And she replied. Wow. It was really her, sending me an email.

A few years ago, when my wife and I moved to Los Angeles, Pauley offered to let us stay in one of her guesthouses—yeah, there are a few—while we searched for an apartment.

"I've been extremely poor and I have been extremely rich," she tells me. "And rich is better."

For one thing, she says, money buys her all the therapy she wants. By her description, she has "severe anxiety depression disorder/severe complex civilian PTSD" and is a "therapy junkie."

Advocacy is Pauley's main gig these days. She's generous with her time and money. But, boy, is she tired of getting mobbed. And also of people wanting to be friends with her only because she's famous. In fact, one of the biggest compliments her (true) friends can pay her is suggesting Pauley join them for an activity in a crowded, public place. It means, for a moment, they forgot she is too famous for that kind of thing. In other words, they see her humanity, not her fame. They're friends with her for the right reasons.

Ironically, the COVID pandemic, which made most people feel lonely and isolated, came with a hidden benefit for celebrities in Los Angeles. Thanks to a mask and a pair of sunglasses, they could finally go out in public without being recognized.

For the first time in over a decade, Pauley could walk past Hollywood tourists on the sidewalk who didn't even notice her. Well, she *could*. But she didn't. Because it turns out she still has more fun sitting on the back steps, watching the dogs.

Pauley resists giving a clear answer to the question of

whether fame has made her more or less happy. It's complicated, she says, and then talks continuously for forty-five minutes about the complications.

But later she texts me an audio message, summarizing her thoughts in more like forty-five seconds.

"I'm grateful for the blessings that have been given to me. I really am. The house I live in, the dogs I take care of, the things I've been able to do for my family and all my nonprofits...I am aware and extremely grateful for the positive things that my job gave me. I mean I know you're actually talking about the fame part which—that sucks." She laughs for a second. "But I never want to come off as ungrateful, because I really, really am not."

★ ★ ★

Face fame happens more often to TV stars than movie stars. It happened to Pauley. And also to RJ Mitte. Like Pauley, he's grateful. But also like Pauley, he's occasionally conflicted.

At age thirteen, RJ heard about a show that was casting a role that seemed tailor-made for him. Not only did his appearance match the description, but also, the character had cerebral palsy, as RJ does in real life. He auditioned and got the part. The show would run five seasons, spawning a successful spin-off series, a stand-alone Netflix movie, and GIFs and memes galore.

The show was called *Breaking Bad*. You know, the one where the high school chemistry teacher cooks meth in the desert wearing only tighty-whities and a gas mask. RJ portrayed Walter Jr., the son of protagonist Walter White.

Fast-forward to today. RJ's a certified grown-up, now in his late twenties. His IMDb entry lists more than twenty post–*Breaking Bad* roles on TV and in movies. And yet: Walt Jr. is still what he's constantly recognized for in public. I asked him if that ever gets frustrating.

"Hundred percent," he said. "I feel that way all the time because at the end of the day, nothing will ever compare to what Walt Jr. did. Nothing. It's impossible." At this point, irritation slips into his voice. This is as clear a description of the downside of face fame as you'll ever hear:

You know, it's hard and I hate it. I hate dealing with *Breaking Bad* bull****. Like, "Hey, I saw that show!"...It's been a decade of the same residual thing, and it's hard not to get bitter. It's hard not to hate a character that you'll never live up to....It's like having an old joke that just doesn't die. Like, I want this thing to go away. I want to be someone else. But no matter how hard you try, it will never leave you.

Don't misunderstand his annoyance. RJ is super-proud of the work he did as a teenager. He's grateful to have had the role of a lifetime. He knows all the acting work he's done since has happened *because* he's face famous. But it's possible to be frustrated and grateful at the same time. Just ask one of your parents how they feel about, you know, being a parent.

Here's the thing about face fame. At first, sure, it's cool. Yay, great, people recognize you. You made it! But eventually, you move on. You change. You grow. The problem is, the memory fans have of you remains frozen in time.

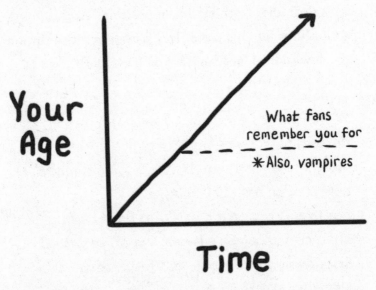

It's like when that uncle you see every couple years at family reunions keeps saying he remembers when you were ONLY THIS HIGH, holding his hand down by his knee.

He addresses you by your toddler-era nickname in a low-key baby voice. And you're like, um hello, let's notice the glow up, please.

I asked what advice RJ would have for a hypothetical person who sometimes kind of always wants to be famous.

"Don't strive for fame. Strive for art. Because at the end of the day, if you build your life on the fame, what is that foundation made of? You'll just burn yourself out if there's no art behind it, there's no passion behind it."

CHAPTER 4

So we have that one more category of fame to define here in English. I also have one last childhood hobby to tell you about: magic.

I learned some basic tricks from how-to books while I was in the hospital for chemo. Then I bought a wooden dowel from the hardware store, spray-painted it black, and dipped each end in a can of white paint, all because my mom's philosophy was to never buy the real thing when we could save money on a janky homemade version. After months practicing, I performed my first (and only) magic show. The audience was other sick kids in the hospital. My hands were so shaky that during a trick involving a ring I borrowed from one of the moms, I accidentally dropped the ring right after it had supposedly disappeared. Oh look it, um, reappeared! Ta-da.

Despite the lo-fi vibe of my illusions, the hospital paid me ten dollars. The crisp Hamilton seemed like a vast sum at the time but was really a minuscule fraction of what my parents were paying for my treatment there. If you break down the math, I'm sure the hospital charged them more for those fifteen minutes of my stay than it refunded to me for my show. Regardless, since I'd been paid to do magic, I guess you could say that I was a professional magician. I mean, I sure told everyone that.

By the time I finished my year of chemo, I'd lost interest in performing magic, but to this day I'm obsessed with watching it. Some people have season tickets to see their favorite team play in a sportsball arena. I myself have season tickets to a weekly magic show at a small theater in my neighborhood. Some say potato, some say shazam, that potato is now a rabbit.

One of my favorite magicians goes by the name Piff the Magic Dragon. He's a short British guy who wears a cartoonish dragon suit and carries around a tiny Chihuahua in a smaller matching dragon suit. (Yes, 100 percent as adorable as you're imagining.) The dog, he claims, is the one who actually does the magic. Piff himself is an ordinary, non-magical dragon.

I'd seen him perform several times on TV but I'd never watched him live. So I was looking forward to attending his show about a year ago while I was in Las Vegas for a conference. Piff has a long-term residency there, right in the middle of the strip, headlining at the Flamingo Las Vegas Hotel & Casino.

But before we meet Piff and his dog, let's define that

final category of fame because Piff has it in spades. We've established that *feat fame* is the result of a truly notable accomplishment. Like, say, you invented something. Or broke something—a world record, maybe, or the patriarchy. And we know *face fame* is when your image is known widely enough that you get recognized at Target. The third kind of fame—which happens to be the best kind—is *name fame*. It means, as you already guessed, name recognition.

✱ ✱ ✱

Name recognition is hardest to build because we all know it's easier to remember a face than a name. I mean, how many times have you seen someone you've met before, and you totally know their face but, as for their name, it's like, "Oh hey there...um, dude...how are you?" It's also easier to remember a story, as in the story of a *great feat*, than the name of the person who achieved whatever it was. Point is, names are just plain hard to remember.

But the good news if you're trying to be name famous is that you don't need everyone to be able to *recall* your name, just to recognize it, in order to experience the benefits of name fame. Like, say, selling tickets to your magic show.

How many times do you think people would need to hear your name to think you're famous? Three times? Five? Twenty?

There's a famous marketing concept called "the Rule of Seven" that says people need to hear about a product seven times before they'll remember and possibly buy it. That's why you see the same ads and YouTube commercials over and over and "click here to skip ad ▶|."

You're probably saying that you get sick of seeing the same ads repeatedly, so actually the more times you see an ad the less likely you are to buy the product. That may be true, past a certain threshold. A psychologist named Robert Bornstein looked at all the experiments on this subject over a twenty-year period and found that, generally, we do like something the more we are exposed to it. Up to a point. After that, more exposure no longer leads to more appreciation. In some categories, we eventually start liking the thing less with each viewing. In various experiments where people were exposed to all kinds of stuff, from drawings to symbols to random nonsense words, after somewhere between ten and twenty exposures, people started saying they liked the subject less each time they had to look at it.

So it turns out overexposure is a real thing. Which might be why we tend to roll our eyes at or mock A-list celebrities, especially the top few whose faces appear on every magazine cover and trending story online. It's not that we're haters. It's just simple psychology.

But back to the original question: How many times do you have to hear a name before you might think it's someone famous? Actually, maybe only once. In one experiment, psychologists showed college students a list of forty non-famous names. Just random first and last names put together. Like these:

1. Sebastian Weisdorf
2. Valerie Marsh
3. Adrian Marr

Not names you're likely to remember. Right afterward, researchers showed participants a second list containing (A) those same forty non-famous names, (B) some new non-famous names, and (C) names of actual celebrities. In total, there were one hundred names on the list, shuffled in a random order. Participants were asked to categorize each name as either famous or non-famous.

Try it for yourself. Doing the test with one hundred names might feel too much like actual school, so let's try just five. Cover up the list above. Which of the following names are famous?

1. Adrian Marr
2. Janet Moreno
3. Valerie Marsh
4. America Ferrera
5. Sebastian Weisdorf

Answer: America Ferrera (4) is famous. Janet Moreno (2) is non-famous. The other three (1, 3, and 5) were on the original non-famous list.

The point of the experiment, though, was not whether students could correctly identify the celebrities as famous. It was about which *non-famous* names participants *incorrectly* said were famous. Turns out the students were more likely to mistakenly say the "new" non-famous names (i.e., Janet Moreno) were famous than the "old" non-famous names they'd just reviewed before the test (Sebastian Weisdorf, etc.). Makes sense, right? You probably didn't say 1, 3, or 5 were famous, either, because you recognized them from the list you'd just read two seconds ago.

But researchers asked a different group of participants to leave right after reading the first list and instead come back to take the hundred-name test twenty-four hours later. The group that came back the next day had the opposite result. They were twice as likely to mistakenly say the random names they'd read the day before (Adrian Marr, Valerie Marsh, Sebastian Weisdorf) were famous. Huh? But it makes sense if you think about it. Those names sounded familiar, but they couldn't quite remember why. Their reasoning went something like: *I feel like I've heard this name, but it's definitely not anyone I know personally. So maybe it's a famous person I've heard of at some point?*

Conclusion: Maybe just hearing your name once is

enough to make people think you're famous—even if you aren't. Now that we've defined all three types of fame, we're ready to look at them together.

So a famous person might possess only one of these three factors. Like when you see someone at the airport who you think might be famous because they look SO FAMILIAR but you can't remember from where? That person has face fame, and face fame only.

But the illustration is a Venn diagram because these traits tend to overlap. Like that thing when you're watching Netflix and you're like, "Hey, that's the girl from [show about blended family forced to live together, teens discovering superpowers, rich people without moral compass, etc.]." You know their face, you know their deed (that is, the show they were on), but not their name. Face fame plus feat fame. But no name fame. Which is the situation our actor friends from the last chapter, Pauley and RJ, are in.

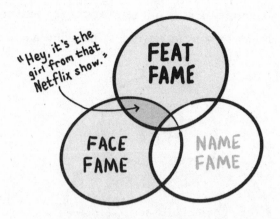

Alternatively, a person could have feat fame (you're familiar with something they did) and name fame (you remember their name), but no face fame (you don't know what they look like). Like a podcast host. Or maybe a writer. I bet there are plenty of authors whose books you really enjoy but who you wouldn't recognize in real life. In fact, quick, turn around! I just walked by! Not really. But that would have been cool, right?

But a real celebrity, a true A-lister, lives at the intersection of all three: They're feat famous, face famous, and name famous.

The A-List

Now look, this Venn diagram is just something I made up one time while I was taking a shower. You don't have to memorize it. It won't be on the exam. But as I've set out on my quest to understand how fame affects happiness, those circles have given me a framework for understanding the different ways fame can manifest.

Speaking of manifesting, it's time to meet Piff the Magic Dragon. Something to know about Piff: He's grumpy. He begins most performances by walking onstage, costumed Chihuahua in hand, frowning at the audience, letting out a long sigh, and saying in a flat voice, "I'm Piff the Magic Dragon. You might have heard of my older brother...Steve."

That's Piff's onstage character: a grumpy dragon. The dragon part is an act. The grumpiness, not so much.

"I come across as a douchebag more often than not," he tells me when I ask about his offstage, real-life personality. "Jade, my girlfriend, orders food in restaurants for me because I'll accidentally say something to upset people."

He upsets people in his shows, too, but that's sort of part of the experience. At the show I watched in Las Vegas a woman who volunteered to help with a trick "ruined it." (She didn't; Piff designed it to fail—no one's trying to say he's one of those kindhearted dragons.) Piff proceeded to shame her by shining a flashlight at her in her seat. Jade, who also plays his assistant onstage, came out and did the same. Sad music played. It was funny. But not to this audience member. She stood up and left the theater.

When I later asked him how often audience members walk out of his shows, he said, "Not often but it happens." Which is the risk you take with performing comedy. More than once, I've had people walk out of my shows, too.

Anyway, while he was onstage, Piff recognized me in the audience.

"Hey, wait!" he said. "You're that comedian from the internet!"

Ah, yes. The strange things that happen when you're semi-famous.

That's how I found myself standing beside a life-size

photo of Piff on the wall by the entrance to his theater in the center of the casino, waiting to meet him to record an episode of his podcast. Piff's dragon suit covers his whole body except for his hands and a hole for his face. I scanned the faces of passing gamblers, searching for Piff in the crowd.

"Hey Josh," said a voice out of nowhere.

I turned and was startled to find this guy I didn't recognize standing RIGHT BESIDE ME. Where had he come from? And how did he know my name? A logical part of my brain knew that it *had to be Piff because who else would be meeting me here and saying my name.* But this didn't look like the face of the Piff I'd seen onstage. Surely, I would have recognized Piff and noticed him standing beside me.

"Hey...dude!" I said, hedging my bets in case it wasn't actually Piff but a long-lost relative or something.

"Come on," he said, pulling out a set of keys and unlocking the doors to the theater. I followed him through another door and then down a spiral staircase into the subterranean darkness. We descended in complete silence other than the sound of our footsteps on the narrow metal stairs. Either this was Piff[11] or I'd accidentally joined up

---

11 Spoiler: It was Piff. But this experience made me finally understand how people who know Clark Kent fail to recognize his face just because he puts on a costume.

with an Ocean's Eleven–type crew and we were escaping through the sewers.

He opened another door and led me into a sizable dressing room. A mirror ran the entire length of one wall, lit by a row of oversized bulbs. Beneath the mirror was a long shelf littered with props I recognized from the show, some dog stuff for the Chihuahua, and some girl stuff for Jade.

Clearly, this was Piff's dressing room. Identity confirmed.

"So, do you get to live upstairs?" I asked, breaking the silence. I'd always imagined that when a performer signs a residency deal at a Vegas casino, it includes a complimentary hotel room. Probably a sprawling penthouse with a grand piano and unlimited room service.

He looked at me like I was crazy. "In the hotel?"

"Yeah."

"No, it's way too expensive," he said.

"Wait, they don't give you a free room?"

He shook his head. "Not even a discount. It's really more like a landlord-tenant relationship." He explained that the arrangement included advertising in the casino, a theater named after him, and use of this nuclear-fallout-shelter-depth dressing room, but no hotel suite.

At the time, I myself was performing a weekly one-man comedy show in my neighborhood in California.

It was at a tiny local theater, just fifty-four seats plus a few rarely occupied overflow stools in the balcony. All week leading up to Friday's performance, I would worry about whether I'd sell enough tickets on Eventbrite and Groupon to fill the room, or at least enough so the show wasn't, like, awkward. Unfilled seats kill the vibe. I mean, have you ever watched a comedy movie in an empty theater?

Some Fridays I couldn't even *give away* enough tickets to fill a few rows. Like, for free. And believe me, I tried. I offered complimentary tickets to friends, Starbucks baristas, homeless people, literally anyone. One Friday night, only eleven people showed up. Which is less like an audience and more like a support group.

Basically, ticket sales were always on my mind. But I'd always imagined that *someday* I could work my way up to a show like Piff's, where the marketing department of a casino megacorporation would take care of everything for me. I could just roll up at showtime and be funny.

Turns out, there's no such thing.

"My room seats two hundred people and they're crammed in there and it's the perfect room," Piff explained. "If you said to me, 'Okay, you can do that show ten times a week. They'll be sold out every night,' I would be happy. Totally done. That's my ambition. Unfortunately it doesn't work like that. You have to win Tournament of Laughs [a comedy competition on TBS that Piff had recently won] to keep having that job. Every time you get on *America's Got Talent* [Piff has, many times], it buys you another three to six months."

That's when I realized a Vegas residency is not the ultimate crowning achievement after all. It's just, like, another thing. Bigger league, same game.

"It's tricky because I love performing and I want to perform," he said. "The unavoidable collateral is you have to tell people, you have to persuade people to buy tickets, which means you have to be famous. It's unavoidable."

The saving grace for Piff, though, is that dragon suit. Because when he's not wearing it, he can hide in plain sight. He can be that third kind of famous, name famous, without being face famous.

As we sat in his dressing room recording an episode of his podcast, I found my eyes glancing back and forth between images of Piff the Magic Dragon—posters from past tours on the wall, novelty merch imprinted with his photo spilling out of boxes on the floor—and Piff the human, sitting in front of me. His real name is John, by the way. Which I always forget. You'll forget it, too, long before you forget the name Piff the Magic Dragon. He's found a niche that's part name fame and part feat fame, the feat fame being that he's the guy who shot a Chihuahua out of a cannon on *America's Got Talent*.[12]

He gets the best of all worlds: a stage name famous enough to sell tickets and perform onstage, but complete privacy when he's offstage. That's how Piff could sneak up on me upstairs, and that's also how he's beaten the fame system. If you can figure out a way to have some feat fame and name fame *without* face fame, you get many of the perks of fame with few of its downsides. Examples: famous author, scientist, or movie director.

Piff shrugs off credit for this cleverness, though. "From an objective point of view, I look at many areas of my act and I go, 'God, that is genius.' And unfortunately, it was one-hundred-percent unintentional." He says *unfortunately* because "if it was intentional, I would be a genius and would be able to tap into that at will and do something useful with it instead of dressing up in a dragon outfit and making children cry."

I asked, probably because despite my disappointment with the unglamorousness of Piff's lifestyle I still wanted to imagine it for myself, what it was like to stand underneath

12 Piff says when he wears the dragon suit in public, people usually ask him if he's "that guy from *American Idol*." Note: He is not a singing dragon.

a giant marquee with your name on it or to see your face on a billboard.

It's bananas....Millions of people have seen my face and there's a billboard in the street [of me] that people just walk past. I can see it. I understand it. But then if I look too long at it, it all falls apart. It just sort of crumbles beneath me. And I'm like, *let's not think about this again.*

Piff recently shared with me a remark he'd heard from a famous comedian: The entertainment industry, this comedian had said, will eventually "chew you up and spit you out."

I asked him why he keeps doing it, if it's as bad as all that.

"It's exactly what life is," he said. "You're born and you die, and there's no exception. So it's embracing that."

Indeed, the death rate for humans has, unfortunately, remained consistently high throughout history. Similarly, every performer eventually reaches an extinction. A final show when they're not famous enough to sell tickets anymore.

"So, like, why not enjoy it while it lasts?" I suggested.

"Happens to everyone so you have to enjoy the present and be super grateful for it," he said. "And acknowledge that we live in a finite world with a beginning and an end."

For a person who "dresses up in a dragon outfit and exploits a Chihuahua for financial gain" (his words, not mine), Piff is a surprisingly deep thinker. The other day I asked Piff directly in an email: Is it possible for a famous person to be happy?

"It's possible," he wrote in a brief reply between multiple live performances packed into a single day. "But hard, I think."

HISTORY

Fame is a bee.
It has a song—
It has a sting—
Ah, too, it has a wing.

—EMILY DICKINSON, 1788

STUFF WE WILL LEARN IN CLASS TODAY:

- In ancient (pre-PFP) history, who had the first widely recognizable face?
- Whose was the first household name?
- Did someone, like, invent being a celebrity?

CHAPTER 5

Okay, class, take a moment to gather up your books, stop by your locker, and check your mentions to see if any of your content blew up during first period. It's time to head to second period: History.

So why study history? Don't we care about experiencing happiness—and maybe fame—like, *right now*? Well, to understand what it's like to be famous and/or happy today, first we have to figure out when and why people started getting famous in the first place. Which turns out to be a story that begins a long, long time ago.

Celebs have been forming power couples since Cleopatra hooked up with Mark Antony,[13] female voices have been getting marginalized since (long before) Joan of Arc, and influencers have been getting into public beefs since Caesar got *et tu*'d by Brutus. Even the word itself has remained nearly the same for thousands of years. The English word *fame* comes from the Latin *fama*. In Greek, the word was *fimi*. So yeah,

---

[13] Marcopatra? Cleotony?

the word has barely changed between Socrates talking about it way back in the day and you reading about it now.

In this class, we'll be searching history for *firsts*. First household name, first famous face, first celebrity. And along the way, we'll examine any clues these individuals left behind about the most important question of all: Were these extremely famous dead people...happy?

Contrary to what you might expect, trolls have existed since long before the invention of the internet comment section. Actually, they've been around as long as fame itself because history's first recorded trolling took place on the birthday of history's first famous person.

Who's history's first famous person, you ask? According to the world's foremost fame historian, Leo Braudy, that distinction belongs to Alexander the Great, who was born twenty-four hundred years ago.

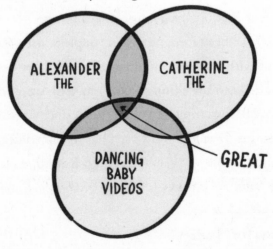

So let's talk about Alexander the Great—which is quite a mouthful, do you think he'd mind if we just called him Alex? Okay, yeah, he probably *would* mind...this is a guy whose last name is "the Great," after all. A guy who literally named seventy cities after himself...but hey, he's dead now, so we can call him whatever we want. Alex it is. Anyway, how could Alex be the first famous person? I mean, before Alex had become great or even been born:

1. King Tut was long buried with his pile of (totally cursed) treasure.
2. Socrates had already reasoned his way to death by hemlock poison cocktail.
3. Siddhārtha Gautama (the Buddha) had already been born (incarnated?) and had died (been reincarnated?).

But according to Dr. Braudy, Alex should get credit for being the first "famous person" because of (A) "his grappling with the problem of fame" and (B) "his constant awareness of the relation between accomplishment and publicity." Which is a fancy way of saying that if Alex was one of my Instagram followers, he would've clicked yes in that survey asking if you want to be famous. Also, if he was on Instagram, he definitely would've been one of those people who are always finding ways to brag on themselves in their feed. *Hey fam, here's a selfie in yet another country I conquered lol #blessedbythegods #thegreat*

We're used to that kind of content today, but back in 356 BCE, vacay selfies and humble brags hadn't been invented yet. Alex was different from rulers who came before him because he tried to make his own name bigger than his job title. Which again, is something we're used to because in modern democracies: Leaders need personal name recognition so you'll vote them into office. But historically, the power was in the name of the office, not the person who held it. Think pharaoh, emperor, chief. It was the title, not the person. The only modern gigs that still work that way are the pope and the English monarchy, both of whom traditionally get rid of their birth name and take a new first name along with the title.

So yeah, that's how power has been passed on for most of history. Dynasty. Lineage. Fame by birthright, not by publicity.

That's why Alexander the Great is the world's first famous person instead of King Tut, Socrates, or Buddha. Because he was a self-promoter in the modern sense. Those other three happened upon fame less deliberately.

1. **King Tut**: King Tut wasn't even a particularly significant pharaoh in his time. He just happened to leave a stash of loot that was discovered

intact in the twentieth century by a media-savvy archaeologist.

2. **Socrates**: He did a lot of talking, sure, but never bothered to write any of it down. So not exactly a media publicity manipulator. It was in fact his protégé Plato who recorded much of his teachings.

3. **Buddha**: That's actually an adopted name meaning "enlightened one." He was born Siddhārtha Gautama. He set out to ease suffering, not become famous. We know very little about his historical life. He certainly didn't have a publicist.

I know you're rolling your eyes. Buddha didn't have a publicist? *Duh.* But guess who did? That's right, our boy Alex. Alex's personal publicist was a guy named Callisthenes, which sounds like the name of a trendy new ab workout but who was actually a close friend who traveled with him to write down his exploits.

Okay, so, back to that troll. Alex was born in 356 BCE, during the month we'd now call July (take note of that name). On the day of his birth, a dude named Herostratus burned down an important temple, the Temple of Artemis. Today it's considered one of the Seven Wonders of the Ancient World, but unfortunately you can't go see it because, like I said, Herostratus the Pyromaniac. He was caught and confessed to arson. They asked him the obvious question:

Why? Herostratus answered—can you guess?—that he did it to become famous. He knew a prince had been born that day and he wanted to go down as the guy who toasted a landmark on the future king's birthday.

What a troll, am I right?

In response to Herostratus's deed, the Greeks actually instituted a new punishment today called *damnatio memoriae* (literally "condemnation of memory"), in which a problematic citizen was not allowed to be mentioned in official inscriptions, carvings, or Instagram stories.

And yet! Here we are twenty-four hundred years later, still recording his name in a book. Which I guess makes me part of the problem? History doesn't remember the names of the people who built the temple, who caught the arsonist, or who passed the law that aggressively failed in its goal to sentence him to oblivion. But we do remember Herostratus, the original troll. In fact, his name today is sometimes used to refer to a person who commits a crime solely to become famous. In the 2018 movie *Assassination Nation* there's a hacker character who leaks people's cell phone data. The hacker's handle? Er0str4tus.

The point is, before the "first famous person" had lived even one single day, history remembers a guy who torched a building to get famous. So which came first, the chicken or the egg? The troll or the celebrity? Arguably, trolling is older than fame itself.

Of course, Herostratus isn't a household name. He's basically only semi-famous compared to Alex, who became...well, *really* famous. He secured himself a legacy by conquering south as far as Egypt and west as far as modern-day India. Many of those cities he renamed after himself are still around, by the way, including Alexandria, Egypt. What he might be most famous for, in fact, is being the guy who supposedly cried when he ran out of places to conquer.

Alex had become a king at the age of twenty. Before he was even old enough to legally drink—in our time, at least—he had left home to pursue (literal) world domination. He would never make it back home, dying at age thirty-two in what's now Iraq. By then, he'd become quite paranoid. He'd had a falling-out with his mentor, Aristotle. He'd had his best publicist/BFF Callisthenes executed for an assassination plot that may or may not have been a product of Alex's imagination. Which seems all the more unfair given that Callisthenes clearly did a bang-up job spreading the word about Alex's life, given how much we know about it today.

Deciding whether a historic figure was "happy" or not is a dicey proposition because the idea that individuals can or should pursue happiness is a pretty modern concept. Further, you never know what's actually going on inside a person, especially if that person is dead and has no actual insides remaining at this point. But still, if I had to describe how fame seems to have affected Alex's mental health, I'd say it was pretty negative. We'll be using emojis to describe the happiness of historic figures in this class.

ALEXANDER THE GREAT'S CELEBRITY EXPERIENCE

If you think about it, we only know hard facts about historical figures if someone was helpful enough to write them down—on a scroll, say, or on the walls of a pyramid. Basically, pics or it didn't happen. The point is, fame can't happen without media, which includes scrolls and pyramid walls. If fame is fire, media is firewood. Or if you prefer a carbon-neutral metaphor, if fame is a Tesla, media is electricity. Or maybe in this metaphor media is actually Elon Musk? Anyway, the point is, media is the essential fuel behind fame.

Media includes: ancient codices; flyers stamped on early printing presses; battery-powered megaphones; praise-hands emojis. Media is how we tell stories, how we communicate, and how we tell each other about someone else. Tell enough people and, well, that someone starts to get famous.

Media is so common today that we forget *there was a time when recorded media was incredibly rare.* Take paintings, for example. Today we see paintings, including very old ones, all the time. Like the *Mona Lisa* or the one where God and David are stretching to touch pointer fingers in the clouds like a socially distanced fist bump. Even if you've never seen them IRL, you've seen photos. It's easy to assume that the people who lived in Europe five hundred years ago when they were first painted would've also seen them. But no. Not only was there no Wikipedia, but public museums are actually a pretty recent invention. So historically, you might've been able to see religious art in a church, but portraits of living people hung exclusively in royal palaces and the dope mansions of the nobles who could afford them.

We often think of paintings as a window into history, but there was a time in that history before painting was invented. Even after it became common, common people didn't get to see much of it. The point is, every type of media had to be invented by someone, somewhere. Whenever a new form of media popped up, voilà, there was a new path to becoming famous.

CHAPTER 6

Alex was the first person to become both name famous and feat famous. Feats were kind of his thing, actually. Long before there was a Sword in the Stone, legend has it there was a Gordian knot. Same deal as that sword: Prophecy had it that whoever could untie the knot would rule all of Asia. Apparently, it was a really, really good tangle. Probably the same knot that any two pairs of wired headphones automatically tie themselves in if you put them in a drawer together. No one could get it untied. Alex couldn't resist a challenge like that. He marched his armies straight over to that knot (in modern-day Turkey), and...sliced through it with his sword. All the aspiring dictators who'd tried and failed to untie it were like, "Wait, you were allowed to just cut it? *Why didn't I think of that?!*"

You know the rest. The prophecy came true. Alex went on to conquer most of the known world at the time, going east all the way into territory in what is now India. Along the way, he became pretty name famous. We know he was aiming for that, too, because those seventy cities. But at the end, when he cried, I wonder if he wasn't secretly crying because even for all the fame he'd achieved, he'd never figured out how to get face famous. I bet he knew that if he went in public without his entourage, no one would recognize him. No selfie requests. For an emperor ruling much of the known world, that's gotta sting a little.

We have to wait a few centuries and cross the Aegean Sea from Greece to Rome to find an individual who figured out how to add face fame to the mix. Long before there was Instagram, before there was printing or realistic painting or any other method to spread your image, the original profile pic was...money. The metal coin. The first person we know for sure who printed their own face on money during their lifetime is one of the most famous people of all time: Julius Caesar.

It seems obvious to us now that if you want to be an A-list celeb, first and foremost you need the plebs to recognize your face. But in an era with very little media, printing your profile on coins was pretty creative. I mean, imagine if everyone's Facebook profile photo had always just been drawings of Greek gods and suddenly one girl comes along and is like, hey, what if I post *my own* photo here instead? She'd get talked about, that's for sure. Definitely get a bunch of friend requests. Other influencers might get jealous.

All of which is approximately how it played out for Julius.

Let's be real: Ancient coin-pressing technology wasn't

exactly 4K. It wasn't even HD. If you saw Julius walking around in normal person clothes, you probably would not have recognized him from the crude profile pic on your money.[14] That kind of face fame wouldn't come along, it turns out, for another fifteen hundred years. But the primitive face fame of Julius Caesar meant everyone at least knew what *a drawing of him* looked like. So even if they wouldn't have been able to pick him out of a police line-up, they could recognize the representation of his image. Which gave him power. For one thing, he paid his vast empire of soldiers with those coins. So just in case there was any question about who your sugar daddy was, the face right there on your denarius was a reminder whose side you should probably keep fighting for.

But as you may have heard, in the end, not quite everyone was on Julius's side. Specifically, I'm referring to the sixty senators, including his BFF, Brutus, who stabbed him. Make that *former* BFF...Brutus was presumably demoted in Julius's mind after the whole stabbing thing. On the other hand, friendship might not have been on Julius's mind at all during his final moments. According to ancient historian Suetonius, after getting stabbed twenty-three times, as he bled out on those steps, Julius took a moment

---

14 Double meaning alert: His coin depictions were literally in profile.

to arrange his toga, to make it *just so*. Talk about a guy with a carefully controlled public image.

JULIUS CAESAR'S CELEBRITY EXPERIENCE

That all happened two thousand years ago. You know how fish don't know they're in water? We're all the fish to Julius Caesar's water. He remains so famous we don't even realize we're all still floating in his legacy. If Alex invented name fame, Julius perfected it. Here are just a few of the ways Julius's name lives on:

- **C-section:** The procedure where a baby is surgically removed from the mother's belly is called a C-section, short for...*Cesarean* section. Why exactly this is named after Julius is a matter of debate (Was *he* born this way? Or was he just good at naming things after himself?), but clearly the name stuck.
- **Leadership titles**: After Julius, the future leaders of Rome started using his last name, Caesar, as their job title. Think about that. It would be like if the leader of the United States was called "the Washington" instead of "the president." But US presidents *do* appoint czars (derived from *Caesar*) to oversee specific

issues.[15] Russian rulers before 1917 were the original czars, or tsars. German emperors were kaisers, also derived from *Caesar*.

- **July**: July is named for Julius. August is named for his heir, Augustus. Those names were adopted after their lifetimes, but while he was alive, Julius invented leap days in February, part of a whole new calendar system called...wait for it...the Julian calendar. It's still used by the Eastern Orthodox church today.

- **Crossing the Rubicon**: This is a great expression you can use to impress your friends. It means passing the point of no return. The Rubicon was a river (it's still there, actually, in Italy) that Caesar led his army through and in doing so entered a civil war that would eventually lead to him becoming emperor.

- **Caesar salad**: Just kidding. It's often credited to Julius, but the salad was actually named for a chef named Caesar, not the emperor.

Clearly, Julius won all three categories of fame. I mean, the dude crushed it.

---

[15] The United States has had everything from drug czar to rubber czar to car czar. "Car czar" might sound more like a tagline in a cringey used car commercial, but Obama appointed one.

I guess that's the kind of fame I was hoping would result from landing a job at MTV. But unfortunately, all my initial efforts at emailing, calling, and snail-mailing Ocean MacAdams got no response. So my last and only hope was to approach him at the *Newsweek* conference, face-to-face.

I think we can agree that "out loud" is by far the most awkward form of talking. Particularly when it comes to something you're nervous about, like asking someone out. Or trying to get a job. In the first category, I've always had my trusty non-question opinion statement "We should hang out sometime," which usually gets a shrug and a casual agreement without me actually having to put my self-esteem on the line by asking a yes or no question. Sadly, no such pickup line exists for getting your first job. "You should put me on payroll sometime" or "We should hang out in your office with me as your employee sometime" just don't have the same ring.

I'd done some part-time work and internships in high school and college—I spent one summer working for a used car salesman (car czar?) and another working for a US senator (similar personality to that car czar, actually)—but working for Ocean would be my first real put-on-pants-and-go-to-an-office-for-money-type gig. So I was super-nervous to ask Ocean out, er, ask him for a job.

In between my two-a-day workouts for that fitness contest, I spent the next several weeks studying music charts and pop culture. I literally memorized the Top 40 charts. I read the music magazines and blogs. Like, all of them. By the day before the conference, I felt like I could do a pretty good impression of a guy who knows about cool music.

My family lived in Virginia. I was going to get up at like 3 AM, drive to Washington, DC, then take the 6 AM train to New York City.

I remember standing with my parents in the kitchen the night before.

"I'm so nervous," I said. "I wish tomorrow was over already."

"I'm sorry," my mom said.

"This is literally the worst feeling," I said, which could not have been true since like I said before, I'd had cancer. Also, by this time my mom had *also* had cancer, so I was basically saying my nervousness was worse than both our cancers.

But if my mom made this comparison herself, she didn't show it. "I'm sure it will go okay."

"Okay? It will be *great*!" said my dad. He's more of what you'd call a glass-is-half-full kind of person, while my mom is more of a glass-is-fragile-don't-break-it-or-we'll-have-to-pay-for-it kind of person.

I lay in bed awake that night, staring at the ceiling, going over scenarios in my mind. Would there even be a chance to talk to Ocean at the conference? Would he have bodyguards to fend off the mobs of other students who wanted the correspondent job?

I wore my coolest outfit: Bright red Nikes with Olympic rings on the side, faded jeans, a well-worn thrift-store T-shirt under a blazer, and a Cub Scout hat with the brim rotated slightly off-center. The hat was meant to be ironic, but I'm actually an Eagle Scout and that had been my real Cub Scout hat ten years before. Sometimes it's hard to know the line between vintage and just, like, old.

At around 3 AM, I got out of bed (I didn't say "I got *up*" because that would imply I'd fallen asleep), showered, and set out for fame. The conference was at the *Newsweek* building in Manhattan, on a high floor with big glass windows overlooking the city.

After the keynote speeches, there were breakout sessions where each speaker, including Ocean, would be doing smaller, informal talks in boardroom-style rooms. I arrived early and got a seat only two chairs away from him.

Ocean was younger looking than I expected. He had a crew cut and wore a suit with no tie.

After some remarks, the big moment arrived.

"Any questions?" he asked.

I raised my hand.

He looked at me. I waited for him to say, "Yes?" or to point at me the way a teacher does when you raise your hand. But he said nothing and pointed at nothing. *Is he actually looking at me or just in my general direction? Does he see that my hand is raised?*

I didn't want to speak out of turn, or worse, start speaking at the same time as the person seated right behind me, like that thing where a stranger waves at you and you wave back only to realize they were actually looking at someone else. So I just waited, hand raised, not sure if we were making eye contact or not. The moment stretched for seconds, hours, days. The icebergs melted, the sun grew cold and collapsed into a black hole, sucking in the entire solar system with it.

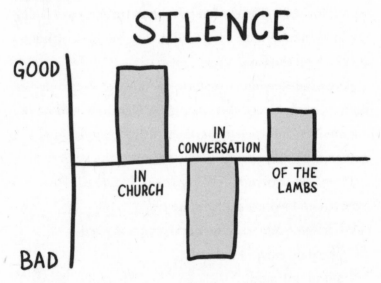

Finally, he raised his eyebrows.

"Yes?" he said, in a tone suggesting he had grown impatient with me sitting there like a waving mannequin.

"Oh, um...," I said, awoken from my trance. "In an interview three years ago, you stated bla bla bla."

Technically, the words were not *bla bla bla*—I was quoting some stuff to show how smart I was and how carefully I'd researched him, Ocean MacAdams, as though he was looking to hire not a news correspondent but a well-qualified stalker. His eyebrows furled, and then he gave an answer that I ignored while my attention returned to the knots in my stomach. *Was that the wrong question? Did I sound uncool?*

After the Q&A session ended, I fiddled with the contents of my shoulder bag on the floor, hoping maybe I'd get lucky and everyone else would exit, leaving Ocean and me alone in the room. Nope. Ocean stood up and walked out right away. I snatched my bag and caught him down the hall.

"Hi, Ocean, I'm Josh Sundquist," I said, extending a shaky, sweaty hand.

He shook it charitably.

Before I could launch into reciting a variation of the cover letter I'd both emailed and paper-mailed him, he said, "Yeah, I recognize you from the materials you sent."

"Oh, great," I said, realizing the whole time when I'd been frozen silently with my hand raised, he'd probably been thinking, *Oh, so THIS is the guy who overnighted photos of himself.*

Ocean was the celebrity. I was the crazed fan.

"So are you still trying to hire someone?" I asked.

"We're always on the lookout," he said noncommittally. My heart sank into my stomach. *Is that a nice way of saying no?*

"Cool, very cool," I said stupidly, as if this was a really fascinating piece of behind-the-scenes MTV gossip. I blinked once and dove in, my last-ditch blunt pitch. "Well, I'd love to talk to you about why I'd be a great choice."

There. Finally. It was out there. I wouldn't have to look back and wonder what if.

"Are you still in school?" he asked.

"Yes," I said.

"Here in New York?"

"No, in Virginia. But I could commute," I said. "Or just finish later."

He frowned. "Okay, well, we'll keep you in mind."

It was a polite but clear rejection.

"Nice to meet you," I said, somehow faking a smile and offering another handshake.

But I don't give up that easily. I might have a hard time working up the nerve to ask someone for a date or a job, but once I've been rejected, I'm really good at awkward follow-up. *Good* probably isn't the right word there because awkwardness isn't a useful skill, like woodworking or cooking or something. That said, persistence past the point of likely failure *can* be useful *sometimes*, like if you're trying to get to the Olympics.

But if you're trying to get famous by being on MTV, it's more annoying than anything else. Like, move on already. And in the case of dating, it's definitely not good. As you'll be aware if you've read my other books, in college I asked for a girl's number and then called her every day for the entire summer—she never picked up—because I didn't know about caller ID or social norms. Yikes.

Anyway, I emailed Ocean pleasantly persistent emails—not daily but, like, monthly—for the rest of the summer. *Hey Ocean, here are eight hot story ideas I think your viewers would be interested in.* My emails were friendly and insightful in all the ways my original I-am-robot-beep-beep cover letter was not. In the fall, after I'd sent in my before-and-after photos for that fitness contest and returned to college, Ocean finally replied to one of my emails.

In the 0.02 seconds it took for me to click open the email, a hundred thoughts ran through my head. Well, the same thought, one hundred times. *Am I going to get on MTV after all?*

"These are good ideas," he said. "I don't think you're right for us on-camera, but if you want, I could put you in touch with the people who hire our PAs."

I've observed that when people describe something as "bittersweet," they usually just mean bitter but want to put a fake positive spin on things. So when I tell you that reading that email was *bittersweet*, know that I choose that word deliberately. It was sweet because, finally, at last, Ocean MacAdams had replied to one of my emails. Not only that, he was essentially offering me a job. Which was what I'd been wanting this whole entire time.

But not "right for us on-camera" was a bitter blow. PA stands for production assistant, the entry-level job in the entertainment industry. PAs fetch coffee and make copies. Which is fine, you have to start at the bottom to come out on top, but PA is the first rung of a career path *behind the camera*, not in front of it. Talent becomes famous. PAs make them so.

It would be like if your goal was to play in the WNBA so you tried out for a team, sent some follow-up emails, and then they were like, "Hey we don't think you can play on the court, but we could use a new janitor." You might still take that job if you were obsessed with working for the WNBA in any capacity, but you'd do so knowing that being a janitor is not a path to a spot on the team someday.

I was devastated. Inside, that is. I never told anyone other than my parents about any of this. My friends had no idea I'd spent the summer studying music and pop culture to try to get a job at MTV. Like I said back in the introduction, admitting you want to be famous feels distasteful, even icky.

To be sure, the MTV News job appealed to me for more reasons than just getting on TV. I thought it would be the most exciting place in the world to work, and I genuinely loved the journalism thing. But it still felt, like, shameful. So I hid it inside. I'm not saying my feelings were special or anything. I'm sure my friends were hiding their own flavor of sad. We humans are all just projecting images of ourselves, and we have been for all of history, except for occasional moments when the mask cracks, and like Alexander the Great, we cry. Famous and non-famous people feel the same under the mask. The only difference is how many times that mask gets photographed—or minted on coins.

CHAPTER 7

If I was to ask you to name the most famous people of all time, some of the names on your list would probably be people who founded religions: Buddha, Jesus, Muhammad, L. Ron Hubbard, etc. And while those first three are undoubtedly among the most famous humans who ever lived, they're different from Alexander the Great because, surprisingly, it's difficult to tell if they actually wanted to be famous.

But before we get into that: I realize I'm stepping into sensitive territory here, but you can't have a book about fame without at least mentioning this group. So let's take a moment to look at religious fame from a historical perspective, operating under the positive assumption that the founders of major religions did so with a genuine intention of making the world a slightly less sucky place to live.

First of all, were these religious founders trying to become famous? It's less clear than we'd assume. For one thing, in historic times it wasn't obvious that a person *could* become famous. Without modern media, the only reliable path to fame was to become a conquering ruler in the mold invented by Alex and Julius.

I am going to focus on Jesus here because, having come up in the Christian tradition myself, he's the figure I feel best equipped to discuss. The Jesus of the Gospels repeatedly rejects attempts by his followers to make him king via a coup. This Jesus is constantly finding ways to slip out of crowds, to escape to the mountains or in a boat to get away from his fans. Furthermore, after he heals people, Jesus specifically instructs people *not to tell anyone* about it. Imagine a TV preacher today who conducted miraculous healings...but only after the lights and cameras are turned off. And then telling the healed person to keep it secret. Not exactly the fast track to big viewership ratings.

In church, I often hear I should be more like Jesus. Which is why I'm always telling people to follow me. Zing! But seriously, folks. Even if you prefer to argue the founders of major religions just did it to be famous, they certainly did not succeed on a large scale in their own lifetimes. There just wasn't a way to transmit information quickly like there is today. In those days, it would take decades or centuries for a new religion to build organizational infrastructure and spread across continents.

The Gospels record a story where Jesus asks someone to hold up a coin. Jesus asks whose face is on it. The crowd tells him Caesar's face is on the coin. (Jesus *and* Caesar in the same story! Was this moment the world's first creator collab?!) The image on this coin could likely have been the heir to Julius Caesar, Caesar Augustus, sometimes called Octavian, or just Gus,[16] who ruled during the time of Jesus.

Here's the fascinating thing, though. During Jesus's lifetime, his fame would pale in comparison to that of Augustus. Like, there were no commemorative Jesus coins. Gus ruled over the largest empire on the planet. He was like the world's number one K-pop act while Jesus was more of a local indie act who sometimes performed at regional festivals. We take it for granted today that the original entrepreneurs of organized religion are some of the biggest names of history. But at the time, no one would have believed images of Jesus would someday be more common than images of Caesar.

Anyway, I know you probably don't want to hear any more about religion. I get it. Religion comes with baggage, and that baggage is stuffed full of controversy. Sometimes, though, the controversy is what helps propel fame. I know because that's how it happened in my first brush with feat fame.

---

16 Actually he's never called Gus, except maybe in the context of his namesake in *The Fault in Our Stars*, a book I bring up solely to mention: Guess whose name is in the *Fault in Our Stars* acknowledgments?

* * *

My before and after photos for that fitness contest turned out pretty great. You've seen images like this in advertisements, and you've always said to yourself, yeah, but look how much of it is just that they're frowning in the before and grinning in the after. And you were completely correct.

So for the "before" picture, I hung up a sad sheet as a backdrop (deliberately droopy and not entirely covering the closet behind it). I wore frumpy gray boxers, adopting a pose that was exactly the opposite of everything your mother taught you about good posture. My hair looked like I'd just narrowly escaped an explosion. I'd been smearing Vaseline on my face for days in an attempt to cause acne.

Over the next eighty-four days, I worked out. Hard. Like three hours a day. And I definitely gained some muscle and whatnot. But for the "after" photo, I also did a bunch of hacks I'd read about on bodybuilder message boards: carb loading, salt depletion, and general dehydration. None of which is healthy, by the way, so, like, don't try this at home. Anyway, photos technically only capture the photons bouncing off your epidermis,[17] which is to say that for a fitness photo, your outer appearance is at least

17 The scientific name for skin. Why does it sound so gross?

as important as what's going on underneath. Which is why the fake tan, the body hair removal, the teeth whitening.

I hired a pro photographer who angled the lights just right to make all those muscles pop. Oh, and the oil! I slathered baby oil on my chest to make the contours better reflect the light. LOL. And also: ick.

In the end, I won the fitness contest. Which was cool. I got a bunch of protein shakes. And enough money to pay for grad school. (Worth it?) Anyway, a couple years later, the photos blew up online, and my Instagram tags have been flooded with re-shares ever since. Literally, to this day, a decade later.

People can't believe how different I looked in the before versus the after. I mean literally, they can't believe it. Whenever they get shared, people accuse me of photoshopping my face onto a bodybuilder's body. Others then come to my defense and say it's a legit and inspiring transformation. These comments escalate into snarky arguments and name-calling until, inevitably, Hitler is mentioned.[18] This used to make me really, really upset. The first time the photos blew up on a site called 9gag, I read thousands of the

---

[18] In case you've never heard of Godwin's law, it states: "As an online discussion grows longer, the probability of a comparison involving Nazis or Hitler approaches one," which is to say, comment wars inevitably devolve into Nazi comparisons.

comments. They accused me of being a liar, a fake, and "not even that good at Photoshop." I would reply: You don't know about the endless hours in the gym, the fake tan, the melted Reese's by the side of the road. But in the entire history of the world, no one's mind has ever been changed by something they read in an internet comment section—though you wouldn't know it from the essay-length political comments your uncle feels compelled to post on Facebook.

My photos even get used without my permission in ads to sell workout equipment or fitness supplements. Which is kind of, you know, infuriating. I mean, at least send me a free sample first.

My name was never on the photos themselves at first, and my body rather than my face was the prime exhibit, so all this was a kind of internet feat fame. A small amount, but enough to expose me to a major downside of fame: Fame is a target. The bigger the target, the more the arrows. People cheer for your fame when it first starts growing, but they will just as happily shoot it full of holes once it's big enough to hit easily. Witness: the indie band that goes mainstream, the small influencer who scores a major brand deal and buys a mansion.

Those arguments in the comments about whether my photos are fake are infuriating, but weirdly, it's the controversy itself that makes the photos so viral. Arguments draw eyeballs, so social media algorithms promote controversial posts. The more people hate on those photos, the more popular they become.

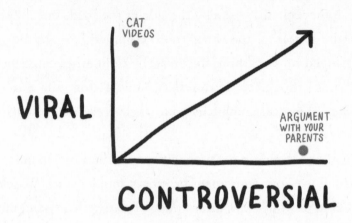

I went to great lengths to manipulate my body to match the image I knew the contest judges were looking for. But interestingly, if this contest had been fifty years ago, or a hundred, or five hundred, the "look" of the perfect body as judged by society would be entirely different. I was recently talking to Dr. Braudy about the history of fame. He observed that the definition of fame mutates over the centuries according to what a culture believes a "perfect person" is.

This morphing definition will help us explain a weird phenomenon. So far in History class, I've name-checked a bunch of people who were born before the year 1 CE. But how many historical figures can you name who lived between 1 and, say, the year 1400 CE? Weird, right?

CHAPTER 8

Yeah, so um…what's up with the Middle Ages?

Sometimes this era is called the Dark Ages. It's so named not because the human experience was such a bummer at the time—although it was that, too; I mean, *Game of Thrones* is set in a fictional version of this era—but because we have so little record of much of anything happening. It's as if humanity went dark for, like, a thousand years.

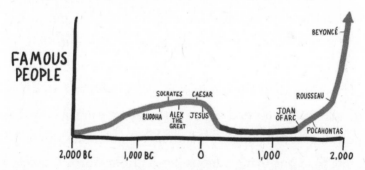

FAMOUS PEOPLE

BEYONCÉ

SOCRATES   CAESAR   ROUSSEAU

BUDDHA   ALEX THE GREAT   JESUS   JOAN OF ARC   POCAHONTAS

2,000 BC   1,000 BC   0   1,000   2,000

I mean, don't get me wrong, some things did happen. Genghis Khan sired millions of descendants. The Mayans built temples. Marco Polo discovered a swimming pool game. But most of us really struggle to name any, you know, *celebs* from the Middle Ages: like the years between

500 and 1500 CE. As Dr. Braudy says, in a time when communication was super slow and people died super young, basically no one became famous—at least not "in the sense of having an immediate audience."

But why, though? Religion was a major factor. Ever heard the word *iconoclast*? It originally referred to people who went around destroying religious images (icons) and the artists who created them. Sounds weird to us since most religions today are basically obsessed with paintings and statues and stained glass, but at one time or another throughout history, all major religions had internal factions of iconoclasts repressing their media. Which can be a real bummer if your goal is to become face famous.

The leading forms of government at the time didn't help, either. There were tribal societies in much of the world, where by definition, it's tough to be famous outside your tribe or community. Larger states were organized into monarchies and dynastic empires. In that kind of setup, where power is concentrated in one person, pretty much only that person gets to be famous. Modern example: Can you name more than one living famous person from North Korea?

Things start to change at the time of the Renaissance. The major game changer: the movable-type printing press, which sparked a long-term decline in the cost of books. By one estimate, the price of a book in the Middle Ages was fifty times higher than the price of a book by the time the

Declaration of Independence was signed in the 1700s. You know when you see the expensive hardcovers in the new release section and you wish you could afford, like, *all* of them? Imagine if they were marked on sale...for 98 percent off. Like I said, game changer. Anyway, that all started in 1450, when Gutenberg invented that movable-type press in the European city of Mainz.

Get this. For scientists and artists born in the hundred years after the printing press was invented, the closer they were born to Mainz, the more likely they are to still be famous today. Why? Access to media lets you get your name out there. That hasn't changed, right? Today, the closer you live to Los Angeles, the more likely you are to become a movie star. Or the closer you live to Silicon Valley, the more statistically likely you are to become an obnoxious tech bro.

Printed words were a big step for fame, but to become a celebrity you need more than text. I mean, no one reads the articles in celebrity tabloids, am I right? Show us the candid photos of the famous people carrying shopping bags and lounging on the beach, please. In order for *celebrity*, not just fame, to blow up, there needed to be a way for the masses to have access to images. The big moment for celebrity was upgraded woodblock printing. Woodblocks are like a rubber stamp, except the rubber part is made out of hand-carved wood. Woodblocks made it cheaper to reproduce images, meaning newspapers could include images alongside their text and regular middle-class people could finally afford to hang portraits of their favorite monarch, enlightenment philosopher, classical composer, or actor. As early as 1675 (!) there were woodblock-printed illustrations in Japan of Kabuki actors performing onstage.

Although our concept of *fame* traces back two thousand years to classical Greco-Roman civilization, the flavor of fame we call *celebrity* first appeared three hundred years ago in Paris, France.

Paris has been the trendsetter of Western civilization since Louis the XIV, aka the Sun King—who also, incidentally, used portraits of himself to make sure everyone knew who was boss. Louis was basically the Steve Jobs of the Renaissance. Here are just a few of the inventions that emerged in Paris under Louis XIV:

- Streetlights
- Mailboxes with pickup three times per day and delivery within four hours—(like, what...modern snail mail doesn't even come close to that)
- Organized public transportation system with set routes and bus stops, er, carriage stops
- A centrally organized urban police force

So yeah, basically every modern thing except the iPhone started in Paris.

There are few things celebrities seem to enjoy more than award shows. So I'd like to turn this portion of today's History class into an award show where we'll honor many of the celebrity-related firsts that happened in Paris during this era. Fun fact: All the people below were born before 1776, so contrary to popular belief, the pop culture system of the United States did not invent celebs. French celebrities were autographing parchment long before anyone got famous by signing the Declaration of Independence.

FIRST TO DEFINE THE WORD *CELEBRITY*
Charles Pinot Duclos (1704-1772)

By the mid-eighteenth[19] century, there was an emerging need to name this new type of person who somehow everyone has heard of and is curious about...*even though*

---

19 Sidenote about the names of centuries: This has always confused me, but the eighteenth century actually means the 1700s. If you see a "teenth" on the century, that means you take that number and subtract a hundred. So the nineteenth century is the 1800s, the twentieth century is the 1900s, etc.

that person isn't royalty. English writer Samuel Johnson proposed *celebriousness* as a synonym for fame. But everyone was like, um, no thanks, autocorrect hasn't been invented yet. Author Charles Pinot Duclos proposed the winner, *celebrity*. Incidentally, it's basically the same word in English as in French except for, you know, the accent(s): *célébrité*.

FIRST CELEBRITY TO BARTER AN IMAGE OF THEIR FACE
Sir Isaac Newton (1643–1727)

If you see an A-lister's face on the cover of a magazine, you can be sure they have something new (movie, album, etc.) to sell you. For celebs, the rights to their image is literally the business model. Probably the first to realize this was Sir Isaac Newton. A Frenchman named Pierre Varignon was asking for a portrait of him, but Newton kept saying no. Giving a portrait, after all, meant sitting still for hours while someone painted you. Eventually, Newton struck two deals with Pierre: one portrait in exchange for help writing a book, another if Pierre got his friend to endorse Newton's new theories about calculus. Pierre hung his limited edition portrait in his home in—where else—Paris.

FIRST INSTA MODEL TO BE BODY-SHAMED
Emma, Lady Hamilton (1765-1815)

Long before gossip blogs were drawing red arrows on celeb bikini photos to call out supposed flaws, Emma, Lady Hamilton, got fat-shamed for profit. Born poor, she hustled her way up from prostitute to model to aristocratic mistress and world-famous pinup model. Engraved prints of her hung in homes across Europe. Historian Antoine Lilti noted, "Emma was not painted because she was famous, she became famous because she was painted. Her face was her fame before being a name." Basically, she was the OG Instagram model. But as she aged, a cartoonist made money from viral drawings of her as deformed and obese. Ugh, trolls. Sidenote: She was born in England but died in France, where celebrities of that era all seemed to congregate.

FIRST CELEBRITY TO TAKE A BREAK FROM TWITTER
Nicolas Chamfort (1740-1794)

Although Nick Chamfort is not especially famous today, he deserves at least an honorable mention here for being the first celebrity to write a lot about *being* a celebrity.

A well-known writer in his time, he wrote, "Celebrity is the advantage of being known to people who we don't know, and who don't know us." That kind of snark would've made Chamfort a hit on Twitter today. Another ironic Chamfort tweet: "I had as much hatred for celebrity as I had love for glory." Just like the Twitter account that goes dark after gaining so many followers that the account holder has a nervous breakdown, Chamfort eventually withdrew from Paris in search of solitude and privacy in the countryside.

FIRST ACTOR TO GET MOBBED WHILE TRYING TO SHOP
Mary Robinson (1758–1800)

Mary Robinson was an actor and novelist from London, not France. But she did live in France for a while. She was the first person to describe a scenario we might otherwise assume was only invented in the recent age of paparazzi: She was too famous to go shopping in peace. "I scarcely ventured to enter a shop without experiencing the greatest inconvenience," she wrote. Long before A-listers couldn't get their car out of the driveway because of the fans camped out there, Mary had the horse-drawn equivalent of the same problem. She wrote, "Many hours have I waited till the crowd dispersed which surrounded my carriage."

FIRST UNAUTHORIZED CELEBRITY MERCH
Benjamin Franklin (1706-1790)

It wasn't until Ben visited Paris that he realized just how world-famous he'd become. In a letter to his daughter, Ben said he'd found images of his face "set in lids of snuff boxes, and some so small as to be worn in rings; and the numbers sold are incredible. These, with the pictures, busts, and prints, (of which copies upon copies are spread every where) have made your father's face as well known as that of the moon." Being that this was a father writing to his daughter, he even threw in a cringey dad joke: "It is said by learned etymologists that the name *Doll*, for the images children play with, is derived from the word Idol; from the number of *dolls* now made of [me], [I] may be truly said, *in that sense*, to be *i-doll-ized* in this country." Um, you lost me at "etymologists," Ben. Stick with inventing electricity.

FIRST LEAKED NUDES
Voltaire (1694-1778)

In 1772, centuries before internet-breaking leaked nudes, artist Jean Huber painted the philosopher Voltaire in a semi-intimate scene: in his bedroom, struggling to pull up a pair of pants over his...yikes...bare thighs! The painting was a sensation. Engravings basically went viral, popular across Europe. You can imagine a similar image on TMZ today. *Celebrities! They're just like us! They pull their pants on one leg at a time!* Voltaire wrote, "The sacrifice one has to make for this unhappy celebrity, which it would be so nice to exchange for peaceful obscurity."

FIRST ONE-NAMER
Rousseau (1712-1778)

Before today's one-name-basis celebrities shed their last names (Oprah! Beyoncé! Zendaya!), *Jean-Jacques* was the original one-namer. History remembers him as Rousseau, but in his day everyone referred to him as Jean-Jacques. Everyone in Paris knew the name. One newspaper described the crowd that formed when he was spotted at a café. "We asked half of the people what they were doing there; they answered that they had come 'to see Jean-Jacques.' We asked them who Jean-Jacques was, and they answered they had no idea, but he was passing by." Basically, he was the original "famous for being famous." Another writer recalled, "We knew that Jean-Jacques frequented a certain café: we rushed there to see him, but he no longer went there."

Fast-forward three centuries, people are still trying to spot celebs at cafés. My wife was recently at a vegan restaurant near where we live in LA. She heard a familiar laugh from the table right beside her. No, it couldn't be! She turned, and it *was*: Jay-Z. He was dining with Chris Martin of Coldplay. Chris's girlfriend, actress Dakota Johnson, was there. Apparently, this was Chris Martin's birthday dinner. There was a birthday cake. They even sang him "Happy Birthday." Imagine that: Hova singing "Happy Birthday" to the lead singer of Coldplay. This being LA, the other diners pretended not to notice. But how could you not?

Ever since that night, my wife has been hinting that we should go back to that restaurant because "we might see a celebrity." It's the exact same effect Rousseau's presence was having on any cafés he visited in Paris nearly three hundred years ago.

This was the point in history when people first became fascinated by celebrities' personal lives, and when the media started covering such things. One time Rousseau's dog went missing. It made the next day's newspaper. Then he found it. Another article. Which maybe sounds weird until you consider that in 2021, Lady Gaga's dogs were stolen and it was *huge national news*.

Rousseau was the original "be careful what you wish for" celebrity. He was born in Switzerland and, like aspiring stars today who move to Hollywood, Rousseau relocated to Paris specifically to get famous. He wanted, in his own words, "to arrive at a celebrity which in the fine arts is always joined with fortune in Paris."

Eventually he did "arrive." Surprise, surprise, it did not make him happy. He hated the constant stream of strangers who knocked on his door. He compared himself to an exotic zoo animal. "Those who only want to see the Rhinoceros should go to the fair and not my home," he wrote. His friend Bernardin de Saint-Pierre recounted a conversation with Rousseau: "I told him they came because of his celebrity. He repeated, greatly irritated: Celebrity! Celebrity! The word infuriated him: the celebrated man had made the sensitive man very unhappy."

Basically, Rousseau had become face famous and was annoyed to discover face fame is only skin-deep. In an unpublished essay discovered after his death, he wrote, "As soon as I had a name I no longer had any friends," which could easily have been written by any celebrity today complaining that once you're famous, people see you for your fame, not for you. Rousseau wrote this in a book called *Reveries of the Solitary Walker* (um, emo title much?): that people knew his face, but they didn't know *him*. Like, they didn't know his actual personality. And that made it hard for him to hang out with anyone.

Rousseau was also disappointed to discover people were more interested in the equivalent of getting a selfie with him than in reading his books.

> Persons who had no taste for literature, nor had many of them read my works...travelled thirty, forty, sixty, and even a hundred leagues [350 miles] to come and see me, and admire the illustrious man, the very celebrated, the great man, etc.

That quote doesn't sound too strange to us today because we are used to the idea that superfans will travel a long distance to meet a celebrity. But this kind of behavior was new. Superfans had just been invented.

Anyway, Rousseau's annoyance at people showing up to meet him even though they'd never read his books is just like when movie stars get tired of interviews where all the questions are about, like, who they're dating, not the craft of acting. Rousseau was the blockbuster actor who shifts to serious roles in small indie movies only to discover everyone still wants to talk about a vampire movie they did a million years ago.

When John Green's book *Paper Towns* was made into a movie starring Nat Wolff and Cara Delevingne, Cara did a bunch of interviews, as movie stars do when their movie releases. She got tired of getting asked the same annoying questions over and over. So she started giving sarcastic answers. "I never read the book or the script, I just winged it," she said after being asked for the umpteenth time whether she'd read the book. But she said it on camera. Surprise, surprise the moment went viral.

John, author of the book she was joking about not having read, wrote a Medium post defending her. He himself had done over *three hundred* on-camera interviews about the movie, and he was tired of hearing the same lazy questions that reduced the complex ideas of his books down to sound bites. He was also tired of seeing the actors asked about whether their co-stars were good kissers or not. Far from being offended by Cara's sarcasm about his book, he was on her side because, he wrote, "The whole process of commodifying personhood to sell movie tickets is inherently dehumanizing."

Maybe Rousseau would've felt better if he could've read John's Medium post and learned that he may have been the first, but certainly wouldn't be the last celeb to have their personhood dehumanized. At any rate, clearly Jean-Jacques's celebrity did not make him happy. Most of the people we looked at in this last chapter didn't leave us enough clues to clearly judge the effect of fame on their happiness, but Rousseau wrote plenty about his disappointment with celebrity.

ROUSSEAU'S CELEBRITY EXPERIENCE

As we've seen, fame happens when media technology happens. As Sharon Marcus writes in her book *The Drama of Celebrity*, "Any invention that increases how far and how fast communications can travel will amplify celebrity culture." Fame has recently blown up bigger than ever before because the internet blew up, phones blew up, social media blew up. If it seems like everyone wants to be famous all of a sudden, it's because compared to the rest of history, all that media tech appeared pretty suddenly, too, offering countless new ways to gain followers.

Just like living near the printing press during the Renaissance made someone more likely to become famous, similar calculations show that in the last century, the more radios and TVs per person in the country where you were born, the more likely you were to grow up to become a famous athlete or performer. This was true regardless of the wealth and total population of your country. More communication devices equals more famous people, period.

Photography was just invented in the 1800s, and photos were pretty rare during that century. Pop quiz: Who do you think was the most photographed American of the 1800s?

Most people would guess Abraham Lincoln. A good guess. In fact, he was the first presidential candidate to use his photo as campaign swag. He made little business cards with his photo on them. Abe credited that photo gimmick as the thing that got him elected. By the way, here's an example of how far media has come since: After Lincoln was assassinated, estimates are that it took months before a majority of the United States population had heard the news. Months! A century later, when John F. Kennedy was shot, the majority of Americans knew about it within *twenty-five minutes*. Imagine how fast news like that would spread today.

Oh, and it turns out the most photographed American of the 1800s (making him, at the time, one of the most photographed people in human history!) was *not* Abraham Lincoln. Yes, he sat for a lot of photos, but not as many as Frederick Douglass, the writer, orator, and abolitionist. Douglass had his photo taken whenever possible, at least one hundred sixty times during his life. I know what you're thinking: a hundred sixty in his entire lifetime? No big deal. I took a hundred sixty selfies...yesterday. But photos were rare back then. Which made them all the more powerful. Douglass saw photos as a way to fight slavery and racism. Unlike drawings and cartoons, which were frequently distorted into racist caricatures of Black people, photos couldn't be edited (oh, the good old days before Photoshop!). So for Douglass, distributing photos of himself—always well-dressed, always staring confidently into the camera, always sporting that signature hair—was a tool of anti-racism. "Pictures come not with slavery and oppression," he wrote, "but with liberty, fair play, leisure, and refinement."

Indeed, like all forms of privilege, fame has been historically concentrated among white guys. Fame is a currency just like money, like power, like privilege within any system. We'll look more specifically at marginalized people and fame in our next class, but in terms of History, the thing to remember is that Frederick Douglass was the first person to harness the invention of photography and the power of face fame for the specific purpose of fighting unjust systems—including the system of fame itself.

SOCIAL STUDIES

Even though I'm happy, I feel like I was a little bit happier two or three years ago when I had less money. I had less people who had opinions about my life. I felt like my life was mine. Now I feel like I don't even own my life. I feel like the world owns me.

—CARDI B

STUFF WE WILL LEARN IN CLASS TODAY:

- In our society, who gets to be famous? Perhaps more important, who *doesn't* get to be famous?

- Are there artists who are just so good at what they do that they can't help becoming popular? In other words, is it possible to be famous against your will?

- Is infamy different from the regular kind of fame?

CHAPTER 9

Okay. Let's say I'm telling you about a famous person's internet content. I tell you about a funny video they made—say, a great sketch that nailed parent-teen relationships. LOL, you say in response. Now I tell you that the creator has something *different* about them, something non-mainstream, something identifying them with a marginalized group. Does this change how you think about the video I just told you about? Does it change how you think about the creator?

Pause and ask yourself this question, because it matters, and it's what we'll be examining in today's Social Studies class. I'm defining social studies as the study of society, especially its structures and institutions that might sort of suck. As you might have heard, society still has some flaws. We're trying to iron them out, but we keep finding more wrinkles.

Look, no one wants to think they are part of the problem. And most of us tell ourselves that we don't judge anyone by the color of their skin or the shape of their body.

Other people, terrible people who live in the dark corners of the internet, do that kind of thing. We are not *those* kinds of people.

Like I said, that's what we like to tell ourselves.

The issues surrounding justice, equality, and racism are too important to ignore in a book about fame because marginalized groups are also marginalized when it comes to the opportunity to become famous. And the problem starts with us, the fans, the consumers of celebrity. Because we do make judgments, even unconsciously.

As a straight white man, I'm not particularly qualified to unpack the impact of systemic racism for you, nor do I have the life experience to examine how LGBTQ+ rights intersect with fame. I'll be bringing in a few other voices that can offer perspectives I don't have.

But I do have one particular area of life experience that's relevant here. I don't want to imply my experience is universal to other marginalized groups, but it happens to be the only one from which I can speak with authority, so it's what I'm going to focus on in this chapter. My hope is that my personal situation might offer some insight when we think about fame in relationship to other problematic structures in society.

Okay, so I was recently at this museum near where I live in Los Angeles. It's called the Getty. It's definitely a "museum famous" museum...if that's a thing. Very picturesque place, up on a hill. Anyway, so I'm looking at the art and I come across this painting by Édouard Manet, who, like the museum itself, is famous among fancy art people. What struck me about the painting was the shape of the subject's body: He had only one leg. We see him from behind, walking along a sidewalk on a pair of crutches. He's actually a small part of the painting. It's mostly a painting of the street itself, which is decorated with French flags to celebrate a French holiday. The painting is named after the street: *The Rue Mosnier with Flags*. The one-legged guy is sort of incidental.

A few things about this.

First, I had never seen a painting with an amputee in it. Like, ever. My wife studied art history in college so she loves, you know, art. And history. Which means that since getting married, I've been to at least the FDA-recommended lifetime dose of art museums. I could not think of another painting—and neither could she—featuring a person who just, like, happens to be going about their life with less than two arms or legs.

Second, I googled it, and weirdly it turns out that five years after he created this painting in 1878, Manet lost his own leg due to gangrene. His left foot was amputated, same as the guy in the painting. Weird, right?

Third, the painting stood out to me because I happen to have one leg. Like the dude in the painting—and Manet at the end of his life—I don't have a left leg, and when I walk down sidewalks, I do it on crutches.

If you know me from the internet, this isn't news to you. But if you randomly picked up this book because you liked the cover design or whatever, this information will come as a bit of a shock. I haven't mentioned it before now because (A) it hasn't seemed particularly relevant up until this point and (B) I wanted you to have the experience of asking yourself this: Does learning that there's something different about me, something that makes me identify with a group outside the mainstream, change the way you think about me? Does it change the way you imagine me sitting at my computer typing this sentence? Does it affect how you might have evaluated me if you were considering me for, say, a job on television??

Of course it does. You have new information, so your perspective has changed. Doesn't make you a bad person.

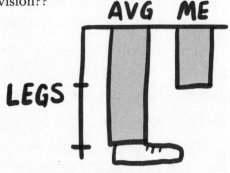

The thing about social studies is we prefer to study the problems of society from afar, thinking the problem is out there, with *them*, not with us. It's easier to go online and call out problematic tweets than to go inside and examine ourselves.

Obviously, there's nothing wrong with assuming I have two legs. But now you know otherwise, so by definition, you picture me differently. I trust you don't think *less* of me—you aren't that kind of person—but it's natural that you think differently about me.

See, even if we have the best of intentions, we can still make assumptions about people's body shapes. Those assumptions may not be negative. But when we group people according to our assumptions, well, that's where prejudice and even injustice take root.

Much better books have been written about these issues. So we will examine social studies narrowly, from the perspective of fame. Even more narrow still: through the lens of my particular experience.

Look, I'm pretty comfortable with myself and my body. I lost my leg, like, a long time ago, as a child.[20] So I'm just used to it.

What I'm not used to, unfortunately, is seeing someone who looks like me in a painting. Which is surprising since it's not like amputees are a recent invention. We've been around, like, for a while. But how many Renaissance

---

20 To answer your question: cancer.

paintings have you seen where anyone was short a body part?

Basically, the development of media hasn't provided equal benefits to all. I've seen few people who look like me on TV or in movies. I mean, there are plenty of characters who have had limbs chopped off—Luke Skywalker, Jaime Lannister, Peeta from *The Hunger Games* (well, in the book version)—but that's amputation as plot device, not disability as an aspect of a character. I mean, how many amputee actors can you name? For that matter, how many famous people from *any* category (singers, athletes, actors, etc.) can you name who have limb differences? It doesn't count, by the way, if they are famous *for* their injury (Bethany Hamilton of *Soul Surfer*, or the *127 Hours* guy).

Disability is underrepresented among famous people. Yes, President Franklin D. Roosevelt used a wheelchair, but he *had to keep it a secret*. America wasn't ready for that. More recently, there have been several people who use wheelchairs elected to Congress. There's even a current state governor who uses a wheelchair. Which is progress. Even so, I'm not sure FDR could win the presidency today, when modern media would prevent the wheelchair from staying secret.

Don't get me wrong. In the history of the world, I firmly believe there's never been a better time or place to be a person with one leg than right here and now. We've got the

Americans with Disabilities Act. There's widespread support for accommodations and equality in this area. Sometimes you even see people represented in the media who have, you know, nontraditional limb configurations.

But for all these reasons, I did have to wonder when I heard from MTV that I "probably wasn't right for on-camera," did he mean...you know? Like, it could be that they didn't need another white guy or that I totally lacked any relevant experience whatsoever, but I couldn't help but wonder if part of what made me not right was having one leg. To be very clear, I have no evidence that suggests Ocean or MTV was thinking this. But if he was, I wouldn't blame him and it would not lower my opinion of him as an overall chill dude who handled my aggressive job-seeking with grace and courtesy. From the few encounters I've had with him, I'm actually pretty sure he'd be super supportive of any person with a disability who had, you know, any training or experience or had done a job like this before. He did offer me that PA job, after all, which was all I was qualified for at the time.[21]

---

21 Ocean has long since left MTV. But while writing this book, I tracked down his current email address via some deep googling and lucky guesswork. I told him about what I was writing. He was kind enough to write back and did seem to remember me. Which was nice. To me, I guess he's always felt sort of like a celebrity.

But looking at the broader TV landscape, regardless of their personal support for people with disabilities, I suspect many entertainment executives worry their audiences are not ready for someone who looks so, you know, different. Otherwise, why wouldn't you see more bodies that look like mine on TV and in movies?

For years, Franchesca Ramsey made Black hair tutorials in relative obscurity. But then she burst into internet fame from her viral video "Stuff White Girls Say...to Black Girls." I'm using the word *stuff* here so PTAs won't ban my book from school libraries, but technically there was a different word there. Anyway, her video was piggybacking on another popular video at the time, "Stuff Girls Say—Episode 1," which was created by the authors of a Twitter account by the same name. Franchesca intended her video to highlight race relations in a funny and relatable way. But you've used the internet, right? So you can imagine that a video with a title and topic like that was, um, a bit polarizing. It gained her a lot of fans. But also a lot of haters.

"Going viral really is a double edged sword because it's brought so many amazing people and opportunities into my life, but there's also a lot of negativity online, and so being exposed to millions of people at once is bound to come with that," she told me.

She used to argue with the haterz, try to change people's minds, to show them how something they said was racist even if they didn't realize it. But not anymore. She's also cut back on how much time she spends on social media.

"These days when something I share goes viral or does 'well' online, I'm appreciative, but it doesn't really impact my day to day. No more crying at my desk over views!" she explained.

Franchesca has continued to make videos about race and social justice both on her channels and for MTV's YouTube channel. She's a cable news contributor. She was a recurring guest star in the final season of NBC's *Superstore*. And she wrote a book about it all titled *Well, That Escalated Quickly: Memoirs and Mistakes of an Accidental Activist*.

The famous names of history are disproportionately white, straight, able-bodied men. But why, though? Well, I decided to ask Franchesca, who identifies as Black and bisexual, how systemic racism has historically contributed to underrepresentation of people of color among celebrities.

One thing that I think is hard for some people to understand is that the systems of oppression go beyond one to one interactions. They permeate in such a way that everything is influenced. It's almost like squeezing a few drops of food coloring into a giant pool. You might not see the dye throughout, but it's still there, changing the color of the water. So for example, schools are funded by the tax dollars of their community. So if you live in a poor neighborhood, your school is going to be underfunded. If your school is underfunded you won't have access to brand new art supplies, instruments, or a state of the art performance space. These are the types of experiences that kids need to cultivate their talents in hopes of one day building a career in entertainment! Now of course you don't *need* to go to a fancy art school to make it or become famous, but upward mobility is about *access*. And unfortunately many POC are barred from that access due to historically racist practices in housing, hiring and education.

I told her that as a person with one leg, I haven't seen many people who look like me in TV or movies, but on the internet, I've had the freedom to build an audience directly. She agreed that the internet has opened similar doors for people of color. Not just to become internet famous, but to use the credibility of viral videos or massive follower numbers to transition to traditional entertainment.

"Without the internet we wouldn't have the likes of Issa Rae, Liza Koshy, and Lilly Singh, three very different women of color crushing it in mainstream media that haven't been relegated to Hollywood's very narrow definitions of what it means to be Black, Indian, or mixed race," she said.

We'll further explore how the internet is changing fame in our final class. But social studies wouldn't be complete without exploring a particular subtype of fame, which we'll discuss in the next chapter.

CHAPTER 10

Is it possible to become very famous without knowing it?

Weirdly, yes. At least, before the internet it was. Consider the strange case of Sixto Rodriguez, an American folk singer who recorded two albums in the early 1970s. They were flops. In the United States, that is. Without him realizing it, though, his albums blew up in South Africa. He and his music became a symbol of resistance to apartheid. In the words of record-store owner Stephen Segerman in South Africa, Rodriguez had recorded "one of the most famous records of all time." To South Africans, Rodriguez was "bigger than Elvis."

But his fans in South Africa heard and believed rumors that he was dead. So no one thought it was weird that, like, he didn't do concert tours or anything.

Decades later, a music journalist wanted to piece together how Rodriguez had died and what had become of the fortune he'd presumably made from his record sales.

So this writer traveled to every country Rodriguez mentions in his songs searching for clues. It's a long story that you can watch in the documentary *Searching for Sugar Man*, but (spoiler alert!) he and the record-store owner eventually tracked down Rodriguez in Detroit, where he was very much alive. Rodriguez had long since given up on music. He was working in construction. He and his children were so poor they'd spent time in homes that lacked indoor plumbing.

At first, Rodriguez couldn't believe he was famous on another continent, but the guys who found him persuaded him to come perform in South Africa. His first concert was in an arena with thousands of seats. It sold out. His fans sang along with every word of the songs he'd recorded nearly thirty years before. Rodriguez had become famous—literally a rock star—without even knowing it.

But is it possible to become famous *against your will*? If we're talking about people who go viral when they're caught on camera behaving badly, sure. But can an artist be so good at their craft that they just can't help but become famous, despite every effort not to be? I'm not sure. You might become famous as a side effect of your craft without *preferring* for that to happen—like Pauley from *NCIS*. But if you are absolutely dead set on staying anonymous, no one can make you a famous artist against your will.[22]

That's always the artist's conflict: Making a living as a musician or painter or actor requires some level of notoriety. So the artist who doesn't want to be famous has to choose between (A) making a living doing their art but losing their privacy or (B) retaining their privacy but not doing their art for a living.

When I asked my followers if they'd want to be famous, many said, "It depends on what I'd be famous for." Like, they would only be interested in fame for "the right reasons." And they'd never want it for the "wrong reasons."

So what are these wrong reasons for being famous? Who is famous but *shouldn't be*?

Your first answer might be, like, a mainstream band with a radio hit that you're sick of hearing. (Not talented! Doesn't deserve it!) Or a famous-for-being-famous-type beautiful person. (Not talented! Doesn't deserve it!)

When Dr. Sharon Marcus, author of *The Drama of Celebrity*, did an AMA on Reddit, this was the second-most up-voted question:

---

22   Don't try to tell me Banksy doesn't want to be famous. Sure, he hides his true identity, but his pseudonym is one of the most famous in the world. Maintaining that mystique requires hard work.

dj_milkmoney: It seems to make sense that people are interested in celebrities that are good at what they do...but what about celebrities like the Kardashians or Paris Hilton who have less definitive talents?

Prof_Sharon_Marcus: Many would say that Kim Kardashian and Paris Hilton are geniuses at being celebrities and that their talent is self-promotion and a keen understanding of how to use media, especially new forms of media.

In other words, anyone who's "not-talented enough" to deserve their massive fame is in fact quite talented—*talented at being famous*. Talented at getting us to look at them, talk about them, and follow them.

But ultimately, the "right" reasons for being famous largely depend on your taste in said talent. If you like a band's music, well, they're probably famous for the right reasons. When it comes to pop culture—actors, social media stars, musicians, authors—the "right" reasons for fame are in the eye of the beholder. So let's just say that as far as the moral rightness of their fame, pop culture celebrities in general fall into a neutral category.

Are there any people we *can* all agree are famous for the right reasons? Sure—individuals who make a great contribution to humanity (Mother Teresa), civil rights leaders (Martin Luther King Jr.), and scientific geniuses (Einstein). Those three have something in common, though. They're dead.

So, um, is there anyone alive right now who is famous for the right reasons? You might suggest, like, Nobel Peace Prize winners, but the sobering reality is: How many living Nobel Peace Prize winners can you actually name? That's what I thought. Winning a Nobel is great, but it's a kind of feat fame that rarely leads to celebrity.

Bottom line, there are few living people who nearly everyone would agree are famous for the right reasons. They're basically all categories of one. You can probably name one famous climate change activist (Greta Thunberg), but can you name two? You might be able to name one wildlife biologist (Jane Goodall), but do you know of any others? If there's a movement you pay close attention to, you might know the names of many of its leaders, but in any category, there's rarely more than one figure who is iconic outside that particular subculture—deserving though they may be.

Now let's compare the number of, say, climate change activists most of us can name (in case you forgot: only one) to the number of social media stars you can think of. Maybe "social media star" is too broad. Let's narrow it to, say, only makeup/beauty gurus. Well, I can name, like, five people who do makeup tutorials and *I don't even wear makeup.* Or compare the number of famous living civil rights leaders to the number of famous comedians or singers or actors or authors you know of.

The point of all this is that even though we *say* we wish we had more celebrities who are famous for the "right" reasons, the reality is that we make people famous by paying attention to them. We vote with our eyeballs and our clicks for who gets to be a celebrity. And most of us follow way more entertainers on Instagram than we do civil rights leaders or Nobel Prize winners.

I'm not judging, by the way. I'm the same. I mean, even wildlife biologists and climate change activists pay attention to the same pop culture you and I do. I know because one of my brothers is a real-life wildlife conservationist (he lives at the beach, protecting baby sea turtles when they hatch and waddle their way to the ocean—yes, that's a real thing you can become when you grow up), but he spends his leisure time watching streamers play video games, not streaming live-cams from endangered eagle nests. My other brother manages Burning Man's giant off-grid ranch in the Nevada desert. He leads projects on renewable energy, land stewardship, and carbon dioxide removal. He has also seen all the Marvel movies.

If we were to plot all the household names you know of on a bell curve according to the moral rightness of their work, there would be a few criminals on the edge of one side and a few humanitarians and scientists on the other, but the vast majority would fall into that morally neutral zone of pop culture and entertainment.

Household Names

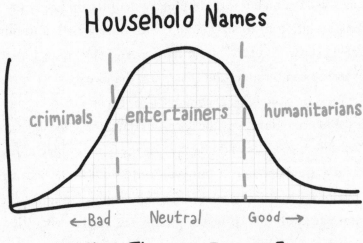

criminals   entertainers   humanitarians

←Bad   Neutral   Good →

What They're Famous For

Interestingly, we don't have a word for good fame, but we do have one for bad fame: *infamy*. And as hard as it is to think of famous humanitarians, it's much easier to think of famous evildoers. Serial killers with great haircuts, eccentric dictators with bad haircuts, or stars of viral videos unwittingly exposing their latent racism. These people are infamous. Infamy ranges from the somewhat terrible—trolls with a big following, mean pranksters, black hat hackers—to the truly evil—terrorists, mass shooters, dictators.

Infamy is a weird word if you think about it because it sounds like it should mean the opposite: in-famy, as in, un-famous. Non-fame.

But it has its roots, like *fama*, in ancient Rome. Fama meant being talked about, but *specifically in a positive way*. Honor, glory, public reputation. There was no neutral pop culture fame back then because there was no mass media.

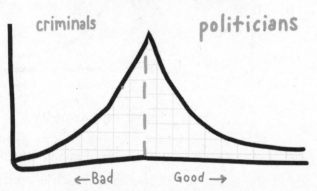

ANCIENT ROME

criminals   politicians

←Bad   Good →

What They're Famous For

I know, I know. What are politicians doing on the *good* side?

Thing is, in ancient Rome, being a politician was a

pretty honorable gig. Of course, a politician could over-stay their welcome and see their reputation switch over to the bad side, which generally resulted in being banished or murdered by a friend on the Ides of March. But there was no "famous for being famous." There were no TikTok stars. There was no neutral fame. There was good fame and bad fame. If people were talking about you, it was either because you had *fama* or because you were *infamis*.

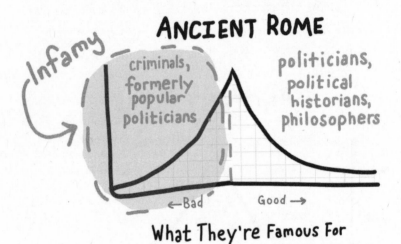

ANCIENT ROME

Infamy

criminals, formerly popular politicians

politicians, political historians, philosophers

←Bad   Good →

What They're Famous For

Today, we have a not-so-great habit of giving infamous individuals the honor of the spotlight, which is unfortu-nate because it's much easier to be a breaker than a maker. We often give more attention to perpetrators than victims. My guess is you'd recognize a photo of the younger of the two brothers who set off bombs at the Boston Marathon back in 2013. But you probably wouldn't recognize a photo of any of the hundreds of injured athletes and bystanders.

You probably wouldn't recognize, for example, Rebekah Gregory.

Even though she's appeared quite a bit in the media talking about her experience that day, she's never had the honor of seeing her face on the cover of *Rolling Stone*. Unlike, say, the remaining bomber—that's how Rebekah refers to him, so I'll similarly avoid using his name—who was on the cover of *Rolling Stone* just a few months after the bombing. He was nineteen. In the cover photo, his face is framed by brown curls. There's a hint of a goatee growing around his chin. He gazes at the camera—it's a selfie, actually—with soft, calm confidence. In other words, this photo is not quite so different from those of the celebrities and pop stars that *Rolling Stone* is known for.

"It was the biggest slap in the face that we could have ever got," Rebekah told me. "We're trying to wrap our heads around the fact that we had just been blown up at the Boston Marathon, and survived one of the largest attacks on United States soil. And then the magazine was almost promoting him in this rock star kind of way. And what that felt like was it was giving more people motivation to do something like he did because he was getting this fame and attention that he wanted from it."

On the day of the bombing, Rebekah and her five-year-old son were unknowingly standing about three feet from a homemade pressure cooker bomb filled with nails and screws. Rebekah's body shielded her son from the explosion, almost certainly saving his life. She lost one of her legs. Today, even after seventy-one surgeries and procedures, many tiny pieces of metal shrapnel remain inside her body.

"Unfortunately, the bad guys and the bad people are always going to get more attention," she said. "That's the problem with this fame thing, because people are getting ideas from what other people have done. And they wouldn't be getting so many ideas if it wasn't broadcasted and these people weren't made to be celebrities."

Rolling Stone, though, isn't in the crime-reduction business. They sell magazines. The issue with the bomber on the cover doubled newsstand sales. It won *AdWeek*'s "hottest magazine cover of the year" award (like, what?).

We humans tend to get our behavior cues from other humans. We acquire language by imitating our caretakers. We learn the ironic use of dank memes by observing peers. The problem arises when we observe bad or straight-up evil behavior. Malcolm Gladwell writes about one sociologist who found that after the school shooting at Columbine—the original mass shooting, after which the shooters became world-famous—six out of the next eleven school shootings were clearly inspired by Columbine. An investigation by *Mother Jones* found seventy-four "plots or attacks" inspired by Columbine—though fortunately many were thwarted by law enforcement. Fourteen of them were planned on an anniversary of that original shooting.

Look, it's easy to blame whatever you don't like in society on some monolithic evil "media" corporation(s). But the problem of criminals being rewarded with fame has been around much longer than the news media. Remember Herostratus, the guy who burned down the temple to get famous...two thousand years ago? That's not to say the media doesn't have a role and a responsibility, but media companies don't crown celebrities. We do, by choosing what names we google and which of their articles we click on. That's literally their business model: attracting your clicks and then showing you ads. The good news is that at least when it comes to mass shootings, the professional media now avoids using photos of the perpetrators. Which probably means selling fewer magazines or newspapers but is also a step in the right direction.

If the *problem* is with us, the good news is the solution is with us, too. We can choose to make more people famous for the right reasons by paying attention to those people. We can help bend the arc of history toward justice by following and clicking on voices that have historically been underrepresented. In doing so, we'll be elevating the sort of people who can be both very famous and very happy—because they'll become famous for the right reasons.

MATH

They all think we should shut the f*** up and stop complaining because you live in a big house or you drive a Bentley....What people don't realize is that fame, whatever your worst experience in high school, when you were being bullied by those ten kids in high school, fame is that, but on a global scale, where you're being bullied by millions of people constantly.

—MEGAN FOX

STUFF WE WILL LEARN IN CLASS TODAY:

- Why do some countries produce more celebrities per capita than others?

- Everyone wants to be famous, but what proportion can be?

- How many celebrities can the average person even remember?

- Do celebrities go through more addiction and rehab than the rest of the population, or are their problems simply more visible?

CHAPTER 11

Get out your graphing calculators, people, because we're in Math class now.

Students love to complain about math. What does it have to do with the real world? How is calculus going to help me when I grow up and become Instagram famous? And so forth.

Fair questions.

But math is important because we need something to tell us when our gut senses are right or wrong. We need it to confirm the assumption we made in our original hypothesis—that fame tends to make people unhappy—by *measuring* both fame and happiness. And you can't measure anything without, you know, numbers.

Turns out it's pretty easy to measure whether someone is happy. You just literally ask them. It's something they feel inside so that's the only way to measure it. Do you feel happy? Say, on a scale of one to ten? There, measurement complete. Easy math.

Measuring fame is the opposite. Happiness is subjective, but we need an *objective* measurement for fame. We need a neutral and reliable fame yardstick. A celebrity centimeter, if you will.

Of course you or I could simply rate how famous we think a celebrity is. But that's not quite precise enough.

Why not? Here's an example. One awkward feature of that tiny theater where I perform my one-man show is that the entrance to the room is on the actual stage, so when people are late they basically join me onstage while I'm performing. And if someone has to leave for a restroom break during the show, everyone in the room knows they are going to pee—and can tell based on how long they're gone whether they did other business, too.

The "backstage" is a closet-sized, curtained-off space right beside that entrance door. That's where I wait for the show to start, so I hear what everyone says as they walk in. Which can make for some uncomfy eavesdropping.

Most audience members have never heard of me. They were just looking for something fun to do on Friday night and ran across a listing for my show. I frequently hear comments like, "So who is this guy?" or "Have you ever heard of him?" or even "How many actors are there in this play?" (Those people are in for a surprise when they discover the entire show consists of one dude talking for an hour and a half.) One time a woman walked out of the theater about ten minutes into my performance. She found my wife in the courtyard.

"When do the other comedians come on?" she asked.

Upon learning there were no other comedians performing, she left.

So, yeah.

To people like her—to most people in the audience, in fact—I'm not at all famous. They don't know my name, my face, anything about me. But every Friday there will also be a few of my internet followers who show up. Sometimes they've traveled long distances to see me perform.[23]

Some followers have planned vacations to California around a performance of the show. One girl with cancer came to see my show on her Make-A-Wish trip. To these people, I am *very famous*. They've been watching my videos online for many years, seeing view counts in the thousands or millions, so my show must be quite popular, right?

They tend to arrive super early, expecting a big crowd. It comes as quite a shock when they walk into a theater that only holds fifty people. Where are the thousands of other fans lining up to get in early? Where are all those internet viewers?

---

23 But unlike Rousseau's reaction to the fans who traveled a hundred leagues to see him, I'm grateful they came. Because, you know, fewer empty seats equals less awkwardness.

I've heard conversations on the other side of that curtain, a mere arm's length away from me, like, "Wow, I thought he was more famous than this!" or "Why is this room so small?" or "Um, why are all these seats empty?"

Yikes.

The point is, fame is in the eye of the beholder. The people who have never heard of me would probably be surprised to know that the group of friends sitting in the front row drove many hours to come see their favorite internet comedian in real life. And that group of friends would likewise be shocked that the rest of the audience had never heard of me before buying a highly discounted ticket to the show. One person's celebrity is another person's WHO DAT.

It's like when you're telling your friends about an influencer you're straight-up obsessed with and you're slowly realizing you're the only one who follows them. "Wait you've *never heard* of ____ ?" Even the biggest names can have limited reach. My best friend watches a lot of sports. I couldn't care less about sports. So athletes who are megastars to him are people I'm like, "Hmm the name sounds familiar, I guess?"

So if fame is in the eye of the beholder, how can we measure it? Is there a number that would represent our *collective* gut sense on how famous a person is?

Possible solutions to this problem:

MEASUREMENT	WAIT BUT NO
Internet followers	Follower count is an easy way to compare the status of two stars. But plenty of A-listers aren't on social media at all: Jennifer Lawrence, Meghan Markle, Eddie Murphy, Emma Stone; the list goes on and on. Quick, name the person who first comes to mind when you think "male movie star." If you said George Clooney or Brad Pitt, you thought of two people who don't have social media accounts. This problem works in the other direction, too: It's possible to have a big following online without being truly, like, famous-famous. Most people couldn't name Jack Dorsey as the founder of Twitter, but @Jack has six million Twitter followers, about two million more than @Jumpman23, aka Michael Jordan—definitely one of the most famous people in the world.
Net worth	It's possible to be rich *and* famous, but it's certainly not inevitable. It's just as possible to be broke and famous, whether by accident ("forgetting" to pay your taxes) or by choice (ever heard of Gandhi?).

Search volume	Here's a clever idea: Could we measure fame by the number of times a name is searched for in a given month? Sort of. But search traffic spikes based on current events, like if a person gets caught in a scandal or has a new movie release. It's also seasonal. LeBron[24] gets way more searches during the NBA Finals than he does in the off-season. Does that mean he's more famous some of the year than other parts of the year? No. Just means he's more on our minds when he's close to winning another championship. It's not like we forget about him over the summer.
Paparazzi interest	What about whether TMZ camps out at the end of their driveway? If so, they must be famous, right? Sure. But paparazzi only pay attention to the celebs that generate the most interesting gossip. Those aren't always the most famous stars. Look at The Rock. He's currently the highest-paid movie star on the planet and also one of the most followed humans on the internet. And yet: When was the last time you saw a paparazzi photo of Dwayne? Meanwhile, the same dozen stars get harassed and stalked day after day by TMZ—because they're the lightning-rod personalities who generate clicks.

---

24 Hey look, another example of a famous sportsball player I've heard of!

Awards	How about awards? Say, Academy Award count? No, because for one thing, awards in one profession don't allow us to compare people in other sectors. Hillary Clinton has won no Oscars, no MVP trophies, and no presidencies. Does that mean she isn't famous?
TV shows and movies	Likewise, appearances in movies or starring roles in TV shows certainly help make an actor more famous. But that metric tells us nothing about athletes, musicians, and vloggers.

So is there *any* method for quantifying this thing? Fortunately, yes. Let's look at two different ways researchers have tried to solve the fame measurement problem using the power of, you guessed it, math.

Obviously, the best method would be to go to everyone in the world, give them a list of eight billion names, and ask them to check off all the ones they'd heard of. Then we'd *really know* who is famous and how famous they are. Unfortunately, surveying every human could cause me to miss my publisher's deadline. Instead, we need to find a way to use existing data.

Two physicists, Dr. Edward Ramirez and Dr. Stephen Hagen, thought of a clever way to do this. They compared several methods for measuring fame, looking for the one that reliably aligns with average gut-sense fame. The winner? Wikipedia page edits, meaning the total number of times a Wikipedia page has been modified. It's conveniently available on every Wikipedia entry.

Using this number, we can see that anyone whose page has been edited a thousand times is, like, pretty famous. Anyone with ten thousand or more edits is probably a household name. Here are the Wikipedia edit counts for a few people we've talked about:

- Beyoncé: **22,093**
- Dwayne "The Rock" Johnson: **17,855**
- Abraham Lincoln: **17,602**
- Julius Caesar: **10,625**
- Me: **197**

Hold up. No surprise Beyoncé is 112.1472 times more famous than me, but she can't possibly be *twice* as famous as Julius Caesar, right? It's not like we have a month named after her.[25] So what's the problem?

Well, there will always be dramatically more internet interest in living people than dead people. Which is how The Rock has more edits than Honest Abe. Plus, the longer it's been since someone died, the less interest the internet will

---

25 Pretty good idea, though, right? How about replacing February with Beyoncuary?

have in editing their page. Like, we've had two thousand years to edit Caesar's Wikipedia. Surely it's about finished by now.

Clearly, fame is too complex to be easily measured by one single attribute. Social media followers, Google hits, wealth, whatever it is, one factor isn't enough, especially if we're comparing celebrities from different spheres. To compare the fame of, say, a tech CEO to an actor, or a living celeb to a long-dead one, what we need is not a single metric but a *formula* that calculates fame using a bunch of different measurements.

Lucky for us, a very smart group of people at MIT's Collective Learning group has developed just such a formula.

Behold!

THE HILARIOUSLY COMPLICATED BUT TOTALLY LEGIT FORMULA FOR CALCULATING HOW FAMOUS SOMEONE IS:

$$HPI = \begin{cases} ln(L) + ln(L^*) + log_4(A) + ln(v^{NE}) - ln(CV) & \text{if } A \geq 70 \\ ln(L) + ln(L^*) + log_4(A) + ln(v^{NE}) - ln(CV) - \dfrac{70-A}{7} & \text{if } A < 70 \end{cases}$$

LOL, wait, what? Really?!

It's actually not as crazy as it looks. Let me break this formula down for you in plain English. I'll take you through each part and, by the end of this chapter, I promise you'll feel like an MIT-level genius.

First, what's this "HPI" thing on the left side of the equation?

$$HPI = \begin{cases} ln(L) + ln(L^*) + log_4(A) + ln\left(v^{NE}\right) - ln(CV) \text{ if } A \geq 70 \\ ln(L) + ln(L^*) + log_4(A) + ln\left(v^{NE}\right) - ln(CV) - \frac{70-A}{7} \text{ if } A < 70 \end{cases}$$

This formula calculates *literal popularity points*. But since the brainiacs at MIT wouldn't want to admit that's what they're after, they're calling their popularity points the "Historical Popularity Index," or HPI for short.

The formula is actually two different equations stacked on top of each other. The top line is for calculating the popularity (okay, fine, MIT nerds, we'll call it the "HPI score") of dead people.

Probably

$$HPI = \begin{cases} ln(L) + ln(L^*) + log_4(A) + ln\left(v^{NE}\right) - ln(CV) \text{ if } \boxed{A \geq 70} \\ \rule{8cm}{0.4cm} \end{cases}$$

Basically, the formula assumes that if it's been more than seventy years since someone was born, they're most likely not living. Example: Since Caesar was born over two thousand years ago, the computer assumes it's a safe bet he's no longer among the living, so Caesar's HPI is calculated using the top line.

The bottom equation is for living people. Example: It's been less than seventy years since Beyoncé was born, so her HPI gets computed using the bottom line.

Since we have a bias toward looking for information on living people, the formula subtracts a penalty from Beyoncé's score. Please don't take offense, Beyoncé fans, it's nothing against her. The problem is that she's alive. Uh, sorry, that sounds wrong—what I mean is, being alive is an unfair advantage if you want to compare her fame to Caesar's.

$$HPI = \begin{cases} \rule{6cm}{0.4cm} \\ ln(L) + ln(L^*) + \log_4(A) + ln(v^{NE}) - ln(CV) - \frac{70-A}{7} & \text{if } A < 70 \end{cases}$$

Probably living →

Penalty for being alive ↑

Otherwise, the same four factors contribute to a person's HPI—let's say it's yours—whether you're alive or dead, or undead. (Question: Would the HPI also work for an undead vampire? Answer: Yes, but their HPI score would be invisible if you held it up to a mirror.)

A   B   C   D

$$HPI = \begin{cases} ln(L) + ln(L^*) + \log_4(A) + ln(v^{NE}) - ln(CV) & \text{if } A \geq 70 \\ ln(L) + ln(L^*) + \log_4(A) + ln(v^{NE}) - ln(CV) - \frac{70-A}{7} & \text{if } A < 70 \end{cases}$$

Let's look at these four parts.

A: Part A gives you points for the number of languages your Wikipedia page is translated into. The more languages, the more famous you are. If your page is only in one language, you're probably only known in one region of the world. If it's in a bunch, you're probably world-famous.

A. Number of languages Wikipedia page is in

$$
HPI = \begin{cases} \ln(L) + \ln(L^*) + \log_4(A) + \ln\left(v^{NE}\right) - \ln(CV) & \text{if } A \geq 70 \\ \ln(L) + \ln(L^*) + \log_4(A) + \ln\left(v^{NE}\right) - \ln(CV) - \frac{70-A}{7} & \text{if } A < 70 \end{cases}
$$

B: What if even though you're not *that* famous—like you're actually just known in one language—but you have a few multilingual stans who translate your Wikipedia into all known languages or something? Part B gives you points for *actual page views* across all those Wikipedia translations.

B. But is it actually getting read in all those languages??

$$
HPI = \begin{cases} \ln(L) + \ln(L^*) + \log_4(A) + \ln\left(v^{NE}\right) - \ln(CV) & \text{if } A \geq 70 \\ \ln(L) + \ln(L^*) + \log_4(A) + \ln\left(v^{NE}\right) - \ln(CV) - \frac{70-A}{7} & \text{if } A < 70 \end{cases}
$$

C: Part C is another age-related score. But instead of a penalty for being alive, this is just a straight-up bonus if it's been a long time since you were born. The longer you're able to avoid being forgotten, the more points you get. So Madame Curie (born about a hundred fifty years ago) gets more bonus points than Beyoncé (born about forty years ago), but Caesar gets *major* bonus points for staying famous for over two millennia.

C. Bonus for being remembered over the centuries

$$HPI = \begin{cases} \ln(L) + \ln(L^*) + \log_4(A) + \ln\left(v^{NE}\right) - \ln(CV) & \text{if } A \geq 70 \\ \ln(L) + \ln(L^*) + \log_4(A) + \ln\left(v^{NE}\right) - \ln(CV) - \frac{70-A}{7} & \text{if } A < 70 \end{cases}$$

D: Finally, since English is disproportionately popular on Wikipedia, Part D gives a bonus to page views in other languages. This helps us to make a fair comparison across regions.

D. Reduces English-language bias

$$HPI = \begin{cases} \ln(L) + \ln(L^*) + \log_4(A) + \ln\left(v^{NE}\right) - \ln(CV) & \text{if } A \geq 70 \\ \ln(L) + \ln(L^*) + \log_4(A) + \ln\left(v^{NE}\right) - \ln(CV) - \frac{70-A}{7} & \text{if } A < 70 \end{cases}$$

See, that wasn't so bad, was it? And don't you feel like a total math boss now that you understand a scientifically valid formula for calculating fame?

Now the fun part! The team at MIT has made a website[26] where you can plug in a famous name and it will tell you that person's HPI. It's called Pantheon. Let's compare the HPI scores of that same list we considered before:

- Julius Caesar: **95.8**
- Abraham Lincoln: **89.1**
- Dwayne "The Rock" Johnson: **74.2**
- Beyoncé: **67.4**
- Me: **Not even ranked**

Since the database includes over 85,000 people (seems like a lot!), I can't say I'm not a little bit disappointed I don't even rank, but then again, there have been over 100 billion humans in the past 50,000 years. Which means Pantheon is only ranking the top 0.000085 percent. Sure, I have some semi-fame, but I'm definitely not in the top 0.000085 percent. I mean, your mom probably hasn't ever heard of me. Or if she has, it was from you. (Thanks! I'm becoming famous, one mom at a time!)

But that list does make gut sense, right? Beyoncé and The Rock are on there, and they have pretty high scores, but Abe has a sizable lead over them—at least until Beyoncé

---

26 It even has a fun URL! Just type this into your address bar: Pantheon.World.

and The Rock run for president, ideally together on the same ticket please. Caesar is more famous still. Which makes sense because, like, July and C-sections.

So! Now we *finally* have an accurate formula to measure and compare any famous individual from ancient history to today, from Alex the Great to Alex Ocasio-Cortez. Which means we are ready to answer some truly fascinating questions about celebrity, geography, money, and more.

What occupation do you think produces the most famous people? Let's start by answering that question for people born in ancient history. What would you guess was the most common career of famous people born before 500 BCE? Politician, of course. It's politicians whose names got written down and memorialized with pyramids and those ancient marble statues where the eyes weirdly lack pupils because the paint has worn off over the years. Of historically popular people born before 500 BCE, over 75 percent were politicians. A distant second place is religious figures—Moses, Abraham, and company—who make up 6 percent of ancient celebs.

In the last hundred years, though, politicians drop to only about 10 percent of memorable individuals. What do you think is number one?

Soccer players. That's right, soccer players. Coming in

at 29 percent. If you happen to be an American, that may surprise you. You might've assumed, as I did, that the biggest group would be actors. And, indeed, they are second place, 16 percent. But if you live, well, literally anywhere else on the planet, you most likely guessed correctly. Americans have a hard time understanding just...how...big... soccer is in the rest of the world.[27]

Speaking of countries, which country do you think is producing the most celebrities per citizen?

From a historical perspective, most of the famous names for the three thousand years before 500 BCE came out of the Middle East. All together, about half were born in what is now Egypt, Iraq, or Turkey. Italy (which is to say, ancient Rome) and Greece were also major celebrity factories in that era, as we know from History class.

But we know a few things have changed between ancient times and today. The printing press, the Renaissance, Hollywood. None of which happened in Greece or Egypt. So Egypt drops from a 22 percent share of ancient fame to just 0.3 percent in the last hundred years. Greece goes from 21 percent to only 0.4 percent.

The Americas (both North and South) don't even show

---

27 The rest of the world, as you are no doubt aware, even has a different (and I would argue more accurate) name for it: "football."

up on the pre-500 BCE list. But it probably won't surprise you to learn that the United States is the big winner in the competition to breed notable humans during the last century. Twenty-six percent of today's famous individuals were born in the USA. A distant second is the United Kingdom, at 8 percent.

This brings us to maybe the most fascinating question: Is the USA actually producing a disproportionate number of celebrities? Or is it just a really big country producing celebs at an average rate? In other words, which country has the highest number of world-famous people per citizen?

I can't write small enough to make you a chart with all of the world's two hundred+ countries,[28] but here are two pie charts to compare the five most populous.

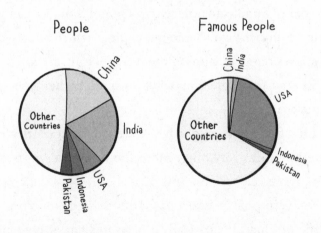

People   Famous People

---

[28] Exact number changes frequently based on, you know, coups and revolutions.

The first chart, entitled "People," shows the five countries with the largest populations. These five alone account for about half of the eight billion of us currently roaming the planet. The second chart, the one called "Famous People," represents the birth country of all the most famous people born in the last seventy years—meaning they're probably alive today.

China and India have over a billion citizens...*each*. But how many celebrities can you name who were born in either of those countries? Maybe an actor or two? Not many. Together, China and India make up over *one-third* of the world's population but have *only 3 percent* of the most well-known people alive today. What's going on here?

Let's dig deeper. If we combine a country's total number of famous people with its population, we can generate a number I call "fame-per-capita," which allows us to compare countries with different population sizes.

So why do some countries produce higher fame-percapita than others?

Your first guess might be money. Rich countries produce more of everything: more food, more exports, and also...more celebs? Yes. Sort of.

You've probably heard of GDP. It stands for gross domestic product. It's basically a measurement of how much stuff a country makes, which also tells you how much wealth is being created there. If you divide GDP by the number of people in a country, you get GDP-per-capita, which tells us how well-off people are, on average, in a given country.

It turns out that in the fifty largest countries in terms of population, there *is* a pretty strong correlation between "GDP per capita" and "fame per capita." In other words, the more money a country's people have, the more famous people tend to be born there.[29]

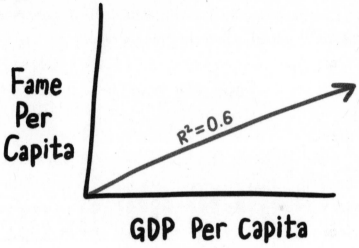

But that doesn't mean the money *causes* more celebs to be created. Just that they're associated. So maybe it's

---

29 Time for a fun math lesson! The "R squared" in that chart is a measurement of correlation. R above 0.50 is considered a "strong correlation," so we can say fame per capita and GDP tend to go together. For even more mind-numbing info on this calculation, see endnotes.

actually that the money buys better education or better technology and those are the reasons children are more likely to grow up to be famous there.

Let's look more closely at the top countries in terms of fame-per-capita. Remember how the USA has the most famous people? Turns out, since our population is pretty large, we don't do as well on fame-per-capita. In fact, we are way down the list at twenty-second. Here's a chart of the top countries in terms of fame per capita.

FAME PER CAPITA

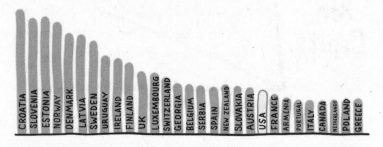

Notice anything in common about the top few countries? Yep, they're all places that seem to produce a disproportionate number of supermodels. Also, they're tiny nations. In fact, each of the top ten fame-per-capita countries have populations of ten million or fewer. That's a smaller population than that of many states here in the USA.

Who are all the famous people coming out of these small countries?

The answer, once again, is soccer. In nine out of those top ten fame-per-capita countries, the largest group of famous people is soccer players.

Here's what I think is going on here. Countries don't have a quota to fill when it comes to, say, singers. But soccer players? Every developed country, regardless of size, has a national soccer team. A given country sends twenty-three players to the World Cup whether it has one billion residents (India) or just one million (Estonia). So the smaller the population, the better your opportunity to excel at soccer. In smaller countries, it's (relatively) easier to stand out by playing in the World Cup, which increases the chances you get noticed internationally. Which may lead to a contract in, say, the Premier League, where you can get really, *really* famous. Soccer famous.

So if you're reading this book in hopes of finding some tips on becoming famous, the data suggests you should move to a very small country and become a very good soccer player.

CHAPTER 12

During my super-senior year of college—the year I got that "you're not right for us on-camera" email from MTV—I was contacted by a nonprofit that gives youth awards for community service. They'd seen me online or something and wanted me to apply.

A few months later, I went to New York to interview for the award. There were twenty-four finalists. Half of us would win. The CEO of the nonprofit stood up at the start of the day and announced matter-of-factly, "We're about to make twelve of you quite famous."

My eyes went wide. *Quite famous?* My adrenaline started pumping. MTV hadn't worked out, but this, *this* could be my shot.

The twelve winners would be honored on an awards show broadcast on the CW. There would be a red carpet. Celebrities. Paparazzi, even. All I had to do was give a better interview than half the other nominees.

In between the interviews, a few of us were standing around the snacks. (Free snacks! Yes please!) We were high up in a New York City skyscraper, not unlike the one where I'd met Ocean MacAdams the year before.

"How'd you hear about this award?" one of the other nominees asked me. He was a teenager, skinny with a tight polo shirt. His community service project: collecting stuff people wanted to get rid of and then dropping it off at prisons to give to inmates.

"They emailed me and asked me to apply," I said. "How about you?"

"Every couple weeks I google 'teen community service awards' and apply for any of the ones I haven't won before," he said.

I paused in case it was a joke. It didn't seem to be.

I coughed back a snort. "Oh, um, cool," I said.

Yikes. He seemed so...desperate for attention. But then again, were my cringey attempts to get on MTV any different? Wasn't I just as desperate for the spotlight?

Anyway, he was chosen as one of the winners. I was not.

I went back to college feeling super-disappointed. But a few months later, the organization reached out again. During the show on the CW, they were giving an honorary award to Lance Armstrong. The CW wanted it to be given by a fellow cancer survivor. Bingo.

A few weeks later, I was back in New York City, trying to follow a map on my phone to the awards show. I knew it was on Times Square. *Will it be near the MTV studio?* When I found the address, I stood in front of the glass doors in disbelief. This show was being recorded in the actual MTV building, in a theater in the basement, just two floors below those glass windows you see in the background of MTV's live broadcasts.

Rehearsal took place in the morning. As I sat backstage memorizing my lines for the show, I kept thinking how Ocean MacAdams was probably working several floors above me at that very moment. What if I walked by him in the hall or something? Would he reconsider if he knew I was giving an award to Lance Armstrong?

It didn't seem implausible. Not only were we filming downstairs, the producer of our show was this guy named Alex Coletti, who I knew from my internet research had produced MTV programming with a certain guy whose name can also mean a large body of water.

It turned out that Lance Armstrong (HPI 68.2) was unable to attend in person. I'd be introducing his video acceptance speech, which is considerably lamer than handing him an award. Oh well. (Mind you: All this was before his cheating scandals. Lance was still a national treasure.)

I'd be able to read my lines on a teleprompter, and it was only like three sentences, but I must've practiced them a thousand times in my head. I was not going to throw away my shot, as Alex Hamilton[30] would say.

That afternoon, the thirteen of us walked into the theater for the first time—the twelve winners and me, the loser—and looked for our assigned seats. The theater was set up so that the front of the room had casual furniture that people would be sitting on. Couches and stuff. I was astounded to find a photo of my face front and center, taped to a two-person love seat beside a photo of Mandy Moore.

I would be sitting with...a *celebrity*? Alone, on a couch, just her and me? I panicked. What would I even talk to her about? I needed some conversation starters.

I couldn't get internet down there in the basement, but up on the balcony I got cell service. I called my friend Judd. Judd had come through in a pinch before. He once loaned me his pants so I could smuggle a two-liter into a movie theater by hiding it inside the left pant leg.

"Yo," he said.

"Dude, are you near a computer right now?" I said.

"Yeah, why?"

"Wikipedia Mandy Moore and TELL ME EVERY-THING!" I said.

"Wait, what?"

"Just do it. I need to know everything about her."

---

30 Well, technically I guess Lin-Manuel Miranda. Not sure if Alexander actually said this.

"Are you stalking her?"

"There's no time to explain, the show starts soon," I said.

"Um, okay," he said. I heard a keyboard clacking. "Okay...so...she's an American singer, songwriter, and actress."

"Yeah, but what else?"

"Oh, check this out: Today's her birthday!"

"That's perfect," I said. "I'll explain everything later, gotta go, thanks."

We went up to the second floor and had our makeup done in a room that overlooked Times Square. I looked through the glass. This was the same view you see in the background of MTV's live shows, which meant the studios—the exact spot where MTV News was recorded—were just on the other side of the wall.

I was supposed to walk the red carpet, which was awkward because first of all, I'd been there all day and this meant pretending I was arriving. Second, there were actual famous people on the carpet. Singer LeAnn Rimes was hosting. Various hip-hop moguls and supermodels were in attendance. More important and impressive to me personally, Malcolm Gladwell, writer for the *New Yorker* and author of books like *The Tipping Point* and *Talking to Strangers,* was in attendance. I mean, the other celebrities were cool, too, but mostly this famous journalist.

Anyway, here's how red carpets work: The normals walk around the carpet and go straight inside the building. Well, they probably aren't exactly normal. They were important enough to get an invite to the event in the first place. Just not quite VIP enough to make it onto the carpet.

The most VIP of the VIPs, the elite of the elite, line up at the entrance to the carpet. There are event-producer types with headsets and clipboards who are basically the bouncers of the red carpet. When you reach the front of the line, you (or if you're important enough to be rolling with an entourage, your handler) tells the bouncer your name. She looks at her clipboard. If your name is on it, you are allowed to pass. But not until the person in front of you has stepped out of the camera area. The first part of the red carpet, where the photographers snap your photo in front of a backdrop of repeating logos, is like a porta-potty: It really only works if one person goes at a time.

The bouncer has an assistant with a stack of pages, each containing a name printed in large letters. The pages are alphabetized and contain the names of every VIP who was invited to the event. The vast majority of these folks won't show up, of course. But just in case they do, there's a sheet of paper with their name on it.

The aid walks out with you on the carpet, holding the sign with your name on it. The flashbulbs start to blink. SNAP SNAP SNAP. Now all the photographers have a reference shot showing you and your name, so their editor can later identify who you are, know how to spell your name correctly, and decide you are not nearly famous enough for your photo to be used.

The aid calls out your name to the photographers like a royal herald presenting a visiting duke, then she steps out of the frame, leaving you in front of the logos. The photographers break out into a chorus of your first name, trying to get a shot of you making direct eye contact with their camera. "Josh!" "Josh, over here!" "Just look here, please!" The flashbulbs blink. You try to act like you've done this a million times and are totally going to hit it off with Mandy Moore, but you're thinking, *This is very sweet of you all to pretend that you want my photo*.

After the still-photo section of the carpet are the interviews. There might be TV journalists as well as print and radio. They're all lined up on the other side of the velvet rope. A handler or event producer will bring you to journalists who want to interview you.

Anyway, there were maybe a dozen famous-enough-to-walk-the-red-carpet types at this award show. Doesn't sound like that many, but getting even one famous person to show up at your event is impressive. There are more events on a given day that want celebrities to grace them with their presence than there are celebrities.

Since this is Math class, let's look at some actual

numbers here. How many celebrities can you name? Let me be more specific: How many living, breathing (not dead, not fictional) individuals can you think of who are household names—that is, who pretty much everyone has heard of? Maybe pause and try to compose a list in your mind or in your notes app.

I asked my followers to do this exercise. Overall the average was eleven names. Can you beat that? If you're having difficulty, here's a hint: Don't start with the basic question (who is famous?) because it's too broad. Instead, take your brain through specific categories: Who are the most famous stars of action movies? How about comedies? Action comedies? Do you know of any well-known football players? How about the other kind of football, aka soccer?

Of course, you'd be able to *recognize* far more famous people than those you could recall off the top of your head. In one study at the University of York, students were paid to try to recall all the famous faces they could think of. Just the faces, not their names. The average student could recall two hundred ninety famous faces. But when shown *photos* of famous people, they could recognize twice as many. (In fact, by adding real-life acquaintances and just random people you'd recognize from the bus or whatever, these scientists estimate that on average, people can recognize an astounding five thousand faces!)

This raises the question: How many truly famous people are there actually out there?

Let's turn to Pantheon and its HPI scores. My personal observation is household names are generally those at HPI 50 and above. To narrow that list to people you and I would probably be familiar with, let's consider only living people born in the USA. That gives us a list of about...drumroll, please...five hundred names. That's it. All the major celebrities, anyone that everyone from this country has heard of. It's a pretty short list, if you think about it, considering the US population is 330 million.

That would mean if a major award show (say, the Oscars) has fifty celebrities walking their carpet, that's a very high proportion. That's basically *10 percent of all the major celebrities* in the country. All in one place at one time.

So if you can get even a few celebrities to come walk the red carpet at a minor awards show on the CW...well, that's pretty cool. And if you want me to walk it with them, well, that's kind of awkward, but sure, why not.

CHAPTER 13

The show was about to begin, and I was still sitting by myself on the love seat in the front of the room. *Is Mandy a no-show?* And then along comes a tech with the headset, escorting a very tall girl in a little black dress across the front of the room.

"Mandy, this is Josh, you'll be sitting together," she said.

"Nice to meet you!" said Mandy, sitting down beside me. She crossed her bare legs, which were very long and shiny, like she'd just oiled them down for a bodybuilding after-photo. For a moment I froze. What could I possibly say to this famous person?

"Happy birthday!" I finally blurted out, which was the equivalent of holding up a sign that said, HELLO I HAVE BEEN STALKING YOU ONLINE!

"Thanks." She smiled.

We both started to speak at the same time. We laughed. "You go first," I said.

"What kind of music do you listen to?" she asked.

"Whoa, I was about to ask you the same question!" I

said. "That was literally what I was about to say when you said you go first!"

I thought, *Are we vibing here? Is this what love feels like?*

"So...what kind of music?" she asked.

"Oh, the radio," I said. Zing! Wham!

I was very pleased with my wit.

A little pro tip for your reference: If you ever meet a famous singer and they ask you what kind of music you listen to, obviously the answer is, *Yours*. Basically, I blew it.

Some drunk Wall Street guys on the balcony started yelling at her, "Hey, Mandy Moore! I'll give you a walk to remember!"

I felt defensive of Mandy. Couldn't these Wall Street douchebags leave her in peace? Why were they invading her privacy? (Though to be fair, they were standing in the exact spot where I'd called my friend to give me facts from her Wikipedia.)

"Oh I forgot you were in that movie *A Walk to Remember*," I said, trying to distract her from the hecklers, but doing a bad job because I was clearly taking a cue from them.

"Yeah," she said.

"I've heard it's great," I said. "I haven't seen it yet, though."

She nodded awkwardly.

"MANDYYYY!" one of the balcony guys was yelling.

Suddenly a woman with a press badge was standing in

front of us with a tape recorder: "Hey, Mandy, any birthday plans tonight?"

The balcony continued: "MANDYYY MOOOOORE!"

Mandy spoke to the journalist. "No, just a quiet celebration with my band."

The journalist continued to ask her questions about her career and love life and such (she was recently single! ANY COMMENTS?) until Mandy politely said she would prefer to just relax and enjoy the show, if that would be possible.

No sooner had she left than a photographer approached. "Mandy, a quick photo?"

She turned toward him and smiled. I put my arm around her shoulder. Not like in a romantic way, just in the way you do when you're posing for a photo. It wasn't a move of confidence. Just habit.

I wondered why there was no security in this building to stop all these journalists from bothering my good friend Mandy. But no, I realized, there *was* security, but the non-profit in charge of this show *wanted* journalists to be able to talk to Mandy Moore. That's how they got the photographers and press to come to the show and publicize their event: by promising them access to celebrities.

That's the perverse math of fame. Mandy Moore was the most famous person in the room. That's why she was sitting front and center: so the cameras could easily capture her reactions, so the journalists could come ask her for quotes during commercial breaks. Because everyone had heard of her, everyone wanted something from her. Including me. I wished her happy birthday, if I'm being honest, not because I wanted her to have a great birthday but because I wanted her, a celebrity, to think I was thoughtful and nice. If I played my cards right, maybe she'd even invite me to the small celebration with her band after the show?

Now that I'm doing this investigation years later, if I could go back in time, I'd be so curious to ask her: Is all this making you happy? From what I saw, though, my suspicion is her honest answer would've been that the more famous you get, the less happy your birthdays are. Mandy Moore is actually the same age as me. Here's an interesting math question: At what age would you guess the average famous person reaches the peak of their fame?

By definition, you can't calculate the answer based on the fame of *living* people. Mandy Moore was crazy famous as a teenage singer. Her HPI was probably lower by the time I met her. But who's to say that twenty years from now, she won't become even *more* famous than she was in her teens? Therefore, finding the average age of peak fame requires combining math and history.

A team at Harvard recently did just that by building a database with the contents of over five million books published in the last two hundred years—about 4 percent of all the books ever published. Their database included over five hundred billion total words in several languages.

To measure peak fame, they made a list of famous people born between 1800 and 1950 and then counted how many times each name was mentioned in all those books. The more often their name was printed in a given year, the more famous that person was in that particular year. They did a bunch of math and made some startling conclusions:

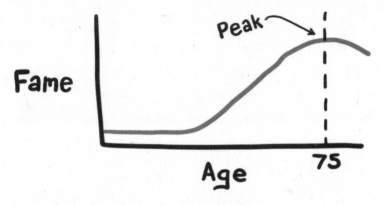

The age of peak fame is seventy-five. Yep, you read that right: seventy-five. How can that be, when most of the celebrities you follow online are not old enough to have children, let alone grandchildren? Well, there's a difference between, like, enthusiastic fandom and general name recognition. The longer a person is around, the more their name tends to get out there, even if they're no longer the hottest celeb. Like, I currently have more YouTube subscribers than ever before, but my videos get fewer and fewer views. Why? Many subscribers move on to watch other things but never bother to unsubscribe. Enthusiasm can fade even as name recognition continues to grow.

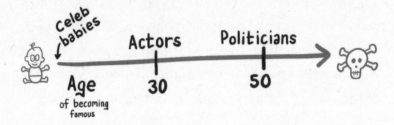

The average age people become famous depends on their profession. The age that people *first* get famous—not their peak of fame, just when people start talking about them in books—depends on their profession. For actors, the age was thirty. But politicians don't become famous until their fifties.

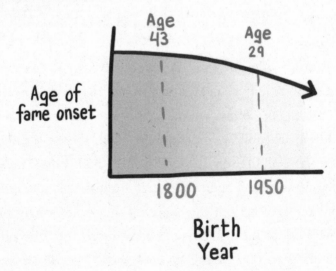

People are becoming famous at a younger age. The age when people *first get famous* is going down over time. On average, people born in 1800 first became famous at age forty-three. Fast-forward to 1950 and the average age had dropped to twenty-nine.

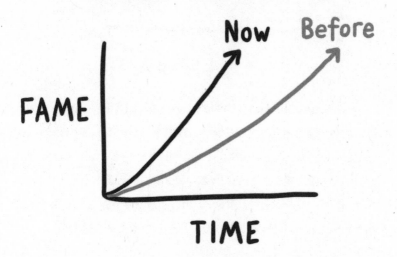

FAME GROWTH

Now   Before

FAME

TIME

People are becoming famous faster. Not only are people getting famous younger, they're getting famous *faster*. In 1800, the average time it took a given level of fame to double was eight years. By 1950, thanks to TV and radio, that was down to three years. Presumably, it's even faster today.

FAME DECLINE

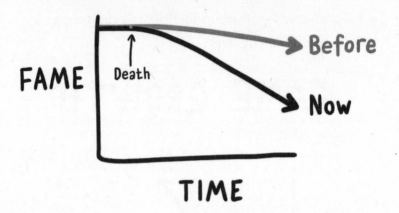

We forget famous people more quickly. How long does it take for a person to become half as famous as they were when they died? In 1800, it took 120 years. Jump forward a century, to those born in 1900, and it was only 71 years. Again, it's even faster now. I mean, how many celebrities can you name who died in the 2000s? In the 1990s?

CHAPTER 14

Suddenly it was my moment to be on TV. Mandy Moore and I were up together onstage. She had just performed a single from her new album. Mandy (we were on a first-name basis by now, obvi) was now introducing me to the audience.

"I want you to meet Josh," she read from the teleprompter. "He's a world-class skier."

She also informed the audience I was a runner-up for the award. *Runner-up.* Is there a sadder accolade? It's like a certificate of participation. Oh, you tried—that's cute.

"It's nice to meet you," she added. I could see on the teleprompter that this phrase wasn't in her script, so it felt like she really meant it. Which helped ease the sting of being an award loser, I mean runner-up.

I smiled at Mandy and turned to face the live audience. I held up a wrist that had one of those yellow bands Lance Armstrong's foundation had been selling to raise money for cancer research.

"Thirty million of you bought these yellow bands so that people like me can...live...strong!" I said. The audience burst into applause. I continued, radiating a confidence that had been entirely missing in my private conversation with Mandy Moore. I didn't even look at the teleprompter. I knew my lines. "Ladies and gentlemen, he kicked cancer's butt and then won the Tour de France seven times... Lance...Armstrong!"

Lance's face faded in on a giant screen behind me.

"Thanks, Josh," he said, beginning a gracious acceptance speech about how many awards he'd won but how especially meaningful this one was.

In the hallway after the show, as I rode the adrenaline high of my national TV appearance, Alex Coletti, the producer, stopped me.

"Hey pal, you should have your own TV show!" he said, pointing at me.

I pointed back at him—just two chill bros bantering in the hallway—and replied with a level of self-assurance that took me by surprise, "You should tell that to your friend Ocean MacAdams!"

Where did that come from? I asked myself.

He nodded. "Okay, I will." He handed me his business card. "Drop me an email about it."

And just like that, my dream of being on MTV felt closer than ever before. *This could actually happen*, I thought. *Finally.*

It all felt meant to be. I mean, Alex Coletti is a real boss—he currently directs *The Tonight Show* with Jimmy Fallon—and he just happened to be buds with Ocean MacAdams.

I emailed Alex the very next morning.

```
FROM: Josh
TO: Alex


Alex—


Hey man, great to see you at the show.
You and your team did a kick ass job.


Your comment that I should have my
own TV show was kind of funny because
I've been trying to get an audition
with Ocean MacAdams to be a News
Correspondent.


When I talked to Ocean last fall, I was
still in college and he was concerned
that I might not be able to graduate if
I was commuting to NYC. So I never got
the chance to audition.


Any help you could provide would be
immeasurably appreciated.


Josh
```

```
FROM: Alex
TO: Josh


Great job last night. Still editing the
footage. I will make Ocean a copy of the
show and touch base with him on your
behalf next week (after I've slept).


You and Mandy make a good couple.
```

I was tempted to inquire more about Mandy Moore. *Wait, did she ask about me? Should you give her my number just in case?* But no, what mattered more than the long shot of dating a celebrity was (the probably even longer shot of) becoming an MTV News correspondent. I waited until a couple days after the show had aired to follow up.

```
FROM: Josh
TO: Alex


Hey dude, I hope you are sleeping right
now.


Great work on the show. I appreciate
you including that shot of Mandy
and me applauding. It proved to my
```

```
disbelieving friends that I was, in
fact, chilling on a couch with Mandy
Moore.

I can't thank you enough for your
willingness to pass along that tape.
```

I refreshed my in-box almost immediately after I had pressed "send" and continued to check my email constantly for the next five days.

While I was still awaiting his reply, the craziest thing happened: The celebrity tabloid magazine *OK!* printed a photo of Mandy Moore and me sitting together on a love seat. We both appear to be laughing. She is wearing the little black dress. I am wearing a cowboy shirt underneath a dark blazer. My arm is clearly draped around her shoulder. The caption on the photo: "Mandy Moore and Josh Sundquist gave an award to Lance Armstrong." As if no explanation was needed about who I was or why my arm was around Mandy Moore.

I immediately forwarded it to Alex. He replied. Finally.

```
FROM: Alex
TO: Josh

You are the man!!!
```

You know she is single?

Gonna speak to Ocean next week

Speak soon.

The week passed. Then another. Weeks turned into months. Nothing. After four months, I figured if Alex was going to be able to persuade Ocean to consider me, it would've already happened. Was it time to give up?

I decided to send Alex one last email.

FROM: Josh
TO: Alex

Hey man!

I wanted to ask for your advice. After
the awards you said I should "have
my own TV show." I realize that the
supply of aspiring television talent
exceeds the demand by a ratio of about
a million-to-one.

What should I do to position myself to

be in the right place at the right time
to get my first break? I've thought
about trying standup. Comedy could give
me television appearances and industry
contacts.

Any advice you can give me would be
appreciated more than you can imagine.

FROM: Alex
TO: Josh

I do not want to give the wrong
answer here. Getting into television,
especially in the on-air capacity is
never easy. For anyone.

You have to ask yourself one very
important question: why do you want to
do it?

For a lot of people I've worked with
at MTV, they never could answer the
question beyond, "to be famous." That's
a dead end path. A lot of them got

> their 15 minutes and were has-beens by
> 30. It's a s****y place to be.
>
> The comedy thing is interesting...*Last
> Comic Standing*?

Alex was referring to the "15 minutes of fame" concept that has become, well, pretty famous. It is most often attributed to a brochure distributed by artist Andy Warhol at a museum exhibition of his work (though the original author of the phrase is itself a kind of famous debate): "In the future, everyone will be world-famous for 15 minutes."

Meaning the spotlight moves on. Quickly.

Question: What percent of the famous people getting significant media attention right now do you think were also getting media coverage, say, three years ago?

Fifty percent?

Twenty percent?

Even less?

A team of sociologists set out to answer just this question by analyzing the names that showed up over a five-year period in newspapers, magazines, blogs, and websites. Many of the names were associated with one-time events. Victim of a freak accident. Criminal who gets caught. Inventor of a viral dance. People getting their fifteen minutes. These names tend to appear briefly, and then never again.

But most media coverage is not given to these folks. Instead, attention is focused on a small group of names that are *already* famous, and 60 percent of media coverage goes to this top 1 percent of names. And here's the answer to that question: 96 percent of famous names were also referenced in the media three years ago—96 percent!

So wait: Is fame gone after fifteen minutes or does it last?

Basically, there's a threshold. Below that threshold, your fame will probably decline over time. Get above it, though, and your fame becomes much easier to hold on to.

It's sort of like gravity. Anyone can jump a few feet off the ground. But they come right back down because, physics. However, if you find a way to shoot up very fast, you can escape gravity. After that, you can float in orbit, staying at that altitude indefinitely with little effort.

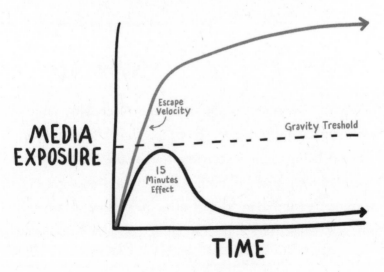

The famous get more famous, and the semi-famous get more...semi. By which I mean less famous. But for true A-listers, those whose names appear in the media thousands of times per year, the chances they'll still be getting media attention three years from now are nearly 100 percent.

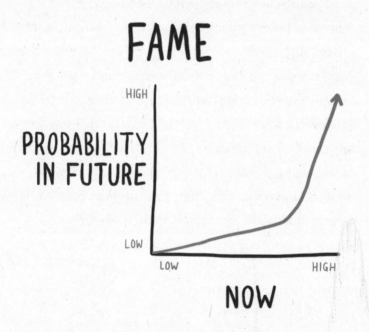

Why? Because, according to these scholars, fame is self-reinforcing. An actor gets a big break and suddenly they're being offered a starring role in another movie and another after that. An athlete gets famous enough to do product endorsements, and now their fame grows even more because they're on TV telling you how fifteen minutes could help you save money on car insurance.

Once they've escaped gravity, everything an A-list star does keeps them relevant. Even the mundane stuff. Especially the mundane stuff. They go to the grocery store? People take photos. They go to a party? Now that party trends on Twitter. They disappear because they went to rehab? Everyone wants to know when they'll be out. Think about that. Even their *absence* from the public eye can make them more famous.

I know what you're thinking: What about such-and-such person who we used to see all the time and now they've dropped off? Doesn't that prove that fame is temporary?

I'd argue the opposite: That person is still *very* famous, so famous in fact you are still thinking and talking about them even though they have not done anything that popped up in your social media feed recently. Sure, they might be less "relevant," they might be a "*former* ____," but hey, we're still curious about them, right?

Take Mandy Moore. She did that appearance on the awards show to promote a new single. After that, though, there was a ten-year period when she didn't release new music or appear in any big movies. A decade! Everyone wondered: What happened to her? She used to be *so* famous!

But the truth was, she was still famous. If she wasn't, no one would be wondering what had happened. It turned out—according to gossip blogs and entertainment news,

which were still covering her because she was still famous—
she had been in a terrible marriage that held her back cre-
atively. But she got a divorce and started working again.
She landed a starring role on the hit TV show *This Is Us* and
put out another album. People called it a comeback, but
if everyone still remembered her, was she ever really gone?

CHAPTER 15

Heads-up. The rest of this chapter and the next will explore some serious subjects like addiction, death, and suicide. Heavy stuff. But we can't really say we've thoroughly explored the intersection of celebrity and mental health without considering these topics. This is still Math class, so we'll be diving deeper into the numbers rather than the emotions, but still, if you think this could be triggering for you, skip ahead to Biology class.

So why talk about this stuff in Math class? As I've said, it's very difficult to measure, on a large scale, what's going on inside the minds of famous people. Because, you know, privacy. But one thing that isn't private: death. Which led me to wonder: Is there anything we can learn in the numbers related to celebrity death?

I eventually took Alex Coletti's suggestion to audition for *Last Comic Standing*. Mind you, I'd never performed in a real comedy club. But how different could it be than giving motivational speeches?[31]

Performance-centered reality shows (*Last Comic Standing*, *American Idol*, etc.) have two kinds of auditions. The first auditions happen in a small room in front of a producer. Producers select which contestants get to appear in the auditions you see on TV in front of celebrity judges. The vast majority of people who show up for an open casting call—sometimes called a "cattle call," which should tell you everything you need to know—are never given serious consideration. The dirty little secret of huge casting calls is that the producers just want to get cool footage of thousands of people standing in line.

Most people who *do* end up auditioning for the celebrity judges skip that line altogether. They get a "booked audition," a scheduled time with a producer. Sometimes it's at an entirely different time and place than the cattle call. Booked auditions happen because the casting people see your content online or because you have an influential agent. Pro tip: You can dig up the email address for the casting people online and send them a video of yourself. That's how I got my booked audition for *Last Comic Standing* at a comedy club in (where else?) New York City.

They liked my video enough that I advanced right to

---

31 Spoiler: It's very different.

the round with the celebrity judges. I'd get ninety seconds to impress them. I waited backstage in a long, narrow hallway with dozens of other comics lined up single file. I felt like I could hear my heart beating.

Suddenly it was my turn. I walked through the curtain and found myself in the main room of the comedy club. The tables and chairs had been removed to make space for the cameras. In the center, right in front of the stage, sat the three judges.

I walked up onstage and grabbed the mic out of the stand.

"Hold on!" yelled a producer. "We might need you to walk in the room again."

"Oh...uh...Okay," I said cluelessly. "I can walk in as many times as you want."

While several producers conferred over their headsets, I stood silently under the spotlights onstage. I looked at the three judges. They were all face famous stand-up comics, meaning people you'd recognize if you saw them on TV, but you might not know their names: Natasha Leggero, Andy Kindler, and Greg Giraldo.

I stood there, silently reviewing my jokes one final time. In hindsight, now that I've actually, like, done some stand-up comedy, I can see that I'd been given a gift: thirty bonus seconds onstage. I could've filled those seconds with improvised lines.

Walk in again? You're gonna make the guy with one leg do extra walking?

Walk in again? Great, I still need to get in more steps today.

You get the idea. Even just saying *Well, this is awkward* would have been a funny tension release. But I just stood there, not realizing my performance had started the moment I entered the room.

I finally got the go-ahead to begin. My nerves made me talk ridiculously fast. Zero laughs. Silence. I finished in far less than my allotted ninety seconds.

"Um, is that it?" said Natasha Leggero. "Can you do a few more?"

Another gift: The chance to do more jokes. But instead of jumping in, I froze. Like an idiot.

"Nah, I've heard enough," said Greg Giraldo. "That's a pass for me."

"Me, too," said Andy Kindler.

Natasha shrugged. I hadn't given her what she needed to say yes. "I like what you're doing, but it's not quite there. Pass for me as well."

I nodded. I'm old enough not to cry from public rejection, but it's definitely what I wanted to do. I pressed my lips together and walked off the stage. Apparently, I would not be getting famous from *Last Comic Standing*.

But as sad as I was in that moment, one of those judges suffered a far sadder ending soon after. Exactly six months and six days later, Greg Giraldo was found dead in his hotel room after he failed to show up for a performance. Cause of death: overdose.

It was no secret that singer Amy Winehouse struggled with addiction. The song she's probably most remembered for, after all, is "Rehab." Which is actually about how she *won't* go to rehab. It was the opening track on her album *Back to Black*, the last song of which was titled "Addicted."

In 2008, when Amy was twenty-five, her former personal assistant claimed that the singer was spending $5,000 a week on drugs. According to the assistant, Amy always feared she would join something called the 27 Club.

"She reckoned she would join the 27 Club of rock stars who died at that age," said her assistant.

Unfortunately, Amy was right. She eventually died of alcohol poisoning. Her age? Twenty-seven.

There's a widespread belief that celebrities suffer from a greater prevalence of substance abuse, mental illness, and overdose than the rest of the population. But this here is Math class, folks, so we won't be taking widespread beliefs at face value. We'll examine the actual numbers. The question is: Are those problems actually more common among famous people, or do we just hear about them more when they affect celebrities? After all, one celebrity's overdose death can trend on Twitter and receive wall-to-wall media coverage, but there are some 30,000 deaths from opioids alone each year in the United States and the vast majority don't get widespread individual attention.

The so-called 27 Club is a long list of musicians who passed away at age twenty-seven. It all started when three famous artists—Jimi Hendrix, Janis Joplin, and Jim Morrison—all died in 1969–1971, all aged twenty-seven. Then, in 1994, Nirvana's frontman Kurt Cobain ended his life at twenty-seven. His mother said, "Now he's gone and joined that stupid club. I told him not to join that stupid club."

That's when it became a "club." Lists were born. Theories were made. Books were written.

Wikipedia catalogs seventy-nine entertainers who died at age twenty-seven. Unfortunately, names continue to be added, including from the world of K-pop. Nicknamed the Princes of K-pop, a group called SHINee is one of the most significant K-pop acts of the last decade. Sadly, one of their members, Jonghyun, died of apparent suicide in 2017. He was twenty-seven years old.

So what's going on here? A team of statisticians in Germany and Australia suggested the following possible explanations. Which would you guess is correct?

1. They found that musicians become famous, on average, at age twenty-six. So maybe the new pressures of fame, that rock-and-roll lifestyle, that access to money and drugs, maybe it all leads to higher-risk behaviors and heightened risk of death the year after making it big.

2. After the 27 Club got rooted in popular imagination, musicians wanting to cement their fame took extra risks—maybe deliberately, maybe subconsciously—or even chose to end their life at this age. (Just to be clear: Although they can both result in death, dangerous risk-taking and attempting suicide are certainly not the same behavior.) So in this explanation, the 27 Club became a sort of self-perpetuating prophecy.

Before we get to the answer, let's look at an entirely different math problem that also relates to celebrity death. There's another viral idea that famous people tend to pass away in clusters, especially in groups of two or three, on the same day or a couple days apart. This "Rule of Three" is mainstream enough that the *New York Times* wrote a piece about it in 2014—after Robin Williams's death occurred one day before that of actress Lauren Bacall (HPI 75). Which was one day before the death of Dutch conductor Frans Brüggen (HPI 63).

More examples:

DECEMBER 25–30, 2006

1. Gerald Ford, US president
2. Saddam Hussein, deposed despot
3. James Brown, Godfather of Soul

NOVEMBER 22, 1963

1. John F. Kennedy, aka JFK
2. C. S. Lewis, *Chronicles of Narnia* author
3. Aldous Huxley, *Brave New World* author

JUNE 23–25, 2009

1. Michael Jackson, moonwalker
2. Farrah Fawcett, TV actor
3. Ed McMahon, TV host

DECEMBER 15–18, 2011

1. Kim Jong Il, North Korean supreme leader
2. Christopher Hitchens, writer/philosopher
3. Václav Havel, Czech Republic president

FEBRUARY 2–12, 2014

1. Philip Seymour Hoffman, actor
2. Shirley Temple, actor
3. Sid Caesar, comedian

Finally, consider the date Greg Giraldo, that *Last Comic Standing* judge, passed away:

SEPTEMBER 29, 2010

1. Greg Giraldo, comedian
2. Georges Charpak, Nobel Prize–winning physicist
3. Tony Curtis, actor (*Spartacus*, *Some Like It Hot*)

The examples are even more eyebrow-raising when you look at pairs of important figures who died within the same week:

- Paul Walker + Nelson Mandela (2013)
- David Bowie + Alan Rickman (2016)
- John Adams + Thomas Jefferson (speaking of coincidence, they died within hours of each other on *July 4th*, 1826, like what even)

We'll get more into psychology next period, but these are as much brain questions as they are math questions. See, our minds instinctively look for patterns and trends. Which is good. Patterns and trends help us predict the future, and those predictions help keep us alive.

Let's say I show you a number:

37

Well, that's just a number. Doesn't mean anything. Like, emotionally. But if I tell you that's how many times your best friend has lied to you, suddenly you *feel* something, right? Patterns are more emotionally resonant than raw numbers. The problem is that they're *so much* more resonant, and so much easier to understand, that sometimes we make up a story to explain numbers when the real story was random chance.

Remember in elementary school how often a pair of students in your class shared a birthday? It always felt like such a crazy coincidence, right? Actually, if you get just twenty-three students in the room, there's a greater than 50 percent chance that a pair of them share a birthday. If you cram in seventy students, the chances of a shared birthday are 99.9 percent![32] Examining the Law of Three is

---

[32] You don't believe me. I get it. If you want to understand the 100 percent legit math behind this, google "the birthday paradox."

just a darker version of the same math. Instead of shared birthdays, we're looking at shared, um, death days.

Using the exact same math, the pair of researchers who used Wikipedia edits to measure fame realized that only twenty-three famous people need to pass away in a given year for it to be more likely than not that two will die on the same day. Using the same math as the birthday paradox, that would mean that if there are seventy such deaths in a year (researchers estimate there are thirty to a hundred each year), the probability of two occurring on the same day jumps to 99.9 percent. So it turns out the Law of Three *is* a real thing. It probably happens most years, actually. But not for any spooky reason. It's just random chance.

What about the 27 Club? Random or real? Well, both.

Those statisticians looked at a list of musicians who'd hit number one on the UK charts in the previous fifty years, comparing their death rates to the UK population as a whole. Conclusion? Musicians have no higher risk of dying at age twenty-seven than they do at, say, age twenty-five or thirty-two.

But! These musicians had a risk of dying *sometime* in their twenties or thirties that was two to three times higher than that of the rest of the population. The risk, in fact, actually peaks in their early thirties, not at age twenty-seven. Then, in later life, musicians' mortality curve matches the general population. So for musicians, there was nothing especially dangerous about age twenty-seven in particular, but there does seem to be a period of heightened mortality risk in early adulthood.

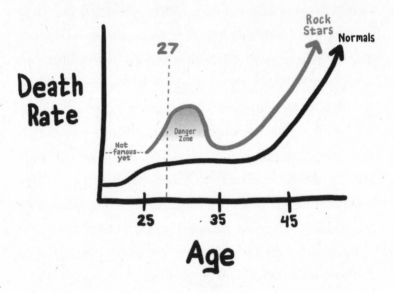

What causes that hump? We can't say for sure—math is great at finding trends but not so much at finding causes—but the authors of the study hypothesize it may be related to the first of those two possibilities we considered before: The pressure of newfound fame. High-stress lifestyle. Money to buy dangerous substances. High-risk environments and decisions.

At any rate, math that links music fame to premature death has definite implications for our overall investigation about happiness. But this study only looked at the risk of death for UK chart-topping musicians. In the next chapter, we'll expand our search to include other sorts of celebrities. Do they also have shorter life spans?

A note, though, before we move on: We've talked about suicide several times in this chapter. If you or someone you love is struggling with these issues and needs help finding support and resources, you can call the National Suicide Prevention Lifeline at 800-273-8255 or visit suicidepreventionlifeline.org. If substance use is a concern for you or a loved one, please visit findtreatment.gov or call 1-800-662-HELP.

CHAPTER 16

This is going to be one of those good news/bad news things. Which do you want first?

Sorry, I'm just making conversation. I already picked for you. I chose to start with:

THE GOOD NEWS

Having your obituary printed in the *New York Times* doesn't mean you were an A-list celebrity, but it at least means your professional accomplishments were significant, meaning you were feat famous. Two scientists in Australia looked at one thousand *New York Times* obituaries over a two-year period. They found that those in creative and performing professions (music, writing, acting, sports, etc.) lived about four years less than business leaders, famous academics, and politicians. But, but, but: All together, the people profiled in the *New York Times* obituaries lived an average of 79.9 years, considerably longer than normal life expectancy. Which suggests that what you are famous for might contribute to how long you live relative to being famous for something else, but *being famous for anything* seems to be associated with a longer life span.

But that doesn't mean the fame *caused* them to live longer. It's also possible fame results from something else—intelligence, great personality, strong jawline—and that something else is linked to longer life.

Here's an astounding fact: Actors who win an Oscar live an average of four years longer than nominees who didn't win. They also live four years longer than actors who were never nominated in the first place. You know how Oscar winners always thank the Academy in their acceptance speeches? Maybe they're thanking them for those four extra years of life they just won.[33] Actors who win *multiple* Oscars live about six years longer. Like, what?

Clearly, winning an Oscar makes actors more famous. But is the fame what makes them live longer? Again, tough to measure causes, but it's probably not the fame itself. The authors of this study suggest the explanation may be in things that happen as a *result* of the fame:

---

[33] Incidentally, four years might not sound like a game changer, but consider this. If every single form of cancer was suddenly cured forever, the increase in human life expectancy would be...four years.

- Being surrounded by agents, managers, and other handlers "who are invested in the person's reputation" and thus tend to encourage "high standards of behavior"
- Increased success and attention, which perhaps also increases the "need to preserve their image by continually avoiding disgraceful behaviors"
- More money, which buys access to the best doctors, nutritionists, chefs, and personal trainers

The money thing definitely matters. Money increases the life span of regular people, too, according to dozens of studies in many countries. But if you're hoping to live longer by getting rich, well, there are plenty of ways to get there without being famous. As Bill Murray said:

> I always want to say to people who want to be rich and famous: "try being rich first." See if that doesn't cover most of it. There's not much downside to being rich, other than paying taxes and having your relatives ask you for money. But when you become famous, you end up with a 24-hour job.

By the way, in another interview, Bill could think of only three advantages to fame.

> There's only a couple times when fame is ever helpful. Sometimes you can get into a restaurant where the kitchen is just closing. Sometimes you can avoid a traffic violation. But the only time it really matters is in the emergency room with your kids. That's when you want to be noticed, because it's very easy to get forgotten in an ER. It's the only time when I would ever say, "Thank God. Thank God." There's no other time.

Oh, and while we're on the subject of good news and math, one other piece of counterintuitive trivia: One researcher found the divorce rate for notable people seems to be below average, at least for men. For eminent women, the rate is the same as the national average: 49 percent. But for notable men, the rate was only 32 percent.

THE BAD NEWS

When a celebrity dies by suicide, it's national news. In that sense, it sometimes feels like suicide might be more common among famous people. Is it possible to use math to determine if this is accurate?

A psychiatrist named Arnold Ludwig spent ten years studying one thousand eminent individuals from the twentieth century. *Eminent*, by the way, is a fancy word for being successful and important in your field. So some of these people were celebrities, others were just feat famous.

With the exception of famous explorers—about half of whom died in accidents, a hazard of the job, I guess—the people on this list had above average life spans. Just like the Oscar winners and the people whose names were included in the *New York Times* obituaries. Beyond that, though, it's mostly bad news for these folks. Just look at the percentage who experience these things at least once in their life:

LIFETIME RATES

	Eminent individuals	US population
Alcohol abuse	20%	13%
Depression	30%	21%
Suicide	4.4%	1.7%

Ludwig also found that 18 percent of the notable people were known to have been hospitalized for psychiatric reasons at least once, although there's no way to find a comparable figure to the general population because psychiatric-health privacy laws vary widely.

I want to be clear that not everyone who dies by suicide is depressed, and not everyone who is depressed dies by suicide. In fact, the vast majority of people who are depressed do not do so. So a suicide rate by no means is the same thing as a depression and unhappiness rate. But while most aspects of what's going on inside a famous person's mind stay private, suicide as a cause of death is often public information, so any difference in the suicide rate of famous versus non-famous people is significant to our investigation into the inner experience of being famous. And there does seem to be a difference in that experience, at least in terms of suicide. The comparison above is 4.4 percent versus 1.7 percent—almost three times higher—which also matches the findings of another study of a hundred celebrities from the 1900s that found stars were three times more likely to take their own lives.

I want to caveat the following by saying there are, well, a lot of caveats due to sample size and selection methods, but Ludwig also divided his list of well-known people by profession. Among poets, a rather astounding 20 percent ended their own lives. The next highest group was musicians (8 percent) and then actors (7 percent). This suggests that how famous you are may be far less significant than *what you are famous for*.

Again, we can't really calculate whether fame *causes* suicide. We can only say based on the (limited) data available, they do seem to be associated.

But could that be because celebrities tend to work in industries that are inherently more stressful, competitive, and/or soul-crushing? Like, perhaps suicide rates are simply much higher in the industries famous people tend to work in, meaning the rate would be equally high for a famous movie star and, say, a non-famous camera operator.

In fact, suicide rates do vary by industry. According to the Centers for Disease Control, one of the following categories has the highest suicide rate of any profession. Which do you think it is?

A. Construction, mining, quarrying
B. Legal
C. Arts, design, entertainment, sports, media
D. Health care

Answer? Construction. Male construction workers end their own lives at twice the national average. For females, it's even worse: four times the national average. The point is, mental health can be a struggle for any person in any profession, whether they are famous or not.

Let's return to the story that got us started on this topic: Greg Giraldo, the comedian who passed away in a hotel room not long after I auditioned in front of him for *Last Comic Standing*. It's unknown whether his overdose was accidental or deliberate, and we certainly don't know what his mental health was like at the time. That's not the point. The point is that he was a person, and although we have been working with numbers in this class, those suffering from mental illness, whether or not they are famous, are not a number or a statistic. They are or were living, breathing people with family members and people who love them.

With that, it's finally time to let go of the heavy subject matter (and heavy math!) of this class and move on to our next subject, where we will try to uncover the stories behind these numbers. We'll do this by looking at the place where happiness and unhappiness actually happen: inside your brain. But first, good news, next period is actually:

LUNCH

So go ahead, put the book down and get your-
self a snack or a glass of water. Enjoy that break.
You've earned it by doing all this thinky reading.
And when you're done eating, turn the page.

BIOLOGY

The biggest surprise of becoming globally famous? On the outside, everybody loves you—but on the inside, everything [feels] the same.

—LIL NAS X

STUFF WE WILL LEARN IN CLASS TODAY:

- Is there something instinctive and biological that makes us want to pay attention to famous people and to become famous ourselves?

- Why do celebrities tend to date other celebrities? Are they following their hearts or making a business decision?

- When celebrities complain about their fame, can't they just, like, move to Kansas and get a regular job? Aren't they choosing to stay in the spotlight?

CHAPTER 17

Hey, students, welcome to Biology class. Biology is the study of life, so in this period we will examine how celebrity affects a person's life: how it changes their brain, their personality, and their way of interacting with the world. We'll also study the life *cycle* of fame. What does it feel like to become famous? What about when your fame starts to disappear?

Let's start with the why of fame, an idea posed to me in that email from producer Alex Coletti:

> You have to ask yourself one very
> important question: why do you want to
> do it?

I spent a long time thinking about that. Here's what I ended up writing back:

> The truth is I'd probably like to
> be famous just as much as the next
> ambitious young person. But I think

it's more than that. If I was offered
an on-camera job on MTV knowing that
somehow no one would ever know my name
or recognize me or even know I worked
there, I would still take the job in a
heartbeat. Why? Because it's not about
fame, it's about excitement.

I can't say for sure whether, deep down, I actually
wanted the fame or if it was truly only "about excitement."
But I sure must've really, really wanted *something* because
I just couldn't quit trying to get on MTV. Or any kind of
TV, for that matter.

I kept auditioning for reality shows as a "comedian." I
put that in quotes because to be a comedian, technically
your jokes should make people laugh. But I didn't let that
stop me. I stood outside all night at a comedy club in San
Francisco for "Standup for Diversity," an NBC talent search
cattle call. I went back yet again to New York City to audition for another major reality show. I can't name it because
I had to sign a scary nondisclosure contract just to be able
to audition, but trust me, you've heard of this show.

Why did I keep flying around the country for these
nerve-racking auditions/humiliating rejections? Why do
I—and so many others—apparently want so bad to become a star?

A psychologist named Dr. David Giles, author of *Illusions of Immortality: A Psychology of Fame and Celebrity*, analyzed a zillion celebrity interviews and found celebs tend to say their reason for being famous was altruistic. Like they wanted to become famous to help people. Non-famous folks who aspire to be famous are no different. I asked my followers why they wanted to be famous. They cited similarly selfless reasons: raising awareness about climate change, promoting animal welfare, or just buying their family a better house. Which is all very nice.

But is that *really* why so many of us want to become a singer or supermodel?

When psychologists dig deep with anonymous, scientific surveys that ask people whether they agree with statements that measure their level of desire to be famous ("I would do anything to become famous," "I would have cosmetic surgery to become famous") as well as their *reasons* for wanting to be famous ("I want to be famous so I can make a difference in the world," "I want to be famous so I can be talked about"), the reasons we claim to want fame don't really check out. Several studies have found a weak association between a strong desire for fame and a goal of creating a positive effect in the world.

Consider this fascinating study: Participants were asked to read profiles of fictional characters and then guess the reasons those made-up people wanted to be famous. On the whole, participants didn't rate factors like altruism or trying to improve the lives of other people as significant motivations. Instead, they tended to say that the fictional characters wanted fame for reasons like glamour, conceitedness, or just plain wanting attention.

This explains how we can be hoping to become famous someday ourselves but simultaneously be criticizing someone else for having the exact same goal. Basically, when it comes to motivations for fame, we're generous toward ourselves and judgy toward others. One moment we're posting an Instagram and refreshing in hopes of seeing a bunch of interaction. The next moment we're seeing someone else's recent post and aggressively judging her photo for trying too hard. *She's only doing that for the likes. Yuck.*

The reasons for desiring fame may vary according to a person's personality. One study found that people who are highly influenced by peers and the media tended to be interested for the perks and status of a celebrity lifestyle, while those with low self-esteem tended to want fame because they thought it would make them feel better about themselves. Another study showed that both narcissists and those with a strong "need to belong" were likely to be people who spend a lot of time fantasizing about being famous—although, fun fact, only the narcissists actually believed those fantasies were likely to come true—but people with strong social connections and relations to others neither fantasized about fame nor thought they were going to become famous.

What about the personalities of people who actually *are* famous? The largest psychological survey I can find ever conducted of actual celebrities—it actually had only two hundred participants, but for a study of celebs, that's impressive—was conducted by Dr. Drew Pinsky, aka Dr. Drew. He asked celebrity guests of his radio show *Loveline* if they would fill out an anonymous survey. The big take-away? Celebrities are about 20 percent more narcissistic than the rest of the population. Let's break it down by pro-fession. Which of the following do you think were the *most* narcissistic: comics, musicians, reality stars, or actors?

Reality stars. I mean, obviously. In their defense, though, they were only slightly worse than comics.[34]

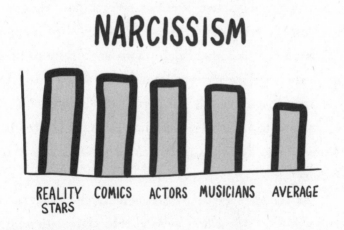

NARCISSISM

REALITY COMICS ACTORS MUSICIANS AVERAGE
STARS

---

[34] As a comic, my narcissism is offended that we comics are not
     number one on this list.

But could it be it's the fame itself that warps normal people *into* narcissists over time? Dr. Drew's survey actually found no correlation between the celebrities' years in the entertainment industry and their level of narcissism. A person who'd been famous for twenty years was no more narcissistic than someone who blew up a year before, suggesting the narcissism was there to begin with. That tracks with those surveys of non-famous people, which show a strong link between narcissism and the desire to be famous.

This doesn't mean all celebrities are horrible people. Dr. Drew points out there are several positive traits associated with narcissism. Narcissists are less likely to experience depression. They're more likable—at least initially, LOL—and perform better in public.

Narcissists also crave attention. Which fame definitely provides. We just can't seem to look away when it comes to fame. An unflattering celeb photo or story pops up in our feed—*click*—we have to know more. Does this make us shallow? Actually, it's just part of our biology. It's not even unique to *our species*, according to a fascinating study by neurobiologist Dr. Robert Deaner at Duke University Medical Center.

Many social species have status hierarchies that determine who gets to eat first, who gets to mate with whom, and, in the case of hens, who literally gets to peck holes in whom. Hence the term *pecking order*. Anyway, Dr. Deaner gave monkeys a choice: They could have a drink of juice—specifically, Juicy Juice, the sweet, sweet nectar that comes in a box—*or* they could look at photos of high-status monkeys. Guess what? The monkeys preferred the photos.

The monkeys (and humans) probably evolved this way because there's survival value in being able to identify and align with high-status individuals. After all, the high-status folks are most likely the ones with food and resources. So don't feel bad when you can't look away from celeb photos. It's in your DNA.

My audition for that nameless reality show in New York took place in a giant convention center. I performed in this temporary room, like a very tall cubicle, for a producer who looked way too young for his all-gray hair. There was a camera guy, too. Zero laughs, per usual.

As I drove back down the interstate that night to my apartment in Northern Virginia, I told myself I was definitely perfect for the show. I'd simply chosen the wrong story to perform. Besides, I got the vibe the gray-haired producer hadn't liked me to begin with.

I emailed the casting people and asked for another audition. They agreed to give me a slot in Miami a week later.

It took place at a nice hotel downtown, in the conference

area on the second floor. While I waited in line for my booked audition, I struck up a conversation with a production assistant. He was around my age, early twenties. It was strange, talking to a peer, but feeling like he somehow had the keys to my future. Like he had all the power.

Turns out the crew travels with the show to each city, organizing all these auditions. He was from LA. He was an actor. His name was Ethan. He wished me luck.

When I reached the front of the line, another production assistant recognized me.

"Hey, didn't you—"

"Yeah, I auditioned in New York," I said, following her down a carpeted hallway.

"Giving it another shot? Good for you."

"Yeah, I think the producer last week didn't like me. So I wanted to give it another try."

"Oh, okay," she said. She was scanning her clipboard. "Let's make sure you're with someone different. Who was it last time?"

"Like his name?"

"Yeah."

"Um, I dunno. He had gray hair?"

"Hmm...both of the producers here today have gray hair." She told me their names. I had no idea. I picked the one that sounded less familiar.

"Okay, come wait at this door," she said. She stood at

the door with me for a while, occasionally putting a finger to her ear to listen to the headset. She was tall and fit, like someone who casually runs marathons on the weekends. Like all production assistants, she wore head-to-toe black.

The door opened and a group of child ballerinas emerged. She held up a hand for me to wait.

"Got it. Ready for Josh Sundquist?" she said into the headset. She nodded at me. "All right, go on in."

I took a deep breath and put on a smile that I hoped hid my nervousness. This was the doorway to everything I'd been dreaming about. Inside I found a small hotel meeting room. Behind the table sat…the same gray-haired producer who had rejected me in New York. My stomach dropped. My smile faltered. Should I walk out? Ask to perform for a different producer? *No, no, don't make a scene. This is okay. I'm doing a different story. I'll win him over this time.*

There were just four of us: him, another producer, a camera operator, and me.

"Nice to see you again," I said. I smiled. The second producer, a woman, smiled back. *There we go. She's my target audience.*

"When you're ready," said Mr. Gray.

I launched into my performance. I got some laughs. Not from Mr. Gray. From the woman and the camera guy.

Yeah, this is going good.

After I finished, I thanked them and walked out.

There. It's over.

It felt like I'd been holding my breath the whole time. I could finally exhale.

The PA girl was still standing at the door. I thanked her, too, as I walked away, back toward the escalator. She put her finger up to her ear and held the other hand up for me to stop.

"Josh, could you hold on a second, please?" she asked. She had a smile on her face, like she was about to deliver some very good news.

"Sure," I said, stepping back to stand beside her.

In my (many? ugh) auditions there had never been a "could you hold on a second, please." I always just walked out of the building and got an email sometime later confirming what I already knew, that I hadn't been selected. So this was new. This was different.

It was weird to know my future was being discussed on the other side of that closed door. No doubt Mr. Gray wanted to dismiss me again. But the other producer was probably telling him viewers would love me. Maybe the camera guy was even chiming in, saying I was funny.

I realized I was holding my breath again.

At last the PA put her finger up to her ear. Big smile on her face.

"All right, Josh! You're free to go!" She gestured down

the hallway toward the escalators, as if she was revealing a prize from behind a curtain on a game show.

Free to go? So...like...had I been selected? The words sounded like I was being dismissed. Like they'd passed again. But her tone made it sound like I'd just won the lottery. FREE TO GO! EVERYONE WANTS TO BE FREE, AND NOW YOU ARE THAT!

I stood there, trying to process it. She nodded in the direction of the escalators, never breaking her big smile.

But the smile was fake. "Free to go" wasn't good. Good would've been *We want you to stick around for an on-camera interview* or *Can you please come back tomorrow to audition for our executive producer*. I looked back at the door, behind which I'd just been rejected. Again.

"Okay...thanks," I said.

I rode down the escalator. I went outside and sat on a bench. On the deck of the hotel, a group of guys—they looked like a dance crew—were being interviewed on camera. From their body language, I could tell they'd been selected to audition in front of the celebrity judges. They were on their way.

I had been *so close*. I just knew it. I was sure that female producer had liked me. If I could just find her again, if she saw me in the hall, maybe she'd bring me to a more important producer who could override my gray-haired nemesis.

So I went back inside the hotel and rode the escalator to

the second floor. I walked past the check-in desk, straight toward the room where I had auditioned before. The tall PA with the clipboard was standing there.

"Oh, hi, Josh," she said. No smile. All the warmth in her voice, that chummy I'm-rooting-for-you vibe was gone. I had been free to go, hint-hint, but I had not gone. Red flag! *Uh-oh! We got another crazy one!*

"Hi again!" I smiled at her. Obviously I would not be welcome to stand there and wait for that producer to emerge, so I just kept walking.

I positioned myself just around the corner, in what seemed to be the most central hallway, right in front of a glass-walled conference room where some PAs were spread out at a long table, eating chips from little snack bags. The crew's break room. If I just stood here long enough, that producer would eventually walk by on her way into that room.

I leaned against the wall and pulled out my phone just to look like I was doing something. I didn't have a crew badge. I wasn't wearing all black. I was definitely not supposed to be there. A security guy was occasionally walking by, eyeing me suspiciously.

"Hey man," I said to him. No one who wasn't supposed to be here would straight up *say hi* to the security guard, right? Surely he'd be fooled.

Just scroll on phone, scroll, scroll, do stuff with thumbs.

On his next pass-by, the security guard stopped in front me.

"What are you doing here?" he asked.

I looked up from pretending to look at my phone.

"Oh, I'm waiting to meet with a producer," I said. Which, technically, was true.

He raised an eyebrow. He didn't seem to be buying it.

"Thanks, though!" I said, as if to say, *Great job keeping this place protected from those desperate people who will do anything to get on TV!*

Looking for an escape hatch, I turned and walked through the glass door into the crew's break room, as if I'd just noticed the person I was waiting for was inside. Would anyone who wasn't supposed to be here do that, Mr. Security Guard?

Turns out Ethan, my friend the actor from LA, was sitting at the conference table. Lucky break!

I sat down beside him.

"Long day, huh?" I said, as if we were just two hard-working crew members on our lunch break.

He nodded.

In my periphery I could see the security guard peering through the glass, trying to decide if I was trespassing or not.

"So when do you get to go back to LA?"

"Not till the season is wrapped," he said.

This was going well! Ethan and I were friends! We could just talk until that producer walked in!

But the next person to walk in was not the producer. It was the security guard.

"You're going to need to come with me," he said. This was no faux-friendly "you're free to go" voice. I was getting ejected from the premises.

I made a last-ditch effort. A Hail Mary that depended entirely on Ethan.

"Oh no, no no," I said. *There's been a miscommunication. I'm not trespassing.* "I'm just talking to my friend Ethan here."

I looked at him, pleading with my eyes. *Please, please say we're friends. I need this.*

The security guard looked at Ethan, waiting for corroboration. Ethan's eyes shifted between me and the security guard. His mouth opened, but nothing came out. It felt like an arrow in my chest.

"Sir, come with me," said the security guard, adding the word *sir* as people do when things are getting heated but they want to pretend to be polite.

I took one glance back at Ethan, but he was looking down at his phone. He grabbed a potato chip from an open bag on the table and popped it in his mouth.

"Now," said the guard, as if to say, *We can do this the easy way or the hard way.*

"Yeah, okay, I'm coming," I said, motioning for him to chill out. *I get it. I lost. I'm leaving.*

I wandered aimlessly around downtown Miami for a while, biting my lower lip. It was early evening, but still quite humid. I sat on some rocks overlooking the bay. *If only I'd picked the other producer's name! I ruined my shot!* Or maybe I just wasn't good at this. Maybe I just wasn't meant to be on TV.

CHAPTER 18

Freshman year of college, back before I got all obsessed with getting on TV, I was interested in politics. Politics was history's original path to fame, after all.

That summer I landed an internship for a US senator. My job was to answer the phone at his office and listen to people complain or yell at me. No one calls their senator with anything positive to say, it turns out.

You'd be shocked by how many people called and just asked me to connect them with the senator, like they were calling my house and asking to speak to my mom. His first name was Frank.

"Is Frank there?"

"Can you put Frank on?"

That sort of thing. And no, I could not. Senators are pretty famous. I mean, I worked for him and I didn't have a way to contact him if I wanted to. I don't think he even knew my name.

At the start of the summer, there was this reception for

all the Senate interns. A couple hundred of us, mostly late teens, were standing around eating cheese cubes and sipping punch, wearing the stiff business attire that we had just purchased the week before. It was a very prom-after-the-lights-come-on vibe.

Anyway, despite there being a few famous senators in the room—I mean, I'm not sure they were famous-famous, but to the political-nerd-type kids who get internships on Capitol Hill, these politicians were straight rock stars—attention was mostly centered on one of the interns, a pretty girl with brown hair. Elbow jabs. *Hey, isn't that...?* Nods, trying not to stare. It felt like the whole room was facing inward, her at the center. But no one wanted to invade her space. *Wait...is that really the girl from the show?*

Having been homeschooled in childhood, with no access to cable TV, I seemed to be the only one who didn't recognize her. Maybe that made me less intimidated. Or maybe the homeschooler part of me was still catching up on social norms. At any rate, I walked right up to her, hovering eagerly on her periphery, close enough that at the next pause in her conversation with another intern, she turned to me. Big smile, even bigger charisma. Dressed like the rest of us, but definitely not quite like the rest of us, either.

I immediately asked her if she was the girl from this TV

show everyone was talking about. I did not even introduce myself. There was no exchange of pleasantries, handshake, or what-senator-do-you-work-for. Just: Hey, are you the famous person?

The smile remained on her face but faded from her eyes. Like she switched from a teenager having a conversation with another teenager to a star being nice to a fan. A pleasant but distant autopilot had switched on.

"Yeah," she said, nodding.

And then she waited. For me to, I don't know, tell her I liked her show or say I was *such a big fan* or ask for something—a photo, autograph, a date. But I didn't have anything to add. I didn't know who she was.

"Oh cool," I said, pleased I could now return to the others and confirm the famous person had correctly been identified. "Nice."

We stood there for another second, awkwardly. I wondered, briefly, if maybe she and I could date. That would be cool, right? Dating a famous person?

I gave her another second to ask me out, but she didn't take the bait.

"Cool," I said again. "Well, nice to meet you."

As I turned away, I sensed a flash of disappointment. Not disappointment I didn't ask for her number—*Dream on, dude*—more like disappointment she'd been recognized.

She had been floating incognito in this sea of teenagers playing dress-up, and I'd come along and ruined her disguise. But looking back on it now, years later, I wonder if maybe it wasn't so much disappointment about being recognized as disappointment about being recognized *without being seen.*

Humans did not evolve to be recognized outside our clan or tribe. Our brains are not wired for being known to millions of people and getting bothered by strangers at intern parties.

"There is little doubt that you and I engage in more relationships than our ancestors did," writes Dr. Giles. "It is estimated that in the Middle Ages the average person only saw 100 different individuals in the course of a lifetime."

A hundred people in a lifetime. Compare that with how many people you see, both in person and online, in a single day. Now multiply that by being a celebrity getting mobbed by thousands.

Bottom line: Evolution hasn't equipped us to handle fame.

Bill Murray, our foremost philosopher of celebrity, put it this way in an interview years ago to promote *Lost in Translation*, a movie about an actor exhausted by the surreal lifestyle of being a movie star:

> You know the theory of cell irritability?...
> If you take an amoeba cell and poke it a
> thousand times, it will change and then re-
> form into its original shape. And then, the
> thousandth time you poke this amoeba, the
> cell will completely collapse and become
> nothing. That's kind of what it's like being
> famous. People say hi, how are you doing,
> and after the thousandth time, you just get
> angry; you really pop.

In other words, stars don't start out being rude to fans. It's just that the fame exhausts you. It changes you.

Here's what a decade of fame will do: In 2010, at age twenty, Taylor Swift said, "There's nothing that hard about [being famous]. It's not that tough. I'm not complaining."

By 2020, at age thirty, Taylor had a pretty different opinion. She said in her *Miss Americana* documentary, "We're people who got into this line of work because we wanted people to like us...because we were intrinsically insecure. Because we liked the sound of people clapping, because it made us forget how much we feel like we're not good enough. I've been doing this for fifteen years. And I'm tired of it!"

If you've seen the movie on Netflix, you might recall this part. Her voice cracks. She starts to tear up. You feel bad for her but also really want her to finish this thought. "It just feels like it's more than music now at this point. Most days, I'm like, okay. But then sometimes, I'm just like…" She pauses. "It just gets loud sometimes."

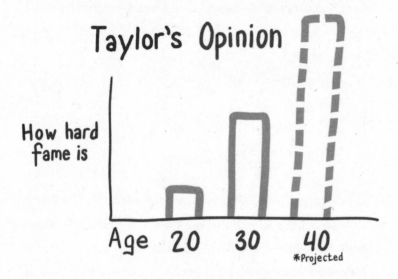

If I were to ask you what particular *type* of fame is most likely to warp a person's brain—or at the very least make them require a bunch of therapy years later—you would probably say: being a child star. I'm going to introduce you to three child actors—one current, one former, and one who's trying to make a comeback—whose paths diverged in their late teens.

Our first actor was performing in Broadway shows by age six. By sixteen, Christy Carlson Romano was *the* Disney Channel star, starring in three Disney shows at the same time: alongside Shia LaBeouf on *Even Stevens*, with Hilary Duff in *Cadet Kelly*, and as the voice of the title role in *Kim Possible*.

In addition to Shia and Hilary, there are many Disney-Channel-stars-turned-mainstream-celebrities:

- Zendaya
- Britney Spears
- Miley Cyrus
- Selena Gomez
- Justin Timberlake

The list goes on, but you get the idea. So if Christy was such a big star—the only one on *three* Disney Shows simultaneously—why isn't she on that list?

When Christy agreed to chat with me as part of my investigation for this book, I'd offered to speak by audio instead of video so she didn't feel any pressure to dress up, to be "on" like she does on camera. But our audio is glitchy—it's probably my fault, I'm nervous about talking to her and fumbling with my AirPods. She switches to FaceTime, camera on. "We'll just do it this way," she says, the sound now crystal clear. She's wearing a pair of glasses that I've never seen in her Instagram photos. They're fun and oversized, like large Harry Potter spectacles. No makeup.

Here's the weird thing about child stars. It's easy to

miss, but being a child actor is a *job*. Like, yes, child actors happen to be doing labor that might make them famous, but fundamentally they are employed. The movie set is their office, and they go to work every day alongside grown-ups who are also doing their jobs—directors, camera crews, agents, etc. The only exposure to peers is, in Christy's words, with other "child stars with momagers."

As with many child stars, Christy's mom was her manager. "I didn't have any real independence from my mom. I had no control over my money in my bank account," Christy tells me. She felt "confined. I felt like I was being held back from living a normal life, a better life."

As a teenager, she had this fantasy. A fantasy about experiencing normal things: Friends. School. That kind of thing. But she was so far removed from ordinary experience that even her view of normalcy was shaped by what she'd seen (or performed!) in movies. She was longing for "the teen-movie happy ending with a group of friends in a Jeep on their way to the beach," Christy writes in *Teen Vogue*.

Senior year of high school, she was accepted at Columbia University, the Ivy League school in New York City. *Even Stevens* ended that same year. "I was told that leaving Hollywood right after *Even Stevens* would ruin my career. In retrospect, it probably did."

What did those Disney-Channel-stars-turned-mainstream-celebrities do that Christy didn't? At the peak of their

Disney Channel fame, they leveled up to mainstream adult celebrity—movies, pop music, critically acclaimed HBO shows, and so forth. But at age eighteen, at the peak of her stardom, Christy left Hollywood in search of that group of friends driving to the beach in a Jeep.

To be clear, some of Christy's peers also went to college, even to demanding Ivy League schools: Natalie Portman to Harvard; Emma Watson to Brown University; Julia Stiles to Columbia. So the career setback wasn't that Christy went to college, but that she went with the intention of leaving Hollywood.

College, unfortunately, didn't live up to her expectations. She had a tough time relating to the other students. "I had been bullied [before I was famous], and I thought that becoming famous would make it better, but it didn't," she tells me. "I was bullied again in college, and I think it was because I didn't really know how to interact with people my own age or how to just slow down and just kind of let myself be a student."

At Ivy League colleges, every freshman was the star student at their high school. Christy's level of success and fame can make others jealous. Plus, it's kind of startling to discover the person you grew up watching on TV is the person sitting beside you in class.

Christy and I are the same age. I tell her that I also got

into Columbia and almost went there. We could've been classmates.

"This is a weird question," I add. "But did you intern on Capitol Hill at some point?"

I ask not knowing if it was her or not. But Christy's eyes widen the same way they did ten years ago when I interrupted her at the reception. Yep, definitely her.

"I did," she responds. "Why...did we meet?"

"Dude. We met, Christy!"

"Oh my God."

I tell her about how it seemed like all eyes were on her at that reception.

"I never really felt like that," she says, which I take to mean she was so used to it that she didn't notice it anymore. Which would mean she also wouldn't notice or recall a conversation like ours. So I tell her about when I approached her and got the impression she didn't want to talk to me—at least not about *Even Stevens*.

"I don't know what I was thinking. I'm so sorry," she says.

"No, I don't think you were rude," I tell her. If anything, I was the rude one.

"I do think it's actually really interesting to kind of unpack because when you saw me, I was coming off of that first year," she says. You know, the year of failing to connect with her peers at college. "So I think I started to get a little bit more standoffish about stuff."

"But I wasn't coming up to you as a fan," I suggest. "I hadn't even watched *Even Stevens*. I was just like, 'Oh! You're the famous person!'"

Christy agrees, explaining that can be threatening, being accosted by someone who recognizes you but doesn't *care about* you. I was like the rando who just wants a selfie to get Instagram likes.

I'm only guessing here, but I bet all Christy wanted at that reception was to be treated like any other intern. She hadn't found normal at college. Now she'd come looking for it in DC. But obnoxious blockheads like me thwarted her normalness wherever she went. Maybe "normal" just wasn't an option?

Soon after the internship, she returned to her Broadway roots as Belle in *Beauty and the Beast*. She was on one of those giant Times Square billboards. She remembers feeling like, "Whoa, I have to be something. The world owes it to me is basically what I was thinking."

She went back to Hollywood. This time, without her mom. Christy was fully in charge.

But here's the part you knew was coming: the troubles.

"I wasn't on time for my auditions. I was not focused, I wasn't prepared mentally. And I was burnt out."

There was drinking. Depression. Experiments with self-harm. By law, child actors' earnings must be put into accounts they can't access until adulthood. Christy had never handled money before, but now she suddenly had access to all her savings. A lot of money went to clubbing. She once spent $40,000 on a crystal that a psychic promised would fix all her problems. The psychic turned out to be a scam artist.

After about a decade of all this, she got sober. She went back to school. Met a guy. Ex-military. Dating him and learning about his own struggles as an adolescent gave her the "empowering realization that famous people aren't unique." Today, they're married with two young daughters.

But she's never quite stepped out of the spotlight. Last year she went public with her mental health struggles, started posting glossy photos on Instagram, and launched a YouTube series where she cooks meals with other former child stars.

I ask if she could ever give up being a public figure.

"I think it's important to figure out a way to bridge the divide between having my career mean something, having my legacy stay intact, but also growing it so that it's more present, rather than something that already peaked. I'm struggling with that still and, you know, the—"

One of her children interrupts in the background, and Christy Carlson Romano has to go.

CHAPTER 19

Christy Carlson Romano's story follows the trajectory we'd probably forecast for a child star. Early fame. Struggles. Substances. And then difficulty figuring out what it means to have "former child star" on your grown-up resume.

CHILD STARS

I want to introduce you to someone who breaks all these stereotypes.

Evelyn Rudie lives about a mile from the star bearing her name on the Hollywood Walk of Fame. It's right at the corner of Hollywood and Highland, the central block of the tourist part of Hollywood. You know, where the Oscars are filmed. Where *Jimmy Kimmel Live!* happens. That sort of thing. For exercise, she likes to walk to the star and back. Recently, though, she discovered it had vanished.

The star had always been a point of pride for Evelyn, a reminder of her childhood fame. She was best known for starring in the TV adaptation of the beloved children's book series *Eloise*. At age six, she was the first child ever nominated for an Emmy. She did *The Tonight Show* seven times.

"I was not able to go to a restaurant without a hundred people sticking their noses in the window, looking and trying to see. 'Oh, look! That's Evelyn Rudie,'" she recalls.

Fame wasn't a priority for her, though.

"If I think back, I was more concerned about: Did the popular girl in school like me? Was I gonna make it when I ran for student body treasurer?

"Which I didn't. I lost."

Her nickname in elementary school: "Evelyn Rudie Cootie."

Remember, this was *Evelyn Rudie*, at that time one of the most famous actors on the planet. Every kid wanted to be like her, right? And yet, *she* wanted to be like someone else.

Evelyn remembers asking her mother why she couldn't be more like her classmate Susie Givens, the most popular girl in school. Her mother said, "You can never be Susie Givens. You'll never be her. And why would you want to? She's got her special things. You've got your special things."

But by age nine, when her star was laid in the sidewalk, *Eloise* was over. She looked around at her actor friends—other child stars—and they were all starring in "their own" series.

She told her parents she wanted a series, too. "My parents said, 'You know what, everything's good. You're wonderful. You get to go to school with your friends. You get to go to birthday parties. You work four times, five times a year. Everything's fine.'"

Evelyn disagreed. And not long after that...she disappeared.

There had been a recent string of high-profile child kidnappings, so her parents assumed she had been abducted. Law enforcement across the country was notified. She was found on a plane headed to Washington, DC. When she landed, the FBI was waiting along with "like nineteen million paparazzi with the cameras and all that." A breathless headline in the *New York Times* announced, "ELOISE" RUNS AWAY.

According to the article, "Evelyn, distressed because she had recently been unable to get choice roles, admitted that the purpose of her flight had been to receive publicity and to bolster her personal popularity."

Sixty years later, Evelyn insists that's fake news. She'd previously met the First Lady, Mamie Eisenhower, on a White House tour. (Perks of being a child star.) Evelyn figured if she knew anyone famous enough to help her get her own series, it would be the First Lady. So she had opened up her piggy bank savings (she got to put $10 in every time she did a TV show—a lot of money in those days), taken a cab to the airport, and hopped on a plane to Washington, DC.[35] Evelyn had even written a note for her parents explaining where she'd gone, but she'd accidentally brought it with her on the plane.

As an actor, Evelyn was approaching "the awkward years" when a child actor is no longer young enough to be cute but not quite grown-up enough to play adult roles. According to Evelyn, this is where things start to go bad for child stars. They've been making a living off being adorable without necessarily studying acting, and suddenly they've outgrown adorableness. "A lot of those kids turn to drugs, alcohol, and promiscuity, anything to make them not feel so rejected," says Evelyn.

Evelyn's parents and agent suggested she take a break and finish high school. Come back to me when you're

---

[35] Later, the local police chief told Evelyn that as a result of her stunt, the law had been changed so that minors could no longer purchase their own airline ticket.

eighteen and we'll talk, her agent told her. In high school, Evelyn got involved in productions at the drama department. There she learned she didn't need to be famous to scratch her itch to create and perform.

After high school, Evelyn met with her agent. He was big-time but also a family friend. So he got real with her.

He said, "I can make you a star again overnight if you want to go that direction. I don't suggest it because your life is then no longer your own. They're going to tell you what you can and can't do. They're going to tell you who you can and can't date. They're going to tell you who you can and can't marry. And basically they will own you for the rest of your life. You will be famous. You will be as wealthy as you can possibly imagine. And that's the trade-off. So you decide." And I just said, "It's not a decision. Thank you very much. Goodbye." And that was the end of it.

At that same age, Christy Carlson Romano left acting to pursue what she saw as a normal, non-famous life. But Evelyn left *fame* to pursue *acting*.

"Being happy was more important to me than being famous," she says. "The work [acting and theater] has always been what drives me...so I think if somebody says, 'Well, over here is the fame and over here is the happiness, which one do you want?' It's the happiness every single time."

And theater is what makes her happy. Evelyn and I are having this conversation on two wooden chairs on the stage of an intimate theater with just six rows of seats. Like a talk show without an audience.

It also happens to be the stage where I perform my one-man show.

Evelyn and her husband have been running this mom-and-pop theater for forty-seven years. When she first met her future husband, he'd just gotten back from fighting in Vietnam. I had previously asked Christy Carlson Romano—who, like Evelyn, married a veteran—why stars often seem to marry other stars.

"I think that celebrities marry other people in the industry because there's an understanding that they're going to work off each other's momentum," she says. There's definitely a bit of "planning" going on in these marriages, according to Christy.

To which we might say, gross! Why not marry for love?

And sure, love seems better. But according to historian and marriage expert Stephanie Coontz, up until the last century, most people didn't have the privilege of marrying for love. You married to create family alliances and arrange for land and wealth to be inherited. There are still many traditional societies where couples don't (or can't) marry for love. So, if anything, when famous people marry to create a strategic business alliance, they're doing what humans have been doing for most of history.

Besides, non-famous people take other factors into account besides love. Do you have a profession you—or your parents—would prefer your future spouse be in? Or *not* be in? Doesn't seem much different from a movie star preferring another movie star.

Anyway, Evelyn didn't marry a movie star, but she did marry a fellow actor. To this day, after Evelyn and Chris perform their original plays—often in front of groups of dozens or even fewer—people ask Evelyn why she didn't continue with film and television. They're perplexed. Even...offended.

"Why didn't you continue?"

"Why do you hide yourself in this little theater?"

"When are you going to move to a bigger theater?"

But these people just don't get it. "What could be better than this?" Evelyn says. "We've got everything that you want."

Evelyn's in her seventies now. There's a highlighted streak in the front of her hair that's changed colors many times since I've known her: magenta, silver, maroon, copper. Evelyn Rudie has no regrets.

"I can look back and say I had it. All the things that everybody just dreams of and desires. I had it. And I loved it. But I don't have to worry about it anymore." Her advice to current child stars and aspiring actors? "You have to worry about the fulfillment that it gives you. If you want to act, act! Act for the rest of your life. But don't act because you want to be famous or because you want to be rich."

Oh, and her Hollywood star? After Evelyn found it missing, she emailed the Hollywood Chamber of Commerce, who oversees the Walk of Fame. Turns out it was being refurbished. Soon it was replaced, good as new. Recently, a group of twentysomething girls were taking photos of one another near the star. Evelyn pointed at it. "That's me!" The girls were all like, "Yeah, right. Ha ha."

So now, when she walks by it, Evelyn just smiles at the star and keeps the memories to herself.

I want to introduce you to one more actor, a girl whose post–high school future hasn't been written yet. If you heard the voices in the audio recordings of my chats with Evelyn Rudie, seventy-one, and Dalila Bela, nineteen, you'd probably guess incorrectly if asked to pick which was the teenager. Dalila (Da-LEE-la) is what you'd call an old soul. She has big thoughts and uses big words. She only joined Instagram recently because the other stars on her TV series (she generally refers to them as "co-workers") were using it to organize a hangout. Dalila is not a natural self-promoter. She goes weeks without posting. But she's quickly gained 1.8 million followers, and I suspect by the time you read this she'll have even more.

Her fans are finding and following her after seeing her roles in the *Diary of a Wimpy Kid* movies, on the PBS Kids show *Odd Squad*, and especially from her portrayal of Diana Barry, best friend of the title character on Netflix's *Anne with an E*.

Even so, Dalila says she's not recognized that often. She was recently in an acting class where some girls were talking about how much they loved *Anne with an E* and the character Diana. Dalila thanked them and told them she portrays that character.

"They didn't believe me and I had to show them a photo of Diana and me side by side," Dalila tells me over Skype.

I ask her if she feels famous. She hesitates.

"Sort of, yeah," she says.

Her newfound influence weighs on her.

"Like with Spider-Man, 'with great power comes great responsibility,'" she says. "With the fame that I've gathered, it's made me really think about how to phrase things and consider the positive and negative ramifications of my actions in a way that I hadn't before."

Dalila did not set out to become famous. But she most certainly set out to become an actor. At age three, she told her parents she wanted "to do what the people on TV did." She booked her first national commercial when she was five. When she was eight, her parents sat her down for a very grown-up conversation.

They told me it could not be achieved if I did it halfway. I would have to give everything. And if that is something that's going to bother me—the not being able to go to my best friend's birthday party, missing out on school pajama day, not being able to go with my friends to the water park because I've got an audition that day or I have to film a movie or I gotta fly out to do this TV show...then I shouldn't do this because my ultimate goal and my happiness are going to clash.

She chose acting. And she doesn't have an ounce of regret...even as her parents' predictions have come true.

"I don't mind if I don't experience prom. I don't mind if I don't experience homecoming," she says. "This is the life that I want. This is what I've always wanted ever since I was young."

The only time Dalila mentions friendships, *plural*, in our conversation is to say that she's lost some of them because of the demands of her job.

"I understand," she says. "The life that I choose does not always allow for a 'normal' life, according to what society considers to be quote normal."

Basically, she's okay with that. So are her parents. Once she decided it was what she wanted, they were 100 percent behind her—and her younger brothers, too, who have also become actors.

Now look, I'm no psychologist, but what jumps out at me about the differences between our three child stars is the *influence of their parents* on their attitudes toward fame around their eighteenth birthday:

- **Christy Carlson Romano** wanted independence from the industry and her mother (who had managed her career during the period when she became famous), so at age eighteen, she left for college.

- **Evelyn Rudie**'s parents persuaded her to stop acting during the awkward years, and then, at age eighteen, their and her agent's description of fame made her permanently quit Hollywood.
- **Dalila Bela**'s parents painted a clear picture of the pros and cons at age eight, but Dalila felt the sacrifices were worth it...and she still does today.

It seems that Christy may have felt some parental pressure, but Evelyn's and Dalila's motivation to become actors came entirely from within. They just really, really wanted it.

Dalila's father is from Panama, and her mother is from Brazil. Her mother has always told her this Portuguese saying, *Antes só do que mal acompanhado*, which means "It's better to be alone than in bad company."

Dalila keeps the company of her family.

"They're my rocks. They always have my best interests at heart," she says. As an actor, you need people who will "keep you from losing yourself because it's very, very, very easy. I will admit it's very easy to get swept up in 'Oh, gosh. I'm famous. Oh, look, I'm going to this party! I'm going to that party! And I'm working with this person and working with that person.'"

Dalila says that fame "can be very taxing on your mental health." Sometimes she'll find she's exhausting herself replying to fans on Instagram.

"All of a sudden I realize, like, 'Oh, my jeez, I'm feeling a little overwhelmed right now. This is a lot. So you know what? I'll set my phone down, listen to music, pet my dog, go spend time with my family, take a walk outside.'"

Dalila's advice for people who want to be famous... but also happy? "Don't think about being famous. Think about what you want. My family has always believed this. If you are doing what you love and giving 110 percent to what you love, you're going to be successful. That doesn't necessarily mean famous, but you're going to be successful. And because you're doing what you love, you're going to be happy."

Being that she's dropping wisdom bombs like that at age nineteen, Dalila may be the rare child star who grows up to have it all: fame, success, and even that elusive thing we call happiness.

CHAPTER 20

If you've ever been unlucky enough to get the thing you most wanted, you've probably had this thought: Hey, wait a second, I thought this would make me feel better? Wasn't this supposed to make me happy? It's made everything worse!

That's what being on MTV was like for me.

It all happened because of that community service award I lost. Which means losing not only led to the CW show with Mandy Moore, it later got me on MTV. Losing was a weirdly big win for me.

It was an MTV show called *America's Best Dance Crew*. They wanted to do an episode honoring outstanding young people, so they teamed up with that nonprofit from the community service award.

Don't get me wrong, it was cool to be selected. I got to work with my favorite dance crew ever (what, you don't have a favorite dance crew?), the Jabbawockeez. You know, the guys who wear the white masks.

At first, I was like: Finally! After all these years, I'm going to be on MTV! Who knows, maybe you-know-who will see it?

But it was crazy stressful. There were endless phone calls with producers, flights back and forth to LA for pre-production. All this between travel to my motivational speeches. I'd recently started making YouTube videos almost every day, too, which were regularly being viewed by tens of people.

The show was broadcast live from a soundstage in LA. It was just like you see in the movies: Giant numbered soundstage buildings, producers driving around in golf carts, all that. Soundstages are basically giant soundproof warehouses. For the show, they'd put up bleachers for the audience members, a gazillion lights, and a stage, all built from nothing in the middle of this cavernous room.

They told us to dress like we were "going out to a club." I wore a tie and a vest, demonstrating how little I knew about going out to clubs. I looked like I'd come straight from an internship on Capitol Hill.

The day of the show, I felt this intense combination of jittery and exhausted. I kept telling myself: This is it! My dream is coming true! I'm about to be on MTV. *Be happy, gosh darn it!*

But that's not how happiness works. The set was loud

and crowded and there was no place to just sit by yourself. I wanted to go home and lie in my bed. Which unfortunately was about two thousand miles away.

Eventually the lights came on, the dance crews performed, and I got to walk across the stage and be on MTV for, like, twelve seconds. I'd planned to walk on with, like, a cool dance move. People would love it! They'd remember me! MTV News would hire me! But I chickened out. I was too nervous. Maybe I just wasn't cut out for this stuff, after all.

Afterward, I slept for what seemed like days. I didn't have the energy to work or hang with my friends. I got sick. It seemed like a bad cold or the flu or something, but it would not go away. I saw a bunch of doctors. I was so tired, I had to cancel speeches. I stopped posting videos. I didn't make plans with friends because I was always afraid I'd feel bad and have to cancel. I just fell apart. All this lasted off and on for *years*. Really, it felt like my life was ruined.

I spent those years looking back on my moment on MTV as one of the worst things that ever happened to me. That's not MTV's fault or anything. It was my fault for getting too stressed and obsessed about the whole thing. Obviously that tiny appearance on MTV didn't make me any degree of being famous, but it did give me a taste of what it *might feel like* to be famous. Which I can boil down to one word for you: *stressful*.

Try something for me. Make a list of the top five things that cause you the most stress.

Okay. Now. Enter Dr. Charles Figley, a mental health expert who specialized in the stress caused by disasters and trauma. He studies populations who experience high levels of stress. First responders. Nurses. Veterans. And yes, celebrities. Dr. Figley was able to survey fifty-one major celebrities about their mental health. He asked what caused them the most stress. These are the top five answers, starting with the most stressful:

1. The celebrity press
2. Critics
3. Threatening letters and calls
4. Lack of privacy
5. Constant monitoring of their lives

No surprises in that list, right? It's all the negative side effects you'd expect to come with fame. What's interesting to me is this: Chances are none of these celeb stressors were on your top five list. Nor are they on mine. So there's clearly a unique kind of stress that comes from being a prominent person.

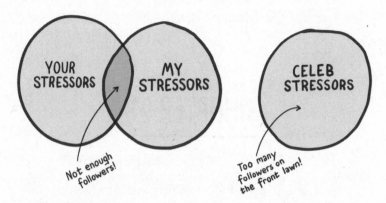

YOUR STRESSORS | MY STRESSORS | CELEB STRESSORS

Not enough followers!

Too many followers on the front lawn!

"To be a celebrity means to have more than the usual assaults on one's ego," Dr. Figley told *Psychology Today.* "You're very vulnerable to the personal evaluations of other people. The public is ultimately in control of whether your career continues."

All this raises the question: If being a celeb is so freaking stressful, why do it then? Why don't these people just, like, quit fame?

CHAPTER 21

As a teenager, Justine Bateman became very famous. Like, *very* famous. Like, chased by paparazzi and hosting *Saturday Night Live* famous. She'd been cast in the sitcom *Family Ties*, a long-running 1980s show that was viewed by twenty-six million people each week. But chances are you've never heard of her. Even though her co-star Michael J. Fox is still a household name. Even though her brother, Jason Bateman, is also now a major star.

So what happened? Why did she let that fame slip away?

Justine describes how it feels to be famous—and to *have been* famous—in her book *Fame: The Hijacking of Reality*, which is by far the most insightful book any celebrity has written about how it feels to be a celebrity. She says fame is like having a sheath over your body. When someone sees you, they don't see you, the person. They see the sheath. When she was twenty-one, a bouncer wouldn't let her into a nightclub even though her valid ID said she was of age. Why? Because the character she played on TV, Mallory, was a teenager.

"You're Mallory. Mallory's not twenty-one," he said.

He literally would not let her pass. He couldn't see the

twenty-one-year-old human underneath the sheath.

When you're that kind of celebrity, every conversation you're in is about...you. If you're standing around on a set, if you're sitting around a dinner table, whatever—you are the center of gravity. Everyone laughs at your jokes. They want to keep you talking, keep you happy, so they keep asking you questions about yourself. Eventually, Justine says, you just forget to ask questions back, to talk about the *other* people in the conversation. Not because you're a terrible person. Just because it's how people act around you.

You're trapped inside the sheath. Buried alive. It's like one of those "psychological thrillers where someone's been given an injection of whatever so that they are alive, conscious, but paralyzed, unable to move at all, while totally conscious of every horror happening to them, watching it."

That's the bad part. The good part is interacting with other famous people:

You are automatically IN when you're dealing with other famous people, people who have your level of Fame. The nod. "Wassup?" The Nod of Recognition. "I see you. You, me. We get it. We get what's going on. I feel you." It's nice. In an airport, at an event, across a room, "Wassup?"

But it's only nice while it lasts.

I felt uncomfy on that red carpet in New York. Turns out, actually famous people feel that, too. Justine says walking a red carpet is like "having your fame temperature taken." You can tell by how long the cameras keep up their click-click-flash-flash how famous you are at that moment. As her fame began to decline, Justine noticed the photographers were less interested. After she'd walked away, the frenzy of shutter clicks would last longer for the next person. The worst was when a photographer said, "Can you just?" and motioned her to step out of the way so he could have a clear shot of another, more famous person behind her.

The secret to the red carpet, she says, is to walk away from the crush of photographers right before they stop snapping. You don't want to be left standing there after they've lost interest. So you listen closely to the shutters, and the moment you hear a drop-off, you say "thank you" and walk away, like removing the popcorn from the microwave before it burns.

Which is also a metaphor for dealing with dwindling celebrity over time. Justine describes it like a bank that's rigged with explosives. It blows when your fame is totally gone. As soon as you notice the countdown on that bomb has started ticking, you have to get in the bank and get out your safe-deposit box: your inner self. Your personal worth. If that stuff is still attached to your fame when the bank blows, you'll be shattered. That's how former stars ends up in rehab, bankruptcies, or worse. Because the bank blew and they didn't know who they were anymore.

After her show ended, at Hollywood parties, Justine noticed that A-list acquaintances, "famous-as-I-used-to-be people," started avoiding her. Averting their eyes. As if her shrinking stardom was contagious. Like it could rub off on them.

Once she was walking across a parking lot and saw actor Aaron Eckhart coming toward her. She smiled, ready to say hi. But he looked down and started walking faster. Not because he's a bad person, but because she looked like a fan and he had somewhere to go. He didn't recognize her. She knew the look on his face because she'd been on the other side of that encounter countless times.

Back when the whole world seemed to know her name, she could get anyone on the phone. Call their office, drop her name, they'd answer. And restaurants! She could call the most popular restaurant on short notice, no reservations available, drop her name, and they'd get a table ready for her right away. But after she became "post-famous," she started making her reservations under a fake name. Not for privacy. She did it to avoid the disappointment, the sinking feeling, of giving her name and having the voice on the phone fail to brighten with recognition.

Whether at social events or with strangers in public, every conversation was the same.

"What are you working on?"

"Are you still acting?"

It's the same conversation you and I have *about* celebrities. *Hey, what's so-and-so been up to? I haven't seen them in anything for a while!* We don't bother to check their IMDb or google them. We used to see them and we don't see them anymore, and therefore they are failing in some way.

It's not that she wasn't doing stuff. Justine got a pilot's license. She started writing and directing and creating digital media. At age forty-six, she was accepted into the UCLA computer science program. Which is, if you think about it, not the kind of thing most forty-six-year-olds are willing to go back to school for. Impressive. But that same year, she also did one day of acting. A small part on an episode of *Modern Family*. Guess which of these events *everyone* cared about? Guess which one everyone congratulated her on?

See, N O T H I N G you do after you've been that famous is E V E R going to be good, or right, or applause-worthy, or impressive, or even f*****g noteworthy. Your obituary will STILL no matter what you've done after that great "achievement" of Fame, will still just list that pinnacle of "accomplishment," to the exclusion of almost everything else you have ever done in your life.

She describes it as an inverse correlation:

HOW INTERESTING ANY OTHER ACCOMPLISHMENTS WILL BE

HOW FAMOUS YOU USED TO BE

Hey, I know what you're thinking. Oh, boo-hoo, a beautiful celebrity has trouble not being quite so famous anymore? I've got *real* problems.

Justine would completely agree with you. She's not saying her problems are worse than yours. She's just saying this is how it feels to become post-famous.

Let's say you're, like, the golden smart kid of your high school.[36] You get great grades, teachers love you. You might not be prom queen, but you're probably student body president or something. The kind of person who if you ask for a bathroom pass or for permission to leave class early to attend a student council meeting, teachers will always say yes. The principal doesn't bother you if he sees you walking the halls during class period. Basically, you're special. Then one day you show up at school and all the teachers have been replaced by new teachers you've never met before. The principal is a complete stranger. None of these people know you. Suddenly, no special privileges or treatment anymore.

That's how declining celebrity works. Getting used to special treatment doesn't always mean you're a narcissist or terrible person, just that you're accustomed to the way people respond to you. When it all goes away, it's like the carpet has been pulled out from underneath you.

---

36 Since you're reading this nerdy semi-scientific book for "fun," this probably isn't even hypothetical.

Recently, Justine started typing her name into Google and it auto-completed to "Justine Bateman looks old." She clicked. Are you familiar with the internet? If so, you can guess the kind of comments she ran across. She wrote in her book about reading comments saying she looked like a "meth addict." She looked "like death warmed over." This was all kind of shocking to Justine because before reading those comments, she thought she looked, well, pretty good.

Which leads us back to that question: If fame is so toxic—and if slowly losing it is even worse—why not just be rid of it once and for all? Move to a small town and get a normal job and don't ever act again, not even one-day gigs on *Modern Family*. This is a fundamental question for us in our investigation into fame and unhappiness. If we all agree that fame tends to make people unhappy, why do so many people seem to want it? Why do celebrities keep doing the thing that makes them famous if it's also the very thing that makes them unhappy?

It's like having a negative relationship with someone close to you, Justine says. Like a boyfriend or girlfriend who you know deep down isn't good for you and doesn't love you for who you are, but you can't seem to quit them. Like a parent who's been terrible to you in the past, maybe even abusive, but you keep trying to make them proud of you because it seems like it's *better to have some relationship than no relationship at all*.

Now look, whether or not you should break off the kind of relationship I'm describing here is between you and a mental health professional. This is just a metaphor. The point is, non-famous people often make the exact same counterintuitive choice that famous people do, deciding that holding on to a broken relationship with a person or with fame—even if it's toxic and receding and taking your self-worth with it—seems better than no relationship at all.

The irony is that if being famous is difficult, *losing* that fame is probably worse. I had a conversation about declining fame with Dr. Donna Rockwell, a psychologist and "fame coach." Yeah, I had the same question: Um, what is a fame coach? It's not, as you might guess, someone who gives you tips on how to get famous—although there are people who do that, too. A fame coach is a person who helps you *deal with fame*. Like a life coach if your life happens to be a famous one.

Besides serving as therapist to some notable individuals, Dr. Rockwell is the co-author of another of the few (really, only two[37]) peer-reviewed, published studies about the psychological experience of being famous.

With the exception of the reliably eccentric Bill Murray,

---

[37] The other being Dr. Drew's....It's surprising how few psychologists study celebrity, given how many of us gawkers would probably want to read about their discoveries.

who for years has had a 1-800- number that rings to his house instead of an agent, most celebrities are protected by layers of guardians whose sole job is to say no to requests and privacy invasions like, you know, filling out a survey. Even if you *could* somehow contact them personally and ask if they'd answer your questionnaire, they'd probably say no because giving a stranger access to their private thoughts would be like allowing paparazzi inside their bedroom.

Unless you happen to be a fame coach, so you have an existing relationship with clients who trust you to keep their insights and stories anonymous. One of the people Dr. Rockwell interviewed was an R&B singer. At the height of her fame, this woman was an A-list superstar who was known around the world. That's the interesting thing, actually. She *still is* known around the world. But she's an older woman now, recognizable but aging and no longer recording hit singles. She made many people wealthy over the course of her career, but sadly none of them happened to be herself, thanks to her faith in the wrong business partners when she signed her early contracts. These days she sometimes struggles to pay the bills.

But no one knows or considers any of this when they recognize her. Strangers interrupt whatever she's doing, inevitably asking for a selfie, a little souvenir piece of her to show off to their friends.

She was recently in public and someone stopped her. The stranger said, "Hey, didn't you used to be _____ ?"

And then he said her name.

Which was still her name, of course. But in his eyes, she was no longer that person. She wasn't herself anymore.

Dr. Rockwell says celebrities experience a common set of psychological phases. First, a "love/hate" relationship with their newfound fame. For years, they've tried so hard to get people to pay attention. Look at me! Please! Watch this thing I do! Now, suddenly, the problem has reversed: The public is paying *too much* attention. People won't look away. Which comes with some cool perks. But also no privacy.

After the *Hunger Games* movies catapulted Jennifer Lawrence to the A-list, she described the adjustment in an interview. "If I were just your average 23-year-old girl, and I called the police to say that there were strange men sleeping on my lawn and following me to Starbucks, they would leap into action. But because I am a famous person, well, sorry, ma'am, there's nothing we can do."

In addition to the crazies camping on your lawn, things are hard when you leave the house, too.

"Everything has to be some sort of strategy," Johnny Depp explained on the *TODAY* show. "To get you into the hotel, to get you out of the hotel, to get you into the restaurant, to get you out of the restaurant." All of it takes planning, maybe security, and a back entrance to avoid causing a riot.

Eventually, you get used to that new normal. Now comes phase two: addiction.

Dr. Rockwell asked her subjects what fame feels like. "One participant said, 'It is somewhat of a high,' and another, 'I kind of get off on it.' One said, 'I've been addicted to almost every substance known to man at one point or another, and the most addicting of them all is fame.'"

If fame is addiction, I suggested to Dr. Rockwell, when you inevitably start to lose it, that must feel like withdrawal from substance use.

"Absolutely," she replied. "You have these neurons

hanging there waiting for what they had before. [But now] there's nothing there. There's nothing to connect to. So they're sad....That's why you find so much depression and anxiety. People become depressed because their neurons aren't doing the jig they've done all these years."

Your brain misses all the attention. Used to be, you couldn't get the paparazzi to leave you alone. Now you can't get them to pay attention. Rock star David Bowie described it like this: "You avoid being photographed and then you'd give your right arm to be photographed."

I recently had a Twitter conversation about this with James Gunn, writer and director of superhero blockbusters like *Guardians of the Galaxy* and *The Suicide Squad*. Not only is he name and feat famous himself, he's worked closely with enough movie stars that I'd call him an expert in the experience of A-list fame.

"People who strive to be famous are usually looking to feel loved from the outside world because they aren't experiencing feeling loved in their lives otherwise," he told me. "This doesn't mean they aren't loved, just that, for whatever reason, they can't experience that feeling."

Striving for fame can feel fun and hopeful, "but when people actually get it, it's disappointing, because it in no way fills that hole of feeling unloved."

If anything, he says, fame makes it worse. You feel alone. Critics and haters emerge.

"At that point many famous people become caught up in a vicious cycle of fighting to maintain their fame while privately despairing at how it feels to be famous," he said.

Dr. Rockwell's subjects opened up to her with "some extraordinarily sad and heartbreaking tales of what it feels like to be in the bubble of fame." But get this. Dr. Rockwell asked each of them: If you could do life all over again, would you give up the fame? None of them said they would. Not one. Zippo. Dr. Rockwell was shocked—"After the heartache, after the emptiness"—none of them wished for a normal life.

Why? They told Dr. Rockwell that being famous meant being "in an exclusive club." You know, the club where Justine Bateman gives you a nod. You're in the room where it happened.[38] You're special.

How come many of us regular folk think it would be cool to try out being famous but *also* have a general sense that it would probably suck? Like, how can we have both thoughts at the same time?

Actually, we human creatures have conflicting drives on the daily. You want to get in a workout, but you also want

---

38   The room where it happened, the room where it happened.

to Netflix. You want to be on time for school, but you also want to go back to sleep. I think the idea of being famous is like the idea of being the president of the United States. We're all curious about it, we've imagined it, and we think it would be fun to try for, like, a day. But overall, we know that the responsibilities, the pressure, the lack of free time to just chill on the couch and look at your phone would all probably add up to a mostly un-fun experience.

And yet: Every four years a bunch of people still run for president.

So yeah, fame is like that.

There's another, deeper reason that might help explain why we humans keep chasing the presidency and/or fame. In *Illusions of Immortality: A Psychology of Fame and Celebrity*, Dr. Giles says being famous means having "symbolic immortality." It's why Alexander named all those cities after himself. He wanted to live forever.

This is Biology, after all, so let's look at this from an evolutionary perspective. You know about survival of the fittest, right? Traits that keep us alive and help us reproduce get passed on. Which means that the desire to replicate is baked in. Life wants to make more life. Which is a poetic way of saying, you know, sex.

For most of human history, people didn't have the option to replicate their image. But even though the average citizen, unlike Caesar, couldn't, say, invent and put their face on their own currency, they *could* make babies. (Which they did, and sidenote, that's why we're here today.) In modern times, though, an ordinary person can create content in seconds that has the potential to replicate their image millions of times.

"Technological developments over time have enabled us to reproduce ourselves in a way that mimics the replication of DNA," writes Dr. Giles. Which is a science-y way of saying that maybe the same drive to make babies also makes us want to become famous. Going massively viral means being everywhere in the world at once. It's almost godlike. Fame feels like immortality.

I'll occasionally get DMs from followers saying I showed up in their dreams. Part of me is like, *Wow, what an incredibly weird thing to hear from a stranger*. But if I'm being really honest, there's also a voice in my brain that's like, *My content makes me show up in people's dreams? Awesome. I'm going to live forever*.

CHAPTER 22

"I would say the most difficult thing about being famous when you are young...is also the greatest thing," John Schneider tells me, describing his life at age eighteen. He mimics an excited crowd of fangirls chasing after him, "*Oh, my God! Oh my God!*"

But: "You can't turn that off. You can't even hide."

He was seventeen when he auditioned for a TV show about backwoods car racing. He arrived in a "dilapidated pickup truck" (he'd borrowed it), spoke in a "big ol' country accent" (he doesn't have one), and performed his audition while "toting a beer" (the beer, I'm assuming, was real). Well, he got the part: Bo Duke in the TV show *The Dukes of Hazzard*. Back in the day, there were only three channels on TV (I know, right). No internet. No Netflix. So everyone watched TV. Being on TV meant being a superstar.

"When *Dukes* was the number one show in a three network world, people could tell by my silhouette who I was because of the way I stand," he says.

But that was all a very, very long time ago.

"Now if I go somewhere and nobody notices me, it hurts my feelings," he says with a sort-of-kidding, sort-of-not chuckle. "It's hard. It's harder to grow accustomed to *not* having a mob than it is to grow accustomed to having a mob."

I met John when I was a child appearing at an event for Children's Miracle Network Hospitals, a nonprofit he co-founded. John has that self-assured Ryan Seacrest vibe. And he has that *look*. You know the one. The hair. The chin. Gotta be a movie star or a senator or something.

Anyway, we've crossed paths at other Children's Miracle Network events over the years, and we caught up the other day by phone to discuss fame and happiness. I asked him how it felt when the mob started, like, receding. Does it feel like your life is going downhill?

"I could see where somebody might feel that," says John. But he's not that kind of somebody. He always believed—*knew*—the mob would return. I guess that's the difference between John Schneider and me: I would see the mob as half empty. He sees it as half full.

He spent fifteen years doing minor TV roles and having modest success in country music until he got his next big role: Superman's adoptive father, Jonathan Kent, in the long-running series *Smallville*.

"But I [always] knew *Smallville* was going to come," he says. After *Smallville*, there was another dry spell. But he "knew there was something else. The trick was just to be ready for it when it showed up, to recognize opportunity. It showed up in the form of *The Haves and the Have Nots*," a Tyler Perry drama on the Oprah Winfrey Network in which John has been a series regular for eight years now.

I suggest his positive expectancy must help him feel better after a show ends. He corrects me: His confidence isn't what helps him deal with the last show ending. It's what helps him *get the next show*. Literally the first thing he says after I start recording our conversation: "You know, Josh, I planned on being famous from about the time I was eight years old."

To John Schneider, becoming famous was always going to be his job. And it always will be. It's all hustle, all the time. "I'm working on the same plan I was working at ten. I'm doing everything I can," he says. He has an indie movie studio now. "We do the music for our movies. I write the movies. My wife produces the movies. I direct the movies. We distribute the movies. We're out on the road promoting the movies, which sounds very highbrow, but it's not. It's no different than a lemonade stand."

John drops phrases like "the gift of celebrity" and "what a gift it is to be famous." I tell him that's unusual. Few famous people are willing to say anything positive about the experience.

"It's wonderful," he replies. At the end of the day, "when

I'm gone, when you're gone," people will remember him. He gets to play characters that impact people. "The secret to happiness in being famous is loving those people who love you." That is, your fans. John loves his fans. "I mean, since long before you were born, I've been going to car shows," he tells me. Car fans are the core fan base of *Dukes of Hazzard*. "I'm out there shaking hands and talking about cars and mingling with the people that keep me here."

John talks to me on Bluetooth while he drives around his property/independent film studio in rural Louisiana on a four-wheeler, getting ready to head out for the next leg of his tour of Southern drive-in movie theaters. At each event, he screens his newest movie (it's car-themed, obviously) and plays a live concert of the country music he wrote for it.

"I believe this next movie will be bigger than anything I've ever done before," he says. Considering the only way to see it right now is to go to one of his drive-in theater tour dates—it's currently not picked up for distribution in traditional movie theaters—this prediction seems unlikely. But that's just not how John thinks.

"Don't second-guess your plan. Don't have a plan B.... Do not have a plan B because plan B yells at plan A that you don't believe in it," he says.

I gotta be honest. I definitely have a plan B. I have, like, a plan C and a plan D. One thing is for sure: John Schneider would be a way better motivational speaker than I am.

We know enough by now to say that John is the exception. Most people find fame to be a burden. But we also know enough by now to say that most famous people, regardless of any chill outward persona, worked very, very hard to get where they are. So why didn't *achieving their dreams* make them happy?

I asked Dr. Giles about this in an email.

"The initial experiences of fame are intensely enjoyable—it opens up those doors that remain closed on the vast majority of people, giving you access to rich and beautiful people and exciting experiences, and most of us would be pretty happy in that phase of the experience," he explained.

But then a couple laws of psychology kick in. The first is the law of diminishing returns, which is the idea that more of a good thing is great, but only up to a point. This is basically the same thing as declining marginal utility.

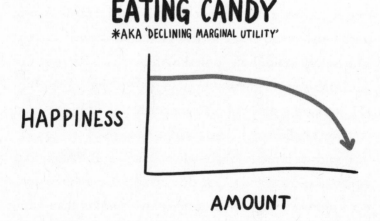

EATING CANDY
AKA 'DECLINING MARGINAL UTILITY'

HAPPINESS

AMOUNT

You can substitute most any pleasant thing and the graph is the same. The first kiss is better than the second. The first time you watch the movie is better than watching it again. And *becoming* famous feels way better than *being* famous.

Why? Because humans are shockingly good at adapting. It's basically our superpower. Adapting keeps us alive. Adapting is evolution in action.

Psychologists call this "habituation." When it comes to negative events, habituation is helpful. Habituation is the sad thing becoming less sad over time. Which is great. Unfortunately, this works in reverse with positive events. Habituation is also the awesome thing that becomes less awesome feeling over time.

Basically, habituation means we are really good at getting used to things. A famous 1978 study showed that both lottery winners and accident victims who became paralyzed anticipated that after a couple years, they would return to the same level of happiness they had before. Dozens of studies show that having more money increases happiness but only up to a point, usually around a middle class standard of living. Beyond that, more money doesn't increase happiness, and it may even decrease it. So if you're poor, money does buy (some) happiness. But if you're rich, *more* money doesn't buy any more happiness.

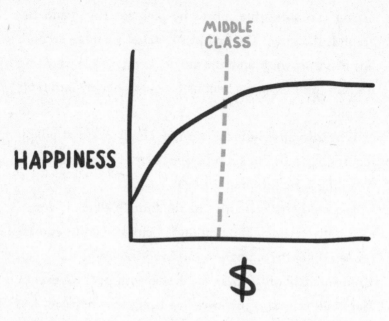

To be clear, I'm not saying that there aren't factors that alter our happiness or life satisfaction. I'm saying that whatever happens, good or bad, our biological default is to get used to it. To habituate.

"The trajectory of fame works a little bit like a drug—euphoria at first, then habituation, followed by repeated attempts to up the dosage in order to generate new highs," said Dr. Giles.

Fame turns us into junkies. It feels great at first. But then you need *more* fame (followers, views, record sales, whatever) to get that same rush as before.

"There are people who manage to be very famous and very happy but they are probably a minority, just as the very happy are probably a minority in society generally,"[39] Dr. Giles told me.

Which is like, *whoa*. This whole time I've been approaching this investigation as if being happy and famous would require a different happiness formula than the one for the rest of us. But why should it? Sure, fame presents a unique set of stressors, but celebs are working with the same standard-issue brains as all *Homo sapiens*. And sure, most celebrities probably aren't happy. But, like, *most people aren't happy*, either.

It's like that thing Russian novelist Leo Tolstoy said. "Happy families are all alike; every unhappy family is unhappy in its own way." Celebs might have unique challenges that can make them unhappy, but the factors that can bring them happiness are the same as for the rest of us.

Just to make sure I was on the right track with this theory, I ran it by bestselling author and happiness guru Shawn Achor. Shawn spent years researching happiness at Harvard. Today he's one of the world's leading positive psychologists. He has a viral TED Talk. He's been on *Oprah*. All of which has meant he's been a happiness consultant to some very famous people. He said this:

---

[39] Depressing aside: Dr. Giles also said some psychologists even "argue that the expectation of happiness is problematic in itself." So there's that.

> I've worked with a handful of Hollywood movie stars who have really struggled to find happiness....We often wrongly believe that we will be much happier if we were rich or famous. But for these movie stars they have all the money they need and they're more famous than they want to be. They often can't go into a Starbucks without being accosted by people asking for autographs or impersonations, so some sit at home alone in their beautiful Hollywood home and feel jaded because the success they thought would create happiness didn't work out.

It's like what Jim Carrey said: "I think everybody should get rich and famous and get everything they dreamed so they can see that's not the answer."

My whole happiness investigation began back when I had dinner with my manager, the guy who wants to make me famous. This is a guy, by the way, who's launched the careers of many, I might even say most, of the biggest names in comedy over the last several decades. Name any top comedian and he's probably worked with them at some point.

More recently, I asked my manager if he could think of any clients he'd made famous over the years who became *more* happy after they made it big. He could think of... none. So I asked: Well, was anyone at least *the same* level of happy after becoming famous?

He thought about it for a few moments. Eventually he named one client, a long-time *Saturday Night Live* cast member, who my manager said stayed the same. Specifically, this comedian was the same level of unhappy both before and after becoming famous.

I thought about this for a few weeks and then went back to my manager: If being a comedian makes everyone unhappy, aren't he and I in the wrong business?

"It's not about this career or this industry specifically," he said. "Successful people can become unhappy in any career."

COMPUTER SCIENCE

Variety: Do you consider yourself famous?
Charli D'Amelio: Definitely not. I consider myself a normal teenager that a lot of people watch for some reason. I mean, it doesn't make sense in my head, but I'm working on understanding it.

STUFF WE WILL LEARN IN CLASS TODAY:

- Does internet fame make you more happy (or less happy) than other types of fame?

- Is social media a positive or a negative for leading members of marginalized groups?

CHAPTER 23

By the time Ocean had sent me that email saying I wasn't right for on camera, I was in grad school at the University of Southern California in Los Angeles, getting a master's in communications. I really didn't even know what that was, but I knew I liked communicating, and I had the money to pay for it thanks to winning that fitness contest. I guess I thought a master's in communications would, like, teach me about being on TV or something. It turns out that's a different degree. That's broadcast communications. The communications program I was in was more about writing corporate newsletters and press releases.

But at least I'd made it to LA, fame capital of the world. I might've given up on MTV, but I hadn't given up on being a TV host. I wrote up a résumé that looked approximately like this and sent it to every TV-host-sounding gig I could find on Craigslist.

Josh Sundquist | Wanna-Be Professional TV Host

SemiFamous@JoshSundquist.com

EXPERIENCE

- Appeared on TV show with Mandy Moore for approximately twelve seconds
- Walked across stage on MTV dance show for even fewer seconds

SPECIAL SKILLS

- Bodybuilding photos, social awkwardness

You get the idea.

I applied to a lot of gigs. No interest. Finally, one place wrote back. It was a start-up network that was weirdly not on TV. They broadcast shows on—get this—*the internet*.

YouTube existed by this point. People were starting to post grainy webcam videos. But this network would broadcast *live* on the internet. There would be no archive or recording. It was basically a low-fi version of TV that had no DVR.

Sounded worthless to me, but hey, they were the only ones who had replied to any of my emails. They said they'd schedule an interview but never did. I did some deep googling and found their parent company and used that to find the address of their studio. When I showed up, the producer was kind of weirded out, but he was like, "Um, okay, since you're here anyway I guess we can do an interview."

I got the job, which would be hosting their news show. They wanted to make the news cool and relatable. It was pretty much the poor man's MTV News. Throughout the whole first episode, a fly kept landing on my face.

We shot a few times per week. One time while we were broadcasting, the script I was reading from the teleprompter started scrolling backward. I just made up stuff to say for the rest of the segment. When we went to break, I asked the producer what had happened.

"Oh, we went out to lunch and the prompter guy got super drunk," he said, like that was a totally normal thing.

The good news is, I'm pretty sure zero people watched the show. Except my mom. But even she got bored and turned it off sometimes.

During that year, I also randomly recorded myself telling a story on my webcam and uploaded it to YouTube. Looking back, it seems obvious that it would be possible to record yourself and share the video. But at the time, cell phone cameras were crap. Vlogging wasn't a word. Internet video wasn't a clear path to fame like it is today. You-Tube was basically a few nerds experimenting with talking to cameras in their bedrooms, a fact that they kept secret from their real-life friends.

Anyway, I uploaded it and forgot about it. A few months later, I was on YouTube and saw that it had several thousand views. Another video I'd posted, a compilation of pranks I'd filmed on my parents' camcorder in high school had over a hundred thousand views. But instead of trying to make more YouTube videos, I thought: *Hmm. That's interesting. Maybe I should check Craigslist for any new job postings for "real" TV shows.*

The earliest internet celebrities were way smarter than me. They saw that people were watching, and they kept making content. By the time I started making content regularly, I was a bit late to the party. But still early enough that the party wasn't crowded yet.

After I finished school, I started posting more on YouTube. Internet video was starting to take off. YouTube had even started paying its creators. I applied a couple times to join the paid program but got rejected. This has been basically the theme of my life: I'm not quite cool enough for MTV—or to be super popular in real life—but also not quite nerdy enough to be super popular on the internet.

Creators had started carrying around little digital cameras and recording their lives. By this time, I'd moved back to the DC area. But all the YouTubers seemed to live in LA and New York. They all hung out with each other, like, all the time. They filmed each other. It was like this big party that viewers got to watch.

I remember watching a vlog where a few famous You-Tubers were hanging out in New York. They all crowded onto an elevator. Each of them seemed to be holding a camera, filming one another. The video had hundreds of thousands of views.

This felt like my chance. Forget TV. If I worked hard enough, maybe I could make it onto that elevator. So I started posting constantly.

Enter Hank and John Green—today they may be more famous as bestselling authors, but at the time they were known online to a niche audience as the VlogBrothers—who announced this conference they were doing. It was going to be like YouTube in real life. They called it "VidCon."

I emailed Hank to introduce myself. I said it seemed like they had the leading creators in each category of videos scheduled to be onstage: the top music stars, the top comedians, the top lip-synchers. Well, I was probably the most popular motivational speaker on YouTube.[40] Shouldn't I be onstage at this conference, too?

Hank watched a few of my videos and then called me. He said he thought I could be "big" on YouTube.

---

40 Technically I was probably the only motivational speaker on YouTube, but hey.

"Not Shane Dawson big, but big," he said.

He offered me a ten-minute spot onstage at VidCon if I could pay for my own plane ticket. I agreed.

The first night of VidCon, I was walking around the hotel, and I spotted several famous YouTubers walking into a ballroom. I followed them. They were speakers at the conference, and so was I, so I should probably be wherever they were. I hadn't gotten an invite, but that was probably because I was a last-minute addition or something...right?

I followed them to the back of this grand ballroom in the basement of a hotel in Los Angeles. There were about thirty of us. I looked around. I recognized...everyone. All of them were famous YouTubers. In fact, these were basically all the famous YouTubers who existed. That was how small internet video was then. You could put thirty famous YouTubers in a room and that was it.

I was starstruck. Here were all the faces I was used to seeing on my computer everyday, except now those faces were attached to bodies. Some of the bodies looked different than I thought. Rhett and Link were way taller than I expected. iJustine was way shorter. Shane Dawson looked about the same.

Everyone else sort of knew each other already. You know, because they'd been riding elevators together and whatnot. These people were famous—if not to people outside the hotel, at least to the attendees inside it.

I was not. When I walked through the lobby, no one recognized me. The next day a conference attendee asked how many subs I had.

"Um, what's a sub?" I asked.

"Subscribers," this kid clarified for me, looking at me like I had asked what the internet was.

"Oh," I said. "I'm not sure. Maybe a thousand?"

I did my ten-minute speech. It was fine. But I wasn't, like, mobbed in the hallway afterward. My name didn't trend or anything. I was kind of disappointed, if I'm being honest. But years later, a YouTube fan who was sitting in the audience told me he saw my speech and was crying by the end of it. He would come back the next year and be onstage himself, going on to amass millions of subscribers. His name was Tyler Oakley. And after VidCon, iJustine gave me a shoutout on her channel, describing me as her "new favorite YouTuber of all time." More shoutouts came. I did some collabs. I started gaining followers.

Then my first book came out in paperback in between the first and second VidCon. I had a book signing at a bookstore in LA and iJustine promoted my signing in a video titled "MEETUP IN LA!" Other famous YouTubers said they were coming, too. Suddenly, it was no longer just a book signing. It was a YouTube thing.

Hundreds showed up. The bookstore ran out of chairs. People were standing several deep in the aisles surrounding the event space. The manager told me afterward that it was the second largest event signing they'd ever had, which was saying something for an LA bookstore that had done plenty of celebrity signings. Number one? Some people called "the Kardashians." I had never heard of them. They weren't YouTubers, after all.

HOW MANY I COULD NAME

KARDASHIANS   VLOGGERS

After I did a little talk and signed all the books, a few YouTubers went to a restaurant next door. Everyone in the group was either a famous YouTuber or the romantic part-ner of one. We were packed into a big, U-shaped booth. It was about the size of an elevator, really. That's when it hit me. I had made it. I was on the elevator.

A guy around my age wandered over to our table. He

hovered there like a waiter, until everyone stopped talking and looked at him. He said hi, that he'd just been at my event next door.

"Cool, thanks for coming," I said.

He nodded but just kept standing there, looking at all these big-time vloggers he was seeing up close in real life. It seemed like he was waiting for us to squish closer together so he could sit down. He looked from person to person around the table. Finally, his gaze settled on me—definitely the least famous person at the table—at the end of the booth.

I looked up and our eyes met. His face was begging for me to vouch for him. *This guy seems cool, everyone, let's have him join us.*

It wasn't so different from the table in the crew-only conference room at that TV show audition. Except now I was the one sitting at the table.

I looked down at my glass of water. I was sitting at the very edge of the booth, after all, barely able to fit there myself. Besides, I didn't even know the guy. Who was I to ask everyone to make room for him?

Finally, after a ridiculously long period of awkward silence, he walked away.

"Well, that was weird," someone said.

The next year at VidCon, the featured creators were instructed to avoid main corridors and use back hallways instead. Safer. Prevents mobs from forming around you. Which I figured was good advice for everyone else. You know, the famous people.

When I checked in at the hotel lobby, I was immediately recognized by someone asking for a selfie. I said yes, of course. It was like that thing Pauley from NCIS calls "the Bees." They swarmed. It wasn't an unruly mob or anything. They formed into a neat, orderly line. But no matter how quickly I took selfies and signed programs, the line kept getting longer. At fan conventions, nothing attracts people faster than a long line. *What are we waiting for? No idea, but they must be famous!*

I shared my story about getting stuck in the lobby with other YouTubers backstage. We commiserated about how hard it was to be famous at VidCon—but secretly, I also thought it was pretty much amazing. All these people, total strangers, knew who I was. They thought I was important. They wanted a photo with me. It felt like everything I'd ever wanted.

Over the next ten years, VidCon grew from that modest convention in a hotel basement to a giant convention of thirty thousand. And it's not just YouTube anymore. There are new platforms every year where people are getting famous—megafamous, mainstream famous.

VidCon now rents out an entire hotel *just* for Featured Creators. There's a security perimeter around the whole block. You can't even walk into the parking lot without a Featured Creator badge. Even so, dozens of young fans, usually middle school age, crowd the sidewalk beside the hotel like junior paparazzi, hoping to snap a photo of a famous creator getting into or out of one of the chauffeured SUVs that whisk creators back and forth to the convention center.

Make no mistake, being a Featured Creator can be stressful, but it's also very, very cool.

Example: The boxes of swag from major brands. One year, I found a giant wooden trunk of merch from a fashion label in my hotel room. But there was a note on top addressed to a different creator. I was kind of crushed. Not because I wanted the clothes—although that, too—but because here I was at the highest tier of internet fame, being invited to VidCon as a Featured Creator and it turns out there's another secret tier where you get even better swag and perks. I found the creator, a fashion and hair influencer from the UK, at a party that night and asked if I could have the trunk delivered to his room.

"Just keep it, mate," he said. "To be honest, I get way more free clothes than I know what to do with."

Those Featured Creator parties, by the way, are amazing. Expensive swag bags, open bar, performances by internet-famous DJs. Everywhere you turn you are literally bumping into people with millions and millions of followers. Sometimes you realize it's a person you're a huge fan of. Honestly, internet creators tend to be really nice, fun people with ridiculously compelling personalities. They have to be; otherwise, why would millions watch them talk into their cell phone camera?

When you do a meet and greet at a fan convention, people line up before the start time, or they get tickets in a lottery to meet you, and at the appointed hour you walk out from behind a curtain to find this queue waiting for you. You can tell how famous someone is not just by how long their line is, but by how loudly their fans cheer when the creator comes out.

Early on, my signings would take three or four hours. But they got smaller each year. Then one year it had dwindled enough that when I walked out, there were smiles and waves, but no cheering. My heart sank. I wondered if anyone else noticed the silence. Maybe not. Maybe it was just my fragile fame ego paying too much attention to such things.

"I'm sorry we didn't cheer for you," said one of my followers when it was her turn to step forward for a photo.

Oh.

The last VidCon I went to was the tenth anniversary.

My meet and greet was so small the convention organizers suggested I meet fans at a table instead of in a line. More personal attention, they said. A more intimate experience. It was a polite spin. Turns out, there weren't even enough people to fill all the seats around the table.

In public these days, people frequently recognize me ("Are you the guy who makes internet videos?") and want a selfie with me, but are clearly struggling to remember my name. I try to make it easy for them. "I'm Josh, what's your name?"

Something else I hear a lot from strangers: "Hey! I used to love your videos!"

I'm never sure how to respond to that. "Um, thanks?"

Basically, this is not an "I struggled for a long time and eventually succeeded" story. This is an "I struggled for a long time and eventually had some experiences on the margins of viral fame" story. It's a story about how all forms of fame, including the semi kind, and especially the internet kind, are temporary. But hey, I am grateful for every single follower, and I consider it a privilege to be recognized—whether or not it happens frequently, whether or not they remember my name—for stuff I've made online. And strangely, these days it turns out what I'm most recognizable for is Halloween costumes. More on that in the next chapter.

CHAPTER 24

The strangest part of my whole internet semi-fame experience might be my Halloween costumes. In 2010 I went to a Halloween party dressed as a partially eaten gingerbread man. I was really just trying to make my friends laugh. I took a grainy bedroom photo of the costume and posted it on this social network that eventually went out of business called DailyBooth.[41]

Anyway, people loved the photo. Which was cool. But I didn't think that much of it. Two years later, my then girlfriend/now wife suggested I dress as the leg lamp from *A Christmas Story*. I posted a photo of it on Facebook. Someone shared it on Reddit. It blew up. Then people found the gingerbread-man costume, and it became a thing. I was the guy with the costumes.

Not something I set out to be. I mean, I wanted to be

---

41 DailyBooth was basically Instagram but on your webcam. Turns out camera phones take way better/more fun photos. Hence, Instagram.

a computer programmer when I grew up. Not a costume guy. But hey, sometimes you stumble across something, and that thing goes viral, and you go with it. Going viral is mostly luck, in my opinion. In fact, the harder you try to go viral, the less likely it is to happen. On the internet, it's more likely some random throwaway photo or video clip you didn't think about is what will be popular.

Costumes weren't my intended goal or career path, but they were the thing I got lucky with. I say lucky because hey, ever since I was speaking into those vents or drawing "Kids' Newspaper," I've wanted to amplify my voice. And it turns out my biggest voice is behind the mask of funny Halloween costumes.

You might have come across some of them online. I've since dressed as a flamingo, Tigger, the Pixar Lamp, and many more. The costumes have been featured on the front page of Reddit pretty much every year, as well as the front pages of BuzzFeed, Yahoo!, and pretty much every other media website you can think of. One year, on Halloween my name trended worldwide on Facebook. The costumes have also been shown on television: the *TODAY* show, *Good Morning America*, ESPN, and more. The costumes are by far the most widely known thing I've ever done.

But the weird thing is, my face isn't visible in most of the costumes. People know my costumes, but not my name. So the costumes are feat fame.

Feat fame is strange. Strangers have told me about my own costumes or DM'd me photos of myself, thinking they're sharing news about someone else. When I wear the costumes in public, I get recognized a lot. "Look, it's the costume guy!" "Hey, were you the flamingo?" "Did you dress as a leg lamp one time?" Basically, I'm recognized way more often when my face and body are entirely covered than when people can see my actual face.

All this is the good side of going viral, of internet celebrity. But there's a downside to a system of fame where anyone can post anything: the trolls, the haters, the racists, the conspiracy mongers.

Sometimes trolls forget that celebrities are also human beings. That's how they can justify the meanness. Sometimes it's the opposite, the troll *does* remember the celebrity is human, and that's part of the thrill: the chance to influence a famous person, to get in their head.

"You can't change your face. You can't change your parents. You can't change any of those things," Willow Smith tells Girlgaze. "So I feel like most kids like me end up going down a spiral of depression, and the world is sitting there looking at them through their phones; laughing and making jokes and making memes at the crippling effect that this lifestyle has on the psyche."

Celebrities are real humans who can and do see what is said about them online. This is the one thing celebrities and trolls have in common: On the internet, it's easy to forget at least some part of them is still human.

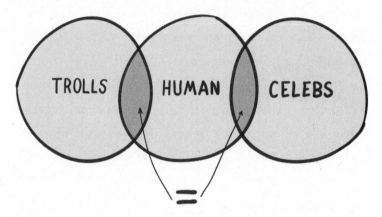

The internet has made fame a two-way conversation, particularly for internet creators. At its best, internet video is kind of magical. You'll happily watch a creator filming themselves in grainy camera footage, but if you saw the same quality video in a movie, you'd give it one star. Internet video makes we the viewers feel like part of the family. Part of the process.

At its worst, though, that two-way conversation can be toxic.

On TikTok, sometimes I film on a selfie cam, sometimes another person films me, and sometimes I record myself in front of a mirror, all of which means the side my leg is on can switch back and forth in the video. I get a lot of comments about this. Most people are making a joke. I mean, you can clearly see that I'm filming into a mirror, and most of us know how mirrors work.

But a teenager recently made a conspiracy-type TikTok about me. He speaks like he's just found proof of a UFO landing, "Guys, I've noticed something VERY STRANGE is going on...." He shows screenshots of me both in front of a mirror and not in front of a mirror to demonstrate that my leg is switching sides. In conclusion, he suggests maybe I'm faking having one leg for the views. This guy doesn't have a lot of followers or anything, but this video was controversial and thus gaining a lot of traction. People kept tagging me in it.

I'm sure you can easily put yourself in my shoe(s) to understand how I felt here. Someone is accusing me of *pretending* to have one leg? As if I'm somehow good enough at special effects to crop out one of my legs but sloppy enough to forget which one? Please.

I was furious, but I decided to deal with it the same way I've always dealt with the social weirdness of having one leg: with comedy. So I made a duet joking about his video.

A few days later, I got a DM from this guy asking me to take down my video about him. I politely suggested he take down his instead. I mean, come on, bro.

He eventually did, but I guess it didn't help. He DM'd

me again a few days later to say he was still getting negative comments on his profile and it was really getting annoying.

Me: I mean, you posted a video accusing a guy with a disability of faking it. What did you expect would happen?

Troll: I guess I hoped I'd get a bunch of views.

Me: Have you gotten a bunch of views?

Troll: Yeah

Me: So haven't you gotten exactly what you were hoping for?

Troll: Well, yeah, but now people are trolling me

Me: Didn't you think people would get mad when you posted that video?

Troll: Yeah

Me: So again, haven't you gotten exactly what you wanted out of this? I don't understand what the problem is?

Troll: The problem is people are trolling me

Me: Bro, that's what it means to get a bunch of views. The more famous you are, the more people will troll you. Happens to me literally every day

People always think, Oh, if I get a viral video then _____ [fill in your goal: you'll make tons of money, kids at school won't bully you anymore, you'll finally be happy]. But going viral just brings a new bag of problems. A certain percentage of viewers won't like any post. Even if it's a tiny percentage, the more views you get, the more people there will be out there who *don't* like it. Especially if your video was meant to make people mad in the first place.

Troll: I guess I didn't think about it that way

Me: Honestly, you're lucky I made a *funny* video about your video. My first instinct was to post an angry video about you. In which case, any complaints you're getting would have been WAY worse. But I didn't want to destroy your life, so I made it funny instead

Troll: Thanks for that, I guess. But can you still take your video down?

Me: You said your goal in making your video was getting views by making people mad. How did you think *I* would feel?

Troll: I guess I didn't think you'd see it

Me: Well, why don't you take a guess at how it made me feel when I saw a video accusing me of faking having one leg?

Troll: Bad, I guess. But I mean you always make jokes about it

Me: I make jokes about it because it SUCKS. I make jokes so I don't get angry about videos like yours. I make jokes because that seems like a better way of dealing with it

Troll: I was joking too I knew you had one leg I just wanted views. But what about that thing at the end of your video where you said maybe I was right? That made me wonder if maybe you were faking after all

At this point, I was really tempted to slam my phone down and make an angry video about this guy. But I reminded myself that just like I wanted him to understand that I was a human person, he was a human person, too.

Me: That was a joke. I'm a comedian. I make jokes

Troll: It made me wonder

Me: Um, OK. I can assure you I have one leg. I had cancer when I was a child

Troll: Sounds like a bummer. Can you take down the video, though?

Me: It was a bummer. And I will take down this video under the condition that you don't post anything like this anymore

Troll: OK, thanks so much

Me: I'm not deleting it, just moving to private. I don't want to come back on your profile and find more mean content in the future. Do you understand?

Troll: Yes, thanks for understanding

So far, he hasn't posted anything else like that since our chat. In fact, most of his content these days is videos promoting Black Lives Matter. Which, for a white teen former troll, seems like a victory for the internet's occasional power to create good—and fame's occasional power to create happy endings.

FINAL EXAM

Fame can be great, fame can be deceiving, fame can also, if you let it, if you get wrapped up in it, it can take you down a long dark road that's very detrimental and damaging to your career, to your life, to your relationships....These days, and it's taken me a long time to get here, I try to be really neutral on fame. I don't hate it, I don't love it, I don't need to be famous. I'm grateful for it, but I keep the meter in neutral.

—DWAYNE "THE ROCK" JOHNSON

ANSWER KEY

Hey, look at the clock on the wall! Finally! The last bell of the day is about to sound. It's almost time to pack up, check your phone, and head out to board the bus—or, if you're lucky, hop in your mom's waiting SUV.

But what kind of school would I be running if there wasn't an exam at the end?

Hold on, don't freak out. This test is ungraded, entirely optional, and even open book. In fact, instead of making you answer any questions, I'm going to just give you the answer key.

Or, at least, my answer key. To be happy in life, regardless of how famous you happen to be, eventually you will have to come up with *your own* answer key. The good news: Unlike in normal school, you are totally free to cheat off mine below. These are the answers I've come up with, personally, after all this research. Maybe you'll agree with them. Or not.

Part of me hoped by the end of writing this book I would have completely lost interest in fame. Not so much, it turns out. Between when I wrote the introduction and now, I've gained a bunch of new followers and even booked my first voice-acting gig, a series regular in an animated show.

Given all we've learned about its association with unhappiness, why would a part of me still want to become famous? It's a question I've asked myself many times during this investigation—and that I've asked many therapists over the years. Like, is there something broken inside me I hope fame will fix?

Maybe I'm just your average attention-seeking narcissist. Or maybe it's because I came close to death when I had cancer as a child—sometimes I feel like I'm still that kid in a hospital bed, not so much afraid of dying as afraid of being forgotten. Fame, after all, means being remembered.

I think both parts of me will always be there, both the wanting and the not wanting of fame. But it's all right to want things we'll never have and to have things we never wanted. Conflicting feels are part of the human experience.

So! The final (self-) examination. What have we learned about the intersection of fame and happiness? Here's my answer key.

1. IF YOU'RE UNHAPPY *BEFORE* YOU'RE FAMOUS, YOU'LL STILL BE UNHAPPY *AFTER* YOU'RE FAMOUS.

After you get famous, guess what? You're still the same person on the inside. The voice in your head is still there, saying the same depressing stuff it was before. You cry the same flavor tears and laugh the same flavor laughs.

It's like what Lil Nas X said: "The biggest surprise of becoming globally famous? On the outside, everybody loves you—but on the inside, everything [feels] the same."

So if you don't get your insides sorted out before the fame, they will still be unsorted after. I'm not saying fame can't affect your happiness one way or the other. I'm saying the major building blocks of your happiness start before and entirely apart from fame.

2. OBSESSION WITH FAME *THEN* ROBS YOU OF HAPPINESS *NOW*.

We humans have this truly unfortunate tendency to always imagine happiness as a thing that exists in the future. Dr. Giles put it this way in an email: "Most of us simply aren't satisfied with ordinary contentment." Instead, we incorrectly have "the belief that we could all be blissfully happy, if only we had X, Y, Z."

It's like a FOMO gap, and it's where most of us spend much of our lives.

Getting the thing—whether it's achieving XYZ-level fame or getting into a certain college or finding a boyfriend or leveling up an avatar—never makes you happy. Trust me. I went to the Paralympics. I won a bunch of contests. I got semi-famous. All of it is cool for a while, but it doesn't permanently change how you feel inside.

Shawn Achor, Oprah's happiness guru, explained it to me this way: "While many of us can tell ourselves that happiness might exist off in the future after a certain level of success, the stars know for a fact that success did not yield the happiness that it promised and they must retool and rebuild if they want to find happiness."

Technically, there's no such thing as *then* because it's always *right now*. So now is the only time you can ever be happy, and the only way to do that is by letting go of the FOMO gap.

3. KEEP THE FAME METER IN NEUTRAL.

I recently reached back out to Alex Coletti, the TV producer, to ask him, as a person who's worked with a lot of famous people over the years, for his thoughts on being famous and happy. He said it's about "separating who you are from what you do."

Did you catch that quote from The Rock?

"I try to be really neutral on fame. I don't hate it, I don't love it, I don't need to be famous. I'm grateful for it, but I keep the meter in neutral."

You are not your fame. Or your grades. Or your job. Or your relationship. So what *are* you? Enough. Already.

4. DON'T BECOME A FAME-AHOLIC.

Celebrities told Dr. Rockwell that fame was like the most addicting drug in the world. Addictions, by definition, make you unhappy. I'm not talking about your "addiction" to cosplay or to your favorite Netflix show. That's just extreme enthusiasm. I mean addiction where you need that next fix so much you can't function.

So if you do happen to become famous someday, appreciate it, use it, grow it in a healthy way, but know that one day, the fame will be gone. Don't cling to something you can't hold on to. James Gunn, the superhero-movie director, told me, "The only happy, famous people I know are those who never wanted to be famous and came upon it by happenstance or those who have worked hard to let go of caring about fame after achieving it."

In other words, those who have rehabbed their fame addiction.

5. BUILD AN ENTOURAGE OF TRUE FRIENDS.

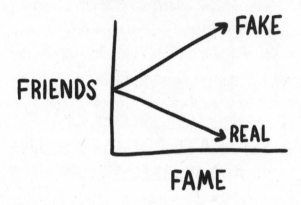

Finding friends is hard. For celebrities, it's even harder. With every new friendship, Pauley Perrette from *NCIS* has to ask: *Does this person like me for me or because I'm famous?*

It's not as simple as just sticking with your OG pre-fame entourage. An A-list actor in Dr. Rockwell's study said that fame had chased many of his old friends away because his fame became "baggage." When he hung out with his old friends, his fame was "like a bloated cod, just sitting there."

Shawn Achor told me, "People often use the rich or famous for their attributes rather than their friendship, so social connection, real social connection, is hard to come by." That's a problem, he said, "because social connection in my research at Harvard is the greatest predictor of long-term levels of happiness."

The temptation when you're famous is to surround yourself with people who keep you in the center of attention, who cater to your every whim and laugh at your every joke. I mean, who wouldn't want that? But those aren't true friends. True friends call you out on your crap, keep you honest and humble, and support you whether your fame is trending up or down. Put those kinds of people in your entourage. And then never let go.

6. SEPARATE PRIVATE STUFF AND PUBLIC STUFF.

100% YOU

PRIVATE PUBLIC

100% REAL

Dr. Rockwell said celebrities naturally tend to create a dual persona: the public and the private. She calls this "character splitting." Which sounds like a serious mental illness, but she actually says it's "the only possible adaptation" that can allow happiness and fame to coexist.

It doesn't mean being fake—in fact, if your public persona is unauthentic, that will lead to unhappiness because, as author Jonathan Franzen says, eventually you will grow to resent the audience for buying "your schtick." It just means you've said: These are the parts of me and my life, the slice of my personality pie, that everyone gets to see, and these other aspects are known only to me and the entourage.

7. FAME IS A CURRENCY, SPEND IT ON SOMETHING GOOD.

FAME STORE

Dr. Rockwell says that people who cope best with being a celebrity are those who see their fame "as a currency that can be used to make the world a better place."

Why? Because, she says, "Happiness comes from feeling part of something larger than ourselves."

Activities can only make us feel happy to the extent those activities feel meaningful. So fame can only contribute to our happiness if that fame is also contributing to others.

8. CHASE PASSION, NOT FAME.

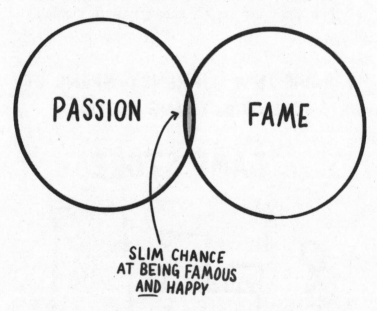

SLIM CHANCE AT BEING FAMOUS AND HAPPY

There are two types of motivation: intrinsic and extrinsic. Let's say you play tennis. You play because you enjoy the thrill of the game, the pleasure of a great serve, and the way a can of tennis balls smells when you first open it. All those are *intrinsic* motivators. Passion fuels your pursuit of the sport.

Then you start playing for your high school team. In competitive, organized tennis, you can win trophies and ribbons and tournaments. Which is cool, and it might even motivate you to practice more, but all that stuff is *extrinsic* motivation, meaning the rewards are all external. Nothing wrong with external rewards. But intrinsic motivation is the more sustainable force because it powers you to push through obstacles and setbacks for the sheer love of the game.

Shawn Achor defines happiness as "the joy we feel when we are striving after our potential." Not the joy we feel when we get the trophy or the millionth Soundcloud download or whatever. Happiness is found within the pursuit of activities that pull us internally regardless of external rewards.

So the only people who have a *chance* at both fame and happiness are those who first become happy as a side effect of following a passion, and then happen to also become famous as a side effect of that same passion. The person who loves tennis so much, and has so much talent, they eventually turn pro. The singer who is obsessed with music and ends up becoming a chart-topping sensation. These kinds of people can be happy and famous because they *got famous doing what makes them happy*.

On the other hand, someone who pursues a sport or music primarily to become famous can never be happy, whether they become famous or not, because they're doing something they don't actually enjoy. If they do happen to get super famous, they'll be even more unhappy because now they have all the problems that come along with fame and they're stuck in a job that *never made them happy in the first place*. That's the problem with extrinsic motivation. It might be enough fuel to get you there, but it doesn't refill itself when times get tough.

You can't become happy by trying to be famous. But there's an outside chance you might become famous by trying to do what makes you happy. Which is the only possible way to be both.

ACKNOWLEDGMENTS

Authors always seem to *conclude* the acknowledgment section by thanking their spouses, but since you probably won't read that far, let me *begin* by thanking my amazing wife, Ashley, who listened to endless hours of me telling her about my research, interviews, and ideas for this book. She also helped me fact-check, build the endnotes, and clean up interview transcriptions. When the first draft was excessively long, Ashley assisted me in deciding which twenty thousand words to cut. Thanks, babe.

My partnership with my fantastic agent, Lucy Carson, is the longest professional relationship I've been lucky enough to have. I've often said I wish everyone I worked with was as thorough, responsive, loyal, and smart as Lucy. This book, indeed my career as an author, would not exist were it not for her. Speaking of the wonderful team at the Friedrich Agency, much appreciation is also due Heather Carr.

Thanks to my editor, Samantha Gentry, who was enthusiastic about this concept from the very beginning and worked closely with me to shape the idea into a manuscript, and the manuscript into a book. YA nonfiction is a relatively small subgenre, so I am thrilled to be paired with an editor who specializes in it. Samantha has been an endlessly supportive and positive collaborator, and anyone who enjoys the book should be grateful to her for making it happen.

This is my third consecutive book to be published by Little, Brown Books for Young Readers. Thanks to everyone at LBYR for supporting me for so many years. Special shout-out to my LBYR marketing champions Stefanie Hoffman, Shanese Mullins, and Savannah Kennelly; production editor Annie McDonnell; publicist Sydney Tillman; and school and library marketers Victoria Stapleton and Christie Michel. Thanks to Sasha Illingworth, Patrick Hulse, and Neil Swaab for a great cover design. Civilians outside the publishing industry don't appreciate how central a role the sales team plays in getting a book into your hands. So I want to thank sales team members Shawn Foster and Danielle Cantarella for their support. Another class of unsung heroes in publishing are copyeditors, whose granular attention to detail and knowledge of language never ceases to amaze me, and without whom my books would be far less readable. So thanks to Chandra Wohleber for her copyediting heroism on *Semi-Famous*.

Much love to my parents, Paul and Linda Sundquist, who were the first/only subscribers to Kids' Newspaper, and who have been equally supportive of all my projects since.

Special note of appreciation to my manager, the great

Barry Katz. I am grateful for his extraordinary insight and advice about all my side hustles, including this one.

This book was a research project, both in terms of examining my own memories and, more importantly, studying what had already been written on the subject by people way smarter than me. *Semi-Famous* was made possible by this existing body of literature, first and foremost of which is the astonishing *The Frenzy of Renown* by Leo Braudy, which traces the history of fame through Western civilization. I highly recommend it to anyone with a great deal of interest in this subject (and time on their hands). Dr. Braudy was also generous enough to record an interview, exchange numerous emails with me, and offer feedback on my chapters about the classical era and the Middle Ages—chapters that I simply wouldn't have been able to write were it not for Dr. Braudy's scholarship and insights.

The chapter about the history of fame in Paris, specifically, owes a great deal to the fascinating *The Invention of Celebrity* by Antoine Lilti. Dr. Sharon Marcus also aided me in thinking about fame in the last several centuries, both through her book *The Drama of Celebrity* and the emails we exchanged. The Pantheon project (Pantheon.world) supplied much of the most interesting data for the Math section, so I'm indebted to Amy Yu, Professor Cesar A. Hidalgo, Ali Almossawi, and Sharar Ronen, as well as the team at Datawheel and MIT's Collective Learning group for creating it. Also, a big thanks to historian Diana Prince, you are a true inspiration.

Props to the absolutely fascinating book *Fame Junkies* by Jake Halpern, which I didn't refer to specifically in these pages but would highly recommend as a next-read for anyone wanting to dive deeper into today's fame culture. A few other notable books I read, some of which are quoted in this text, others which merely helped me think about this subject, include *Stargazing* by Kerry O. Ferris and Scott R. Harris; *Starstruck* by Jib Fowles; *Fame: the Psychology of Stardom* by Andrew Evans and Dr. Glenn D. Wilson; *The Price of Greatness* by Arnold M. Ludwig; and *Fame: The Hijacking of Reality* by Justine Bateman. These are just a few highlights. If you really want to nerd out on my research (or read this stuff for yourself), check out the endnotes section, which is long enough to be a book in itself. I'm grateful to each and every one of those sources.

I was also fortunate enough to have specific input from experts who allowed me to interview them and/or replied to emails from a random guy asking follow-up questions about their books. These individuals include Dr. Leo Braudy, Dr. David Giles, and Dr. Sharon Marcus. A special thanks to Dr. Diana Rockwell, who was one of the first people I interviewed—early in this project and early in the pandemic—and whose paper was especially insightful. Thanks to mental health expert Jessie Borkan for her extensive feedback on the chapters dealing with sensitive subjects. A big thank-you to James Gunn. I'm such a fan of his movies, so to have a conversation with him on Twitter (a conversation he even broadcast to his followers!) was a thrill and a privilege.

Many semi-famous and even truly famous people generously shared personal and honest experiences about themselves in recorded interviews. These include the brilliant Pauley Perrette, the talented RJ Mitte, the hilarious Piff the Magic Dragon, the incisive Franchesca Ramsey, the wonderful Rebekah Gregory, the wise-beyond-her-years Dalila Bela, the delightful Christy Carlson Romano, the inspiring Evelyn Rudie, the always-energized John Schneider, and the fascinating Euodias. Massive thanks to Dwayne "The Rock" Johnson. I didn't interview him or anything, but wow, is this guy awesome or what? I did get to interview the wonderful Erik Stolhankse, and though I don't quote him directly, a thought he shared—specifically, that his ideal level of fame would be just enough to allow him to do the work he loves—has had a great deal of influence on this text and on me personally.

Speaking of which, I wouldn't be able to do the work I love—that is, writing these books—without you, my reader. So thank you for giving me the chance to write another book. I'm incredibly grateful that you took the time to go on this adventure with me. Thanks also to everyone who follows me online. Having an audience on social media is a primary reason I get to do creative projects like this one, so I'm grateful to each follower. And if you don't follow me yet, um, what are you waiting for? Stop reading this boring acknowledgments section and follow me so I can maintain my status as a semi-famous internet comedian.

ENDNOTES

INTRODUCTION

5   A recent survey of one thousand people under age eighteen showed: Jacob Dirnhuber, "Vlog's a Job: Children Turn Backs on Traditional Careers in Favour of Internet Fame, Study Finds," *The Sun*, May 22, 2017. Accessed August 16, 2021. thesun.co.uk/news/3617062/children-turn-backs-on-traditional-careers-in-favour-of-internet-fame-study-finds/.

PERIOD 1

17   "Sometimes I'm in denial that I'm really famous": Scott Mills and Chris Stark, Britney Spears: *"I would do the Super Bowl!,"* BBC, August 24, 2016. Accessed June 11, 2021. bbc.co.uk/programmes/p045qsjx.

CHAPTER 1

20   According to fame historian Antoine Lilti, another characteristic of celebrity: Antoine Lilti, trans. Lynn Jeffress, *The Invention of Celebrity* (Cambridge, UK: Polity Press, 2017), 6.

21   Let's travel to South Korea to meet a girl: Euodias (@euo.couer), Instagram. Accessed August 16, 2021. instagram.com/euo.coeur/.

21   The job she'd do anything for, the job that could make her famous: "MY EX K-POP TRAINEE EXPERIENCE (2 Years) + Audition | Euodias," YouTube, November 23, 2017. Accessed August 16, 2021. youtube.com/watch?v=gUitdNgpFVA&feature=youtu.be.

21   Idol trainee auditions are like the open casting calls: Euodias, as told to Elaine Chong, "'I could have been a K-Pop idol—but I'm glad I quit,'" *BBC News,* February 13, 2020. Accessed August 16, 2021. bbc.com/news/stories-51476159.

22   In Japan—which has its own set of idols: "Japanese idol," Wikipedia, s.v. Accessed August 16, 2021. en.wikipedia.org/wiki/Japanese_idol#cite_note-:1–52.

22   The *New Yorker* asked Girls' Generation how they felt about: John Seabrook, "Factory Girls: Cultural Technology and the Making of K-Pop," *New Yorker*, October 1, 2012. Accessed June 22, 2021. newyorker.com/magazine/2012/10/08/factory-girls-2.

25   "Good for her! She wants it so much!": Euodias, "'I could have been."

27   The agency might decide your debt is a few hundred thousand dollars: Lucy Williamson, "The dark side of South Korean pop music," *BBC News*, June 15, 2011. Accessed August 16, 2021. bbc.com/news/world-asia-pacific-13760064.

27   According to the *Wall Street Journal*, talent agencies might invest: Jeff Yang, "Can Girls' Generation Break Through in America?," *Wall Street Journal*, February 6, 2012. Accessed August 16, 2021. wsj.com/articles/BL-SEB-68860.

27   The average successful K-pop idol group lasts about five years: Seabrook, "Factory Girls."

27   During that time, you may get a base salary of around $30,000: "Average annual incomes for K-pop idols rise significantly thanks to the Hallyu Wave," Allkpop, January 22, 2015. Accessed August 16, 2021. allkpop.com/article/2015/01/average-annual-incomes-for-k-pop-idols-rise-significantly-thanks-to-the-hallyu-wave.

27   If you're thinking all this is sounding a little like a real-life *Hunger Games*: Ben Beaumont-Thomas, "Kim Jong-Hyun: SHINee star dies amid an unforgiving K-pop industry," *Guardian*, December 18, 2017. Accessed August 16, 2021. theguardian.com/music/2017/dec/18/kim-jong-hyun-shinee-star-dies-amid-an-unforgiving-k-pop-industry.

27   In fact, after a recent investigation by the Korean Fair Trade Commission: SBS PopAsia HQ, "Major K-pop agencies to reform unfair contract clauses," *SBS PopAsia*, March 8, 2017. Accessed August 16, 2021. sbs.com.au/popasia/blog/2017/03/08/major-k-pop-agencies-reform-unfair-contract-clauses.

28   She shaved her head and posted a long, weepy apology video: Ian Martin, "AKB48 member's 'penance' shows flaws in idol culture," *Japan Times*, February 4, 2013. Accessed August 16, 2021. japantimes.co.jp/culture/2013/02/01/music/akb48-members-penance-shows-flaws-in-idol-culture/#.XrWDixBlChB.

28   The celebrity apology video is an art form: Alex Blumberg, PJ Vogt, and Alex Goldman, "#126 Alex Jones Dramageddon," *Reply All*, podcast, September 13, 2018. Accessed August 16, 2021. gimletmedia.com/shows/reply-all/mehwa6.

29   Like, say, Coachella, where Blackpink became planetwide-level stars: Evan Real, "Blackpink to Make History as First K-Pop Girl Group to Play Coachella," *Hollywood Reporter*, January 3, 2019. Accessed August 16, 2021. hollywoodreporter

.com/news/general-news/blackpink-makes-history-as-first-k-pop-girl-group
-play-coachella-1172860/.

30   Former idols report years of working seven days a week, no days off: Sonia
     Kil, "Korean Talent Agencies Ordered to End Slave Contracts," *Variety,* March
     9, 2017. Accessed August 16, 2021. variety.com/2017/artisans/asia/korea-talent
     -management-agencies-ordered-to-end-slave-contracts-1202005310/.

30   Seventeen-, eighteen-hour days—shooting endorsement commercials: Ellie Har-
     rison, "K-pop stars in training work for 18 hours a day and encouraged to starve
     themselves," *Independent,* February 13, 2020. Accessed August 16, 2021. indepen
     dent.co.uk/arts-entertainment/music/news/k-pop-stars-training-starving-exhau
     stion-gay-lgbt-south-korea-a9333071.html.

30   About sixty groups are debuted per year: Seabrook, "Factory Girls."

31   "That would definitely be": Euodias, email message to author, June 13, 2020.

CHAPTER 2

36   You've heard about the legendarily high-calorie diets of Michael Phelps: Kath-
     leen M. Zelman, "The Olympic Diet of Michael Phelps," *WebMD,* August 13,
     2008. Accessed June 11, 2021. webmd.com/diet/news/20080813/the-olympic
     -diet-of-michael-phelps.

CHAPTER 3

49   Pauley appeared in an astounding 352 episodes of the show: "Pauley Perrette,"
     IMDb.com. Accessed August 16, 2021. imdb.com/name/nm0005306/.

49   Consistently the number one most viewed: Travis Clark, "The 41 Most Watched
     TV Shows of the Last Year, according to Nielsen ratings," *Business Insider,* May 29,
     2020. Accessed August 16, 2021. businessinsider.com/most-popular-tv-shows-of
     -2019-2020-season-nielsen-ratings-2020-5#1-ncis-cbs-41. See also: "And the world's
     most watched TV drama is..." Entertainment.ie. Accessed August 16, 2021. enter
     tainment.ie/tv/tv-news/and-the-worlds-most-watched-tv-drama-is-218761/.

50   At one point, her Q Score: Mandi Bierly, "Pauley Perrette as appealing as Tom
     Hanks and Morgan Freeman? Kinda awesome," *Entertainment Weekly*, March
     22, 2010. Accessed August 16, 2021. ew.com/article/2010/03/22/pauley-perrette
     -mike-rowe-q-scores/.

50   "Such a familiar pose": Author discussed fame and its consequences with Pauley Perrette in several conversations from December 14, 2020 to June 17, 2021.

56   The show would run five seasons, spawning a successful spin-off series: "Breaking Bad," Wikipedia, s.v. Accessed August 16, 2021. en.wikipedia.org/wiki/Breaking _Bad.

57   "Hundred percent": RJ Mitte, interview with author, May 20, 2020.

CHAPTER 4

63   There's a famous marketing concept called "the Rule of Seven": "How Many Contacts Does It Take Before Someone Buys Your Product?," *Business Insider,* July 12, 2011. Accessed August 16, 2021. businessinsider.com/how-many-contacts -does-it-take-before-someone-buys-your-product-2011-7.

69   "I come across": This and the following quotes come from an interview the author had with Piff the Magic Dragon, August 12, 2020.

73   "You have to win Tournament of Laughs": "Tournament of Laughs," *TBS.com.* Accessed August 16, 2021. tbs.com/shows/tournament-of-laughs.

74   He's the guy who shot a Chihuahua out of a cannon on *America's Got Talent*: "Piff the Magic Dragon," Wikipedia, s.v. Accessed August 16, 2021. en.wikipedia.org /wiki/Piff_the_Magic_Dragon.

CHAPTER 5

77   "Fame is a bee. It has a song—It has a sting": Emily Dickinson, *The Poems of Emily Dickinson*, edited by R.W. Franklin (Cambridge, MA: Belknap Press of Harvard University Press, 1998), 3:1527.

80   According to the world's foremost fame historian, Leo Braudy, that distinction belongs to Alexander: Leo Braudy, *The Frenzy of Renown: Fame and Its History* (Bridgewater, NJ: Replica Books, 2000), 5.

81   A guy who literally named seventy cities after himself: Nate Barksdale, "8 Surprising Facts About Alexander the Great," History.com, August 29, 2018. Accessed August 16, 2021. history.com/news/eight-surprising-facts-about-alexan der-the-great.

81   But according to Dr. Braudy, Alex should get credit for being: Braudy, 32.

82   The only modern gigs that still work that way are the pope and the English monarchy: Braudy, 574.

82   King Tut wasn't even a particularly significant pharaoh in his time: "Tutankhamun," History.com, July 20, 2020. Accessed August 16, 2021. history.com/topics /ancient-history/tutankhamen.

83   It was in fact his protégé Plato who recorded: "Socrates," History.com. Accessed August 16, 2021. history.com/topics/ancient-history/socrates.

83   He was born Siddhārtha Gautama: "Gautama Buddha," Wikipedia. Accessed August 16, 2021. en.wikipedia.org/wiki/Gautama_Buddha.

83   Alex's personal publicist was a guy named Callisthenes: Braudy, 46.

83   On the day of his birth, a dude named Herostratus burned down an important temple: "Herostratus," Wikipedia. Accessed August 16, 2021. en.wikipedia.org /wiki/Herostratus.

83   Today it's considered one of the Seven Wonders of the Ancient World: "Temple of Artemis," Wikipedia, s.v. Accessed June 11, 2021. en.wikipedia.org/wiki /Temple_of_Artemis.

84   He knew a prince had been born that day: Kaushik Patowary, "The Arsonist Who Set Fire to an Ancient Wonder of the World So That People Would Remember Him," Amusing Planet, March 9, 2019. Accessed August 16, 2021. amusingplanet .com/2019/03/the-arsonist-who-set-fire-to-ancient.html.

84   In response to Herostratus's deed, the Greeks instituted a punishment: Harriet I. Flower, *The Art of Forgetting: Disgrace and Oblivion in Roman Political Culture* (Chapel Hill: University of North Carolina Press, 2017).

84   In the 2018 movie *Assassination Nation* there's a hacker character: *Assassination Nation*, written and directed by Sam Levinson (USA: Neon, 2018).

85   What he might be most famous for, in fact, is being the guy who supposedly cried when he ran out of places to conquer: "r/AskHistorians—How Old Is That Story About Alexander Crying Salt Tears Because There Were No More Worlds to Conquer?" Reddit. Accessed August 16, 2021. reddit.com/r/AskHistorians/comments/1agohz/how_old_is_that_story_about_alexander_crying_salt/.

85   He would never make it back home, dying at age thirty-two: Braudy, 48.

85   He'd had his best publicist/BFF Callisthenes executed for an assassination plot: Braudy, 47.

87   Like the *Mona Lisa*: Leonardo da Vinci. *Mona Lisa*, oil on poplar panel, 1503–1519. Musée du Louvre, Paris, France.

87   Where God and David are stretching to touch pointer fingers in the clouds: Michelangelo di Lodovico Buonarroti Simoni, *Creazione di Adamo*, fresco, 1508–1512. Cappella Sistina, Vatican City, Italy.

CHAPTER 6

88   Long before there was a Sword in the Stone, legend has it there was a Gordian knot: Evan Andrews, "What Was the Gordian Knot?," History.com, August 29, 2018. Accessed August 16, 2021. history.com/news/what-was-the-gordian-knot.

89   The first person we know for sure who printed their own face on money: Leo Braudy, *The Frenzy of Renown: Fame and Its History* (Bridgewater, NJ: Replica Books, 2000), 105.

90   According to ancient historian Suetonius, after getting stabbed twenty-three times: Braudy, 89.

91   C-section: The procedure where a baby is surgically removed from the mother's belly: "Caesarean Section," Wikipedia, s.v. Accessed August 16, 2021. en.wikipedia.org/wiki/Caesarean_section.

92   The United States has had everything from drug czar to rubber czar: "List of U.S. Executive Branch Czars," Wikipedia. Accessed August 16, 2021. en.wikipedia.org/wiki/List_of_U.S._executive_branch_czars.

92   Russian rulers before 1917 were the original czars: *Merriam-Webster.com*, s.v. "czar." Accessed August 16, 2021. merriam-webster.com/dictionary/czar.

92   German emperors were kaisers: *Merriam-Webster.com*, s.v. "kaiser." Accessed August 16, 2021. www.merriam-webster.com/dictionary/tsar and merriam-webster.com/dictionary/kaiser.

92   It's often credited to Julius, but the salad was actually named for a chef: Daven Hiskey, "Caesar Salad Was Named After Caesar Cardini, Not a Roman Emperor," *Today I Found Out,* September 1, 2010. Accessed August 16, 2021. todayifoundout.com/index.php/2010/09/caesar-salad-was-named-after-caesar-cardini-not-a-roman-emperor/.

CHAPTER 7

103   The Jesus of the Gospels repeatedly rejects attempts by his followers to make him king via a coupe: John 6:15, New International Version Bible (Grand Rapids, MI: Zondervan, 2011).

103   Furthermore, after he heals people, Jesus specifically instructs people *not to tell anyone* about it: Matthew 8:4, New International Version Bible (Grand Rapids, MI: Zondervan, 2011).

103   The Gospels record a story where Jesus asks someone to hold up a coin: Matthew 22:21, New International Version Bible (Grand Rapids, MI: Zondervan, 2011).

104n16   Actually he's never called Gus, except maybe in the context of his namesake: John Green, *The Fault in Our Stars* (New York: Dutton Books, 2012).

106n18   In case you've never heard of Godwin's law, it states: Mike Godwin, "Meme, Counter-meme," *Wired,* October 1, 1994, wired.com/1994/10/godwin-if-2/.

CHAPTER 8

109   Genghis Khan sired millions of descendants: Hillary Mayell, "Genghis Khan a Prolific Lover, DNA Data Implies," *National Geographic,* February 14, 2003. Accessed August 16, 2021. nationalgeographic.com/culture/article/mongolia-genghis-khan-dna.

110   As Dr. Braudy says, in a time when communication was super slow and people died super young, basically no one became famous: Leo Braudy, *The Frenzy of Renown: Fame and Its History* (Bridgewater, NJ: Replica Books, 2000), 207.

110   Ever heard the word *iconoclast*: *Merriam-Webster.com,* s.v. "iconoclast." Accessed August 16, 2021. merriam-webster.com/dictionary/iconoclast.

110   By one estimate, the price of a book in the Middle Ages was fifty times higher: Gregory Clark, "Lifestyles of the Rich and Famous: Living Costs of the Rich Versus the Poor in England, 1209–1869," International Institute of Social History, August 2004. Accessed August 16, 2021. iisg.nl/hpw/papers/clark.pdf.

111   Anyway, that all started in 1450, when Gutenberg invented that movable: "Printing Press," Wikipedia, s.v. Accessed August 16, 2021. en.wikipedia.org/wiki/Printing_press.

111   For scientists and artists born in the hundred years after the printing press: C. Jara-Figueroa, Amy Zhao Yu, and César A. Hidalgo, "How the Medium Shapes

the Message: Printing and the Rise of the Arts and Sciences," *PLoS One* 14, no. 2 (February 20, 2019), doi.org/10.1371/journal.pone.0205771.

111 The big moment for celebrity was upgraded woodblock printing: "Wood Engraving," Wikipedia, s.v. Accessed August 16, 2021. en.wikipedia.org/wiki/Wood_engraving.

112 As early as 1675 (!) there were woodblock-printed illustrations in Japan: Howard Link, *The Theatrical Prints of the Torii Masters* (Tokyo: Tuttle, 1977), quoted in Sharon Marcus, *The Drama of Celebrity* (Princeton, NJ: Princeton University Press, 2019), 128, 253.

112 Streetlights, mailboxes: Joan DeJean, *How Paris Became Paris: The Invention of the Modern City* (New York: Bloomsbury, 2014), 14, 124.

112 Organized public transportation system with set routes and bus stops: "Public Transport," Wikipedia, s.v. Accessed August 16, 2021. en.wikipedia.org/wiki/Public_transport.

112 A centrally organized urban police force: "Police," Wikipedia, s.v. Accessed August 16, 2021. en.wikipedia.org/wiki/Police.

114 English writer Samuel Johnson proposed *celebriousness*: Antoine Lilti, trans. Lynn Jeffress, *The Invention of Celebrity* (Cambridge, UK: Polity Press, 2017), 104.

114 Eventually, Newton struck two deals with Pierre: Patricia Fara, *Newton: The Making of Genius* (London: Macmillan, 2002), 36–37, quoted in Lilti, 53. The first portrait is in the permanent collection at the Metropolitan Museum of New York; the second is at the National Portrait Gallery in Washington.

115 "Emma was not painted because she was famous": Lilti, 65.

116 "Celebrity is the advantage": Lilti, 107.

116 Mary Robinson was an actor: Mary Robinson, *Memoirs of Mary Robinson* (Philadelphia: Lippincott, 1895).

116 "I scarcely ventured": Robinson, 178.

117 In a letter to his daughter: Franklin to Sarah Bache, June 3, 1779, in *The Private Correspondence of Benjamin Franklin*, ed. William Temple Franklin (London, 1817), 1:42.

118 The painting was a sensation. Engravings basically went viral: Lilti, 19.

118 "The sacrifice one has to make for this unhappy celebrity, which it would be so nice to exchange for peaceful obscurity.": Lilti, 17.

118   "We asked half of the people": Lilti, 112.

118   "We knew that Jean-Jacques frequented a certain cafe": Lilti, 113.

119   One time Rousseau's dog went missing: Lilti, 111.

119   Lady Gaga's dogs were stolen: Alex Stone and Emily Shapiro, "5 Arrested After Lady Gaga's Dog Walker Shot, Pets Kidnapped," ABC News, April 29, 2021. Accessed June 11, 2021. abcnews.go.com/Entertainment/arrests-made-kidnapping-lady-gagas-dogs-police-sources/story?id=77402499.

120   "To arrive at a celebrity": Lilti, 134.

120   "Those who only want to see the Rhinoceros": Lilti, 136.

120   "I told him they came because of his celebrity": Lilti, 136.

120   "As soon as I had a name I no longer had any friends": Lilti, 135.

120   Like, they didn't know his actual personality: Lilti, 143.

121   Persons who had no taste for literature: *The Confessions of Jean-Jacques Rousseau, Newly Translated into English* (London, 1891), 2:298.

122   John, author of the book she was joking about not having read, wrote a Medium post: John Green, "But Did You Read the Book?," *Medium,* July 30, 2015. Accessed June 22, 2021. medium.com/@johngreen/but-did-you-read-the-book-2e2dad0ebab1.

123   "Any invention that increases how far": Marcus, 217.

123   Just like living near the printing press during the Renaissance: Jara-Figueroa, Yu, and Hidalgo, "How the Medium Shapes the Message."

124   Abe credited that photo gimmick as the thing that got him elected: Braudy, 494.

124   A century later, when John F. Kennedy was shot: Braudy, 497.

124   Yes, he sat for a lot of photos, but not as many as Frederick Douglass: Jennifer Beeson, "Who's the Most Photographed American Man of the 19th Century? HINT: It's Not Lincoln," *Washington Post,* March 15, 2016, Accessed June 11, 2021. washingtonpost.com/news/in-sight/wp/2016/03/15/douglass/.

124   Douglass had his photo: John Stauffer, "Picture This: Frederick Douglass Was the Most Photographed Man of His Time," interview by Michel Martin, *All Things Considered,* NPR, December 13, 2015. Accessed June 11, 2021. npr.org/2015/12/13/459593474/.

125   "Pictures come not with slavery and oppression:" Frederick Douglass to Louis Prang, June 14, 1870, in Katharine Morrison McClinton, *The Chromolithographs of Louis Prang* (New York: Clarkson N. Potter, 1973), 37, quoted in Braudy, 453.

CHAPTER 9

127   "Even though I'm happy, I feel like I was a little bit happier": Kathryn Lindsay, "Cardi B Isn't Shy in Pinpointing the Dark & Unexpected Side of Fame," Refinery29, January 29, 2018. Accessed August 16, 2021. refinery29.com/en-us/2018/01/1893/cardi-b-cr-fashion-book-interview-dark-side-of-fame.

136   But then she burst into internet fame from her viral video: Franchesca Ramsey (chescaleigh), "S*** White Girls Say...to Black Girls," YouTube, January 4, 2012. Accessed on August 16, 2021. youtube.com/watch?v=ylPUzxpIBe0.

136   Which was created by the authors of a Twitter account by the same name: Brad, "S*** People Say," Know Your Meme, 2011. Accessed August 16, 2021. knowyourmeme.com/memes/shit-people-say.

136   "Going viral really is": Franchesca Ramsey, email message to author, December 23, 2020.

137   I decided to ask Franchesca, who identifies as Black and bisexual, how: Raffy Ermac, "Franchesca Ramsey Opened Up About Being Bi on National Coming Out Day," Pride.com, October 12, 2020. Accessed on June 15, 2021. www.pride.com/comingout/2020/10/12/franchesca-ramsey-opened-about-being-bi-national-coming-out-day.

CHAPTER 10

140   Consider the strange case of Sixto Rodriguez, an American folk singer: Sugarman.org: The Official Rodriquez Website. Accessed June 15, 2021. sugarman.org/.

140   In the words of record-store owner Stephen Segerman: *Searching for Sugar Man*, written, edited, and directed by Malik Bendjelloul (Sony Pictures Classics, 2012).

142   When Dr. Sharon Marcus, author of *The Drama of Celebrity*, did an AMA: Sharon Marcus, "Science AMA Series: I'm Professor Sharon Marcus, from Columbia University, and I Study Celebrity Culture in the Past and in the Present, AMA!" Reddit, March 17, 2015. Accessed June 22, 2021. reddit.com/r/science/comments/2zca5c/science_ama_series_im_professor_sharon_marcus/. I'm indebted to Dr. Marcus for raising this excellent point both in the AMA and

in her book *The Drama of Celebrity* (Princeton, NJ: Princeton University Press, 2019). She was also kind enough to lend me further insight by emailing with me about this topic.

148 But there was no "famous for being famous": Daniel J. Boorstin, *The Image, or What Happened to the American Dream* (New York: Atheneum, 1962). This phrase is a variation of a phrase that originated with Boorstin's definition of a celebrity as "a person who is known for his well-knownness."

149 "It was the biggest slap": Rebekah Gregory, interview with author, August 9, 2020.

150 The issue with the bomber on the cover doubled: Steve Annear, "The Dzhokhar Tsarnaev 'Rolling Stone' Cover Won Adweek's 'Hottest Cover of the Year,'" *Boston Magazine*, December 4, 2013. Accessed June 15, 2021. bostonmagazine.com /news/blog/2013/12/04/adweek-hot-list-2013-dzhokhar-tsarnaev/.

150 Malcolm Gladwell writes about one sociologist who found that: Malcolm Gladwell, "Thresholds of Violence," *New Yorker,* October 12, 2015. Accessed June 15, 2021. newyorker.com/magazine/2015/10/19/thresholds-of-violence.

150 An investigation by *Mother Jones* found seventy-four "plots or attacks": Mark Follman and Becca Andrews, "How Columbine Spawned Dozens of Copycats," *Mother Jones,* October 5, 2015. Accessed June 15, 2021. motherjones.com/poli tics/2015/10/columbine-effect-mass-shootings-copycat-data/.

CHAPTER 11

153 They all think we should shut: Stephen Marche, "Megan Fox Saves Herself," *Esquire*, January 15, 2013. Accessed August 16, 2021. esquire.com/entertainment /interviews/a18000/megan-fox-photos-interview-0213/.

159 If you said George Clooney or Brad Pitt, you thought of: Kali Coleman, "18 Celebrities Who Are Not on Social Media," *Best Life*, November 18, 2019. Accessed August 16, 2021. bestlifeonline.com/celebrities-not-on-social-me dia/?nab=0&utm_referrer=https%3A%2F%2Fwww.google.com%2F.

159 Most people couldn't name the founder of Twitter: Jack Dorsey, Twitter. Accessed January 21, 2022. twitter.com/jack.

161 Two physicists, Dr. Edward Ramirez and Dr. Stephen Hagen, thought: Edward D. Ramirez and Stephen J. Hagen, "The Quantitative Measure and Statistical Distribution of Fame," *PloS One*, Public Library of Science, July 6, 2018. August 16, 2021. ncbi.nlm.nih.gov/pmc/articles/PMC6034871/?report=classic.

162 Here are the Wikipedia edit counts for a few people we've talked about: Wikipedia, accessed January 21, 2022: Beyoncé, xtools.wmflabs.org/articleinfo/en.wikipedia.org/Beyonc%C3%A9#general-stats; Dwayne "The Rock" Johnson, xtools.wmflabs.org/articleinfo/en.wikipedia.org/Dwayne_Johnson; Abraham Lincoln, xtools.wmflabs.org/articleinfo/en.wikipedia.org/Abraham_Lincoln; Julius Caesar, xtools.wmflabs.org/articleinfo/en.wikipedia.org/Julius_Caesar; Me, xtools.wmflabs.org/articleinfo/en.wikipedia.org/Josh_Sundquist.

163 Lucky for us, a very smart group of people at MIT's Collective Learning group has developed just such a formula: "Collective Learning," MIT Media Lab. Accessed August 16, 2021. media.mit.edu/groups/collective-learning/overview/.

163 THE HILARIOUSLY COMPLICATED BUT TOTALLY LEGIT FORMULA FOR CALCULATING: Amy Zhao Yu et al., "Pantheon 1.0, a manually verified dataset of globally famous biographies," *Scientific Data* 3, 150075, January 6, 2016. Accessed August 16, 2021. nature.com/articles/sdata201575.

168 There have been over 100 billion humans in the past 50,000 years: Wesley Stephenson, "Do the dead outnumber the living?," *BBC News,* February 4, 2012. Accessed August 16, 2021. bbc.com/news/magazine-16870579#:~:text=So%20what%20are%20the%20figures,billion%20people%20have%20ever%20lived.

169 What would you guess was the most common career of famous people: Information about the careers of famous people from 3500 BCE to 2020 comes from "Occupations of Memorable People," Pantheon database developed by Amy Zhao Yu et al. Accessed June 15, 2021, and August 13, 2021. pantheon.world/explore/rankings?show=occupations.

170 From a historical perspective, most of the famous names: Information about where famous people from 3500 BCE to 2020 were born comes from "Birth Places of Memorable People," Pantheon database developed by Amy Zhao Yu et al. Accessed August 13, 2021. pantheon.world/explore/rankings?show=places|countries.

171 Is the USA actually producing a disproportionate number of celebrities?: According to Pantheon, a disproportionate number of the world's currently living famous people were apparently born in Europe or North America—that is, the cultural region we'd call "the West." Why? It might simply be a by-product of privilege. Despite the Pantheon formula's efforts to control for the language bias, it can't control for the fact that speaking a certain language, like being born to a certain region, socioeconomic class, or ethnicity, must affect your chances at fame from the start. A 2014 study showed that the number of famous people who come from a certain country is strongly correlated with the languages associated with that country (Shahar Ronen et al., "Links That Speak:

The Global Language Network and Its Association with Global Fame," *Proceedings of the National Academy of Sciences* 111, no. 52 [December 15, 2014], pnas.org/content/111/52/E5616) I asked Dr. Braudy why fame might be more historically concentrated in certain regions. He suggested it could be a factor of what point in history a region moved from isolated tribal society to unified people group, or that it could be a result of media development. Dr. Braudy predicts that as internet access increases around the world, all countries will eventually "resemble what developed first in Western culture," which is to say, once the entire globe has internet access, the distribution of fame (and fandom) will even out.

172   The first chart, entitled "People," shows the five countries with the largest: Worldometer. Accessed August 16, 2021. worldometers.info/world-population/population-by-country/.

173   Strong correlation between "GDP per capita" and "fame per capita." DISCUSSION: This is my original research and calculations, but in case a mathematically inclined reader wishes to duplicate or verify my findings, I ran a regression on fame per capita and publicly available GDP per capita data (en.wikipedia.org/wiki/List_of_countries_by_GDP_(PPP)_per_capita, via International Monetary Fund). Fame per capita is an original metric. I derive it like so: (publicly available population data * proportion of global population) / (share of living famous people born in this country) = "fame-per-capita." Population data comes from worldometers.info/world-population/population-by-country.

174   Notice anything in common about the top few: All the fame per capita and country stuff is original research based on the Pantheon database developed by Amy Zhao Yu et al. According to my calculations, there's a very small inverse correlation between population size and fame per capita, meaning the bigger a country, the *lower* its fame-per-capita.

CHAPTER 12

183   In one study at the University of York, students were paid to try to recall: R. Jenkins, A. J. Dowsett, and A. M. Burton, "How Many Faces Do People Know?," *Proceedings of the Royal Society B: Biological Sciences* 285, no. 1888, October 10, 2018. Accessed August 16, 2021. royalsocietypublishing.org/doi/10.1098/rspb.2018.1319. On average, the students could recall 290 such faces. That sounds like a lot, but students were given an hour to brainstorm, and they got paid for each face they were able to recall. (Note: When given a cleverly designed test of photos of famous people, participants could recognize 775 famous faces.) Researchers also gave the students an hour to think of all the faces they could recall of people they'd seen in real life. Anyone they'd recognize from personal contact, including people whose

name they didn't know (e.g., elementary school bus driver, that guy who always misspells your name at Starbucks). Students were able to think of an average of 362 faces from memory. The researchers assumed that, given more than an hour, the participants would've come up with even more names. They did some additional calculations to estimate that the average person can recognize 5,000 faces.

CHAPTER 13

188   A team at Harvard recently did just that by building a database: Jean-Baptiste Michel et al. "Quantitative Analysis of Culture Using Millions of Digitized Books," Digital Access to Scholarship at Harvard, American Association for the Advancement of Science, 2011. Accessed August 16, 2021. dash.harvard.edu /handle/1/8899722. They took the top fifty most famous people born each year from 1800 to 1950 as judged by the length and views of their Wikipedia page. To judge "age of peak fame," they counted the mentions of a person's name each year in all those books. The more often their name was printed, the more famous they were in that particular year.

CHAPTER 14

200   "In the future, everyone will be world-famous for 15 minutes.": "15 Minutes of Fame," Wikipedia, s.v. Accessed June 15, 2021. en.wikipedia.org/wiki/15_minutes _of_fame.

200   A team of sociologists set out to answer just this question: Arnout van de Rijt et al., "Only 15 Minutes? The Social Stratification of Fame in Printed Media," *American Sociological Review* 78, no. 2 (March 27, 2013): 266–89. Accessed August 16, 2021. doi.org/10.1177/0003122413480362. Out of all the names that appeared in these articles, they created a random selection of 100,000 names. From there, they calculated the number of articles that mentioned each name in a given year. "Famous" is defined as at least one hundred media mentions. By the way, the researchers found this phenomenon even when they limited the calculations to just entertainers. So there's not an effect where entertainers come and go significantly more often than, say, politicians. The Mandy Moores will always be able to make a new splash, even after a ten-year absence. The research team also crunched the numbers on blogs only, and also TV only, and the effect was the same: The names showing up a lot today are largely names that were also showing up three years ago. The rankings within these names might change year to year—the release of a hit movie might spike one actor's mentions in a given year—but a celebrity dropping off the list completely turns out to be quite rare. The only ones who actually drop off are the people who were only semi-famous to begin with.

204   She had been in a terrible marriage that held her back: Allison Stewart, "Mandy
       Moore Thought Her Career Was Over. Now She's Living Out Her Music
       Dreams," *Washington Post*, March 13, 2020. Accessed August 16, 2021. washing
       tonpost.com/entertainment/music/mandy-moore-thought-her-career-was-over
       -now-shes-living-out-her-music-dreams/2020/03/12/056e91aa-63ab-11ea-acca
       -80c22bbee96f_story.html.

CHAPTER 15

208   Exactly six months and six days later, Greg Giraldo was found dead: Larry Get-
       len, "The Midlife Vices of Greg Giraldo," *Vulture,* February 2, 2011. Accessed Au-
       gust 16, 2021. vulture.com/2011/02/the-midlife-vices-of-greg-giraldo.html.

209   In 2008, when Amy was twenty-five, her former personal assistant claimed:
       "Ex-Manager Claims Amy Winehouse Spent £3,500 a Week on Drugs," *New Mu-
       sical Express,* December 28, 2008. Accessed June 15, 2021. nme.com/news/music
       /amy-winehouse-248-1324550. Her assistant specifically alleged Winehouse was
       spending £3,500 a week. To put this in better context for my primarily American
       readership, I've taken the liberty of converting the US dollars, which at the cur-
       rent exchange rate would be approximately $5,000 USD.

209   "She reckoned she would join the 27 Club of rock stars who died at that age":
       Amy Winehouse died after 'Ecstasy binge' (+ photos, video)," *NZ Herald*, July 24,
       2011. Accessed June 15, 2021. nzherald.co.nz/world/amy-winehouse-died-after
       -ecstasy-binge-photos-video/V5AY76VC2YUZISJHPAMNS65AEY/.

209   She eventually died of alcohol poisoning: "Amy Winehouse Inquest: Singer
       Drank Herself to Death," *BBC News,* January 8, 2013. Accessed June 22, 2021.
       bbc.com/news/uk-england-london-20944431.

210   "Now he's gone and joined that stupid club": Dee Norton et al., "Nirvana's Co-
       bain Dead—Suicide Note, Shotgun Near Body of Musician at His Seattle Home,"
       Seattle Times, April 8, 1994. Accessed August 16, 2021. archive.seattletimes.com
       /archive/?date=19940408&slug=1904521.

210   Wikipedia catalogs seventy-nine musicians who died at age twenty-seven: "27
       Club," Wikipedia, s.v. Accessed August 16, 2021. en.wikipedia.org/wiki/27_Club.

210   Nicknamed the Princes of K-pop," a group called SHINee: "SHINee," Wikipe-
       dia, s.v. Accessed June 9, 2021. en.wikipedia.org/wiki/Shinee.

210   Sadly, one of their members, Jonghyun, died of apparent suicide: Zoey Phoon,
       "Jonghyun from SHINee Commits Suicide, Here's His Final Letter to the World,"

World of Buzz, December 19, 2017. Accessed August 16, 2021. worldofbuzz.com/jonghyun-shinee-commits-suicide-heres-final-letter-world/.

210   A team of statisticians in Germany and Australia suggested: Martin Wolkewitz et al., "Is 27 Really a Dangerous Age for Famous Musicians? Retrospective Cohort Study," *BMJ*, U.S. National Library of Medicine, December 20, 2011. Accessed August 16, 2021. ncbi.nlm.nih.gov/pmc/articles/PMC3243755/.

211   Robin Williams's death occurred one day before: The death dates and HPI scores for Lauren Bacall and Frans Brüggen come from the Pantheon database at pantheon.world. Accessed August 16, 2021. The database was developed by Amy Zhao Yu et al., "Pantheon 1.0, a Manually Verified Dataset of Globally Famous Biographies," *Scientific Data* 3 (January 5, 2016): 150075, doi.org/10.1038/sdata.2015.75.

211   This "Rule of Three" is mainstream: Alan Flippen, "No, Celebrity Deaths Do Not Come in Threes," *New York Times,* August 14, 2014. Accessed August 16, 2021. nytimes.com/2014/08/15/upshot/no-celebrity-deaths-do-not-come-in-threes.html?mcubz=0.

212   December 25–30, 2006: Flippen, "Celebrity Deaths."

212   November 22, 1963: Edward D. Ramirez and Stephen J. Hagen, "The Quantitative Measure and Statistical Distribution of Fame," *PloS One*, Public Library of Science, July 6, 2018. Accessed August 16, 2021. ncbi.nlm.nih.gov/pmc/articles/PMC6034871/?report=classic.

212   June 23–25, 2009: Ramirez and Hagen, "Quantitative Measure and Statistical Distribution of Fame."

212   December 15–18, 2011: Flippen, "Celebrity Deaths."

213   September 29, 2010: On This Day. Accessed August 16, 2021. onthisday.com/date/2010/september/29.

213   The examples are even more eyebrow raising when you look at pairs: Jessica Lawshe, "Celebrities Who Died in Pairs (and Trios)," Ranker, June 14, 2019. Accessed August 16, 2021. ranker.com/list/celebrities-who-died-in-pairs-trios/jessica-lawshe.

215   Using the exact same math, the pair of researchers who used Wikipedia: Ramirez and Hagen, "Quantitative Measure and Statistical Distribution of Fame." The researchers used a thousand Wikipedia edits as the baseline for being famous.

218   Two scientists in Australia looked at one thousand *New York Times* obituaries: C. R. Epstein and R. J. Epstein, "Death in the *New York Times*: The Price of Fame Is a Faster Flame," *QJM: An International Journal of Medicine* 106, no. 6 (April 12, 2013): 517–21. Accessed August 16, 2021. academic.oup.com/qjmed/article /106/6/517/1540882.

219   Actors who win an Oscar live an average: Donald A. Redelmeier and Sheldon M. Singh, "Survival in Academy Award–Winning Actors and Actresses," *Annals of Internal Medicine* 134, no. 109 (May 15, 2001): 955–962. Accessed August 16, 2021. pubmed.ncbi.nlm.nih.gov/11352696/ This was one of the most mathematically rigorous studies I came across on the topic of fame. Researchers calculated that four-year difference by analyzing the life span of every deceased Oscar nominee since the Academy was founded in 1929. The longevity difference between winners and "losers" (a slightly unfair term because aren't all movie stars basically winning?) holds up regardless of the year the actor was born, gender, or ethnicity. Winners still live longer even if you remove everyone from the list who passed away before age sixty-five to control for unusual deaths and accidents. The number of people who win multiple Oscars is small, so that average of six years longer is technically not statistically significant.

219n33   If every single form of cancer: Olshansky SJ, Carnes BA, Cassel C. "In search of Methuselah: estimating the upper limits to human longevity." *Science*. 1990;250:634-40. [PMID: 2237414]. And Detsky AS, Redelmeier DA. "Measuring health outcomes —putting gains into perspective." [Editorial]. *New England Journal of Medicine*. 1998;339:402-4. [PMID: 9691111].

220   More money, which buys access to the best doctors, nutritionists: Since acting salaries are always confidential, the only numbers we know about their pay are estimates or leaks. So it's tough to guess exactly how much an Oscar is worth in terms of future pay for an actor. The Oscar statue itself is worth very little—when they win, actors aren't given the statue until they've signed a contract saying if they ever want to sell it, they can only sell it back to the Academy...for $10 (Olivia Bahou, "How Much Money Do You Get When You Win an Oscar?," *InStyle*, March 4, 2018. Accessed August 16, 2021. instyle.com /awards-events/red-carpet/oscars/how-much-money-do-you-get-when-you-win-os car). Estimates for pay bump on the movie following an Oscar win, though, are in the millions—though I should note that, like many industries, actor pay is highly slanted against females. One study found that Best Actor winners made $3.9 million more per movie whereas Best Actress winners made $500,000 more. (Stephen Follows, "How Much Do Hollywood Campaigns for an Oscar Cost?," Stephen Follows Film Data and Education, January 15, 2015, stephenfollows

.com/much-hollywood-campaigns-oscar-cost/). Across the board, a commonly cited estimate is that winning actor's agents ask for 20 percent more on their next movie following a win.

220   Money increases the life span of regular people, too: Raj Chetty et al., "The Association Between Income and Life Expectancy in the United States, 2001–2014." *JAMA*, U.S. National Library of Medicine, April 26, 2016. Accessed August 16, 2021. ncbi .nlm.nih.gov/pmc/articles/PMC4866586/#idm139631873012512title. But as with all studies related to health, there are so many complex factors affecting our wellness that we should be careful about drawing any broad conclusions from a single study. The same team that found Oscar-winning actors lived four years longer, later analyzed writers and found people who won an Academy Award for writing a screenplay lived 3.6 years *less* than those who didn't. (Donald A. Redelmeier and Sheldon M. Singh, "Longevity of Screenwriters Who Win an Academy Award: Longitudinal Study," *BMJ* 323, no. 7327 [December 22, 2001]: 1491–96, doi.org/10.1136/bmj.323.7327.1491). On that note, if you happen to be judging this book for a potential award, maybe do me a favor and vote for someone else? Which is weird since not only is that the opposite of what happens to actors who win the same award, it's the reverse effect of what happens to successful people in all other professions. But at least compared to the acting Oscar winners, we can say this: Can you think of any Oscar-winning actors? Like, can you recall any awkward acceptance speech that got uncomfortably political or went too long and they got drowned out by the music? Probably you can. Now: Can you name any Oscar-winning screenwriters? Hmm. So one simple explanation might be that if you win an Oscar for acting, you get more famous, but if you win an Oscar for writing…you're still basically anonymous. To the extent that fame itself may help explain the longevity of Oscar-winning actors, writers simply may not enjoy that benefit. They get more pressure to follow up their winning screenplay with more work of equal quality without the social prestige of fame. Or maybe there's some biological factor that makes you a great screenwriter but also dooms you to an early grave. Bottom line: Although maybe not for screenwriters, getting famous means you'll probably live longer.

220   "I always want to say to people who want to be rich and famous: 'try being rich first.'": Geoffrey Macnab, "Bill Murray: 'I Know How to Be Sour,'" *Guardian*, December 31, 2003. Accessed August 16, 2021. theguardian.com/film/2004/jan/01/1.

220   Bill could think of only three advantages: Scott Raab, "Bill Murray: The ESQ+A," *Esquire*, May 23, 2012. Accessed August 16, 2021. esquire.com/entertainment /interviews/a14156/bill-murray-interview-0612/.

221   One researcher found the divorce: Alison Aughinbaugh, Omar Robles, and Hugette Sun, "Marriage and divorce: patterns by gender, race, and educational

attainment," *Monthly Labor Review*, U.S. Bureau of Labor Statistics, October 2013. bls.gov/opub/mlr/2013/article/marriage-and-divorce-patterns-by-gender -race-and-educational-attainment.htm.

222   Just look at the percentage who experience these things: Arnold M. Ludwig, *The Price of Greatness: Resolving the Creativity and Madness Controversy* (New York: Guilford Press, 1995), 137, 146, 276, 295. Ludwig's study has received some criticism for its retroactive diagnosing of mental illness. I've tried to steer clear of his categorization of specific mental illness and use only the objective measurements (e.g., known suicide). A study like Ludwig's can fall prey to confirmation bias, though his selection standards were relatively rigorous and specific in their neutrality. He studied a thousand individuals from the twentieth century who had a biography written about them that was reviewed in the *New York Times Book Review*. It's not just that a person's life was notable enough to be in the obituaries, but that there were books written about them, and furthermore those books were important enough to get written about in the newspaper. Additionally, anyone famous *for* their substance use, mental illness, or cause of death was eliminated. For more of his methodologies, check out his book.

222   13%: Christopher Ingraham, "One in eight American adults is an alcoholic, study says," *Washington Post*, August 11, 2017. Accessed August 16, 2021. washington post.com/news/wonk/wp/2017/08/11/study-one-in-eight-american-adults-are -alcoholics/.

222   21%: Deborah S. Hasin et al., "Epidemiology of Adult DSM-5 Major Depressive Disorder and Its Specifiers in the United States," *JAMA Psychiatry* 75 (4) (April 2018):336–346. doi:10.1001/jamapsychiatry.2017.4602. Accessed August 16, 2021. jamanetwork.com/journals/jamapsychiatry/fullarticle/2671413.

222   1.7%: "Data table for Figure 2. Number of deaths, percentage of total deaths, and age-adjusted death rates for all causes and the 10 leading causes of death in 2018: United States, 2017 and 2018," National Center for Health Statistics (NCHS) Data Brief o. 355, January 2020. Accessed August 16, 2021. cdc.gov/nchs/data /databriefs/db355_tables-508.pdf.

223   In fact, the vast majority of people who are depressed do not do so: Ronald C. Kessler et al., "Prevalence, Severity, and Comorbidity of Twelve-Month DSM-IV Disorders in the National Comorbidity Survey Replication (NCS-R)," *Archives of General Psychiatry* 62(July 2005):617–627. Accessed August 16, 2021. pubmed .ncbi.nlm.nih.gov/15939839/.

223   Which also matches the findings of another study of a hundred celebrities: Jib Fowles, *Starstruck: Celebrity Performers and the American Public* (Washington, DC: Smithsonian Institution Press, 1992), 237.

224   One of the following categories has the highest rate of suicide of any profession: Cora Peterson et al., "Suicide Rates by Industry and Occupation—National Violent Death Reporting System, 32 States, 2016," Centers for Disease Control and Prevention, January 24, 2020. cdc.gov/mmwr/volumes/69/wr/pdfs/mm6903a1-H.pdf.

CHAPTER 17

229   "The biggest surprise of becoming globally famous?": James Patrick Herman, "Lil Nas X's Wild Ride From Obscurity to Grammy Nominee," *Variety*, January 22, 2020. Accessed August 16, 2021. variety.com/2020/music/news/lil-nas-x-grammys-old-town-road-1203469735/.

233   A psychologist named Dr. David Giles: David Giles, *Illusions of Immortality: A Psychology of Fame and Celebrity* (London: Palgrave Macmillan, 2000).

233   Several studies have found a weak association between a strong desire for fame and a goal of creating a positive effect in the world: John Maltby, "An Interest in Fame: Confirming the Measurement and Empirical Conceptualization of Fame Interest," *British Journal of Psychology* 101, no. 3 (December 24, 2010). Accessed June 15, 2021. scottbarrykaufman.com/wp-content/uploads/2013/09/Mfame BJP2009.pdf. See also Dara Greenwood, Christopher R. Long, and Sonya Dal Cin, "Fame and the Social Self: The Need to Belong, Narcissism, and Relatedness Predict the Appeal of Fame," *Personality and Individual Differences* 55, no. 5. (April 17, 2013). Accessed June 15, 2021. This routes here: sciencedirect.com /science/article/abs/pii/S0191886913001931?via%3Dihub.

233   Participants were asked to read profiles of fictional characters and then guess the reasons those made-up people wanted to be famous: John Maltby et al., "Implicit theories of a desire for fame," *British Journal of Psychology* 99(2) (2008): 279–292. Accessed June 22, 2021. shura.shu.ac.uk/6051/4/Day_desire_for_fame.pdf.

234   People who are highly influenced by peers and the media: Maltby, "An Interest in Fame."

234   Another study showed that both narcissists: Greenwood, Long, and Cin, "Fame and the Social Self."

235   It actually had only two hundred participants, but for a study of celebs: S. Mark Young and Drew Pinsky, "Narcissism and Celebrity," *Journal of Research in Personality* 40, no. 5 (2006): 463–71. Accessed August 16, 2021. sciencedirect.com /science/article/abs/pii/S0092656606000778?via%3Dihub.

235   He asked celebrity guests of his radio show: "Loveline," Wikipedia, s.v. Accessed June 15, 2021. en.wikipedia.org/wiki/Loveline.

236   Dr. Drew points out there are several positive traits: Young and Pinsky, "Narcissism and Celebrity."

236   It's not even unique to *our species*, according to: Robert O. Deaner, Amit V. Khera, and Michael L. Platt, "Monkeys Pay Per View: Adaptive Valuation of Social Images by Rhesus Macaques," *Current Biology*, Cell Press, March 28, 2005. Accessed August 16, 2021. sciencedirect.com/science/article/pii/S096098220500093X.

CHAPTER 18

249   "There is little doubt that you and I engage in more": David Giles, *Illusions of Immortality: A Psychology of Fame and Celebrity* (London: Palgrave Macmillan, 2000), 92.

249   Bill Murray, our foremost philosopher of celebrity: Geoffrey Macnab, "Bill Murray: 'I Know How to Be Sour,' " *Guardian,* December 31, 2003. Accessed August 16, 2021. theguardian.com/film/2004/jan/01/1.

250   In 2010, at age twenty, Taylor Swift: Jocelyn Vena, "Taylor Swift Says 'There's Nothing That Hard' About Being Famous," *MTV News,* September 29, 2010. Accessed August 16, 2021. mtv.com/news/1648958/taylor-swift-says-theres-nothing-that-hard-about-being-famous/.

250   By 2020, at age thirty, Taylor had a pretty different: Emily Yahr, "In Taylor Swift's Netflix Documentary, Two Emotional Scenes Are Especially Jarring," *Washington Post*, February 3, 2020. Accessed August 16, 2021. washingtonpost.com/arts-entertainment/2020/02/03/taylor-swifts-netflix-documentary-two-emotional-scenes-are-especially-jarring/.

252   "We'll just do it": This and the following quotes come from several conversations the author had with Christy Carlson Romano in December 2020.

253   She was longing for "the teen-movie happy ending": Christy Carlson Romano, "Christy Carlson Romano: My Private Breakdown," *Teen Vogue*, May 28, 2019. Accessed August 16, 2021. teenvogue.com/story/christy-carlson-romano-my-private-breakdown.

257   She once spent $40,000 on a crystal: "Christy Carlson Romano: My Private Breakdown."

CHAPTER 19

259   "I was not able": Evelyn Rudie, interview with author, November 24, 2020.

260   A breathless headline in the *New York Times* announced: "'ELOISE' RUNS AWAY; Young TV Actress Admits Flight Was for Publicity," *New York Times,* November 5, 1959. Accessed June 15, 2021. nytimes.com/1959/11/05/archives/eloise-runs-away-young-tv-actress-admits-flight-was-for-publicity.html.

263   Most people didn't have the privilege of marrying: Stephanie Coontz, *Marriage, a History: How Love Conquered Marriage* (New York: Penguin Books, 2006).

266   "They didn't believe": Dalila Bela, interview with author, November 25, 2020.

267   She booked her first national commercial when she was five: "Dalila Bela," Wikipedia, s.v. Accessed June 15, 2021. en.wikipedia.org/wiki/Dalila_Bela.

269   Dalila's father is from Panama and her mother is from Brazil: "Dalila Bela," Wikipedia, s.v. Accessed June 15, 2021. en.wikipedia.org/wiki/Dalila_Bela.

CHAPTER 20

275   "To be a celebrity means to have more than the usual assaults": Mary Loftus, "The Other Side of Fame," *Psychology Today*, May 1, 1995. Accessed August 16, 2021. psychologytoday.com/us/articles/199505/the-other-side-fame.

CHAPTER 21

276   Justine describes how it feels to be famous: Justine Bateman, *Fame: The Hijacking of Reality* (New York: Akashic Books, 2018).

277   It's like one of those "psychological thrillers": Bateman, 79.

277   You are automatically IN: Bateman, 68.

279   After her show ended, at Hollywood parties, Justine noticed: Bateman, 187.

281   See, NOTHING you do after you've been that famous: Bateman, 187.

283   She wrote in her book about reading comments saying she looked like a "meth addict.": Bateman, 111.

284   Dr. Rockwell is the co-author of another of the few: Donna Rockwell and David C. Giles, "Being a Celebrity: A Phenomenology of Fame," *Journal of*

Phenomenological Psychology, October 2009. Accessed August 16, 2021. researchgate
.net/profile/Donna-Rockwell/publication/233667622_Being_a_Celebrity_A
_Phenomenology_of_Fame/links/5a0a154845851551b78d2dc2/Being-a-Celebri
ty-A-Phenomenology-of-Fame.pdf.

284   With the exception of the reliably eccentric Bill Murray: Eric Kohn, "Bill Murray
Explains Why He Created a Secret 1-800 Number to Be Reached About Roles,"
IndieWire, June 10, 2019. Accessed June 15, 2021. indiewire.com/2019/06/bill
-murray-1-800-number-explained-1202148757/.

287   "If I were just your average 23-year-old girl, and I called the police": Jonathan Van Meter, "'The Hunger Games' Jennifer Lawrence Covers the September Issue," *Vogue,* August 11, 2013. Accessed June 15, 2021. vogue.com/article
/star-quality-jennifer-lawrence-hunger-games.

287   "Everything has to be some sort of strategy": Randee Dawn, "'Transcen-
dence' Star Johnny Depp Still Hates Being Famous: It's 'Living like a Fugi-
tive,'" *The Today Show,* April 4, 2014. Accessed August 16, 2021. today.com
/popculture/transcendence-star-johnny-depp-still-hates-being-famous-its-living
-2D79484613.

287   "One participant said": Donna Rockwell, interview with author, April 22, 2020.

288   "You avoid being photographed and then you'd give your right arm to be photographed.": "r/DavidBowie—Do You like Being Famous?," *reddit,* July 2, 2020.
Accessed June 15, 2021. reddit.com/r/DavidBowie/comments/hk74rg/do_you
_like_being_famous/.

288   "People who strive to be famous are usually looking to feel loved from the outside world": James Gunn (@JamesGunn), Twitter, October 30, 2020. Accessed
June 15, 2021. twitter.com/JamesGunn/status/1322276235985055744.

291   "Technological developments over time have enabled us to reproduce ourselves
in a way that mimics the replication of DNA": David Giles, *Illusions of Immortality:
A Psychology of Fame and Celebrity* (London: Palgrave Macmillan, 2000), 53.

CHAPTER 22

292   "I would say": This and the following quotes come from an interview the author
had with John Schneider, November 24, 2020.

292   He was seventeen when he auditioned for a TV show about backwoods car racing: For more information on the show, see IMDb, s.v. "The Dukes of Hazzard,"
imdb.com/title/tt0078607/.

292   He arrived in a "dilapidated pickup truck": Mary Shaughnessy, "His Dukes Days Over, Ex-Hayseed John Schneider Moves Out of Hazzard County into Country Music," *PEOPLE*, October 21, 1985. people.com/archive/his-dukes-days-over-ex -hayseed-john-schneider-moves-out-of-hazzard-county-into-country-music-vol -23-no-17/.

293   I met John when I was a child appearing at an event for Children's Miracle Network Hospitals: "Our History," Children's Miracle Network Hospitals. Accessed August 16, 2021. childrensmiraclenetworkhospitals.org/history/.

296   "The initial experiences": David Giles, email message to author, November 11, 2020.

297   A famous 1978 study showed that both lottery winners: Philip Brickman, Dan Coates, and Ronnie Janoff-Bulman, "Lottery Winners and Accident Victims: Is Happiness Relative?," *Journal of Personality and Social Psychology* 36, no. 8 (August 1978): 917–27, doi.org/10.1037/0022-3514.36.8.917. This study gets cited all over the place by people who haven't read it. The methodology was not rigorous. To prove that, say, lottery winners returned to a "baseline," you'd need to measure them before the win, immediately after, and then once again after the given interval to measure whether their happiness changed over time. Instead, this study merely interviewed them *once* after the win and asked how happy they *predicted* they'd be in a "couple years." This is a flawed method because ample research proves conclusively that our memories of the past are heavily influenced by intervening events, and further, that we are inept at predicting what will make us happy in the future (Daniel Todd Gilbert, *Stumbling on Happiness* [New York: Vintage Books, 2007]). Same with the victims of accidents: They were interviewed once, soon after the accident and simply asked to predict how they'd feel in the future. Further, they weren't even interviewed for this study, but as part of a different study. The sample sizes of both groups were small (between 20–30). Finally, plenty of research since then has questioned the idea of a "set-point baseline" of happiness. For example, chronic illness has been associated with a permanent reduction in happiness while marriage tends to result in a sustained increase in happiness. (Bruce Headey, "Life Goals Matter to Happiness: A Revision of Set-Point Theory," *Social Indicators Research* 86, no. 2 [April 2008]: 213–31, doi.org/10.1007 /s11205-007-9138-y).

297   Dozens of studies show that having more money increases happiness, but only up to a point, usually around a middle class standard of living: "Google Image Search: Effect of Income on Happiness," Google. Accessed June 15, 2021. google.com/search?rlz=1C1CHBF_enUS723US723&sxsrf=ALeKk02CkRdu 0jNZuEhPcBplgj0fMasZDg%3A1607721445406&source=univ&tbm=is ch&q=effect%2Bof%2Bincome%2Bon%2Bhappiness&sa=X&ved=2ahUKEwjqu JqN7cbtAhWHt54KHS_kDKcQ7Al6BAgmEEs&biw=1918&bih=1447.

299 "Happy families are all alike; every unhappy family is unhappy": Leo Tolstoy, *Anna Karenina*, eds. Leonard J. Kent and Nina Berberova (New York: Modern Library, 2000), 3.

300 "I think everybody should get rich and famous and do everything they ever dreamed of so they can see that it's not the answer." This statement is famously attributed to Carrey, but it's been quoted so many times on the internet that the original source isn't clear. It may be apocryphal. That said, it's a very similar sentiment to the ideas Carrey discusses in this video, Absolute Motivation, "Jim Carrey—What It All Means: One of the Most Eye Opening Speeches," YouTube, November 4, 2017. Accessed August 16, 2021. youtu.be/wTblbYqQQag.

CHAPTER 23

303 "Definitely not. I consider myself a normal teenager that a lot of people: Meg Zukin, "How Charli D'Amelio, TikTok's Biggest Star, Is Balancing Fame in Quarantine," *Variety*, August 5, 2020. Accessed August 16, 2021. variety.com/2020/digital/news/charli-damelio-tiktok-quarantine-1234726394/.

320 "You can't change your face": Maria Pasquini, "Willow Smith Says Growing Up Famous Is Hard but 'You Can't Change Your Parents,'" *People*, November 24, 2017, people.com/celebrity/willow-smith-growing-up-famous-cant-change-parents/.

FINAL EXAM

327 "I don't hate it, I don't love it, I don't need to be famous": Philip Ellis, "The Rock Admits He Acted Like an 'Asshole' When He Got His First Taste of Fame," *Men's Health*, April 17, 2020. Accessed June 15, 2021. menshealth.com/entertainment/a32185986/the-rock-dwayne-johnson-fans-fame-instagram/.

ANSWER KEY

332 "Most of us": David Giles, email message to author, November 11, 2020.

332 "While many of us": Shawn Achor, email message to author, January 13, 2021.

333 "Separating who you are": Alex Coletti, email message to author, November 22, 2020.

334 I mean addiction where you need that next fix: Mark D. Griffiths, "The Myth of the Addictive Personality," *Psychology Today,* May 11, 2016. Accessed June 15,

2021. psychologytoday.com/us/blog/in-excess/201605/the-myth-the-addictive-per
sonality.

334   "The only happy, famous people I know are those who never wanted to be famous": James Gunn (@JamesGunn), Twitter, October 30, 2020. Accessed June
15, 2021. twitter.com/JamesGunn/status/1322279914150666240.

337   It doesn't mean being fake: Jonathan Franzen, *Farther Away* (New York: Farrar,
Straus, and Giroux, 2012).

Ashley Sundquist

JOSH SUNDQUIST

is a Paralympian, social media star, comedian, motivational speaker, and Halloween enthusiast. He is the author of *We Should Hang Out Sometime*, *Love and First Sight*, and the best-selling *Just Don't Fall*. As a motivational speaker, Josh speaks to schools, conventions, and corporations across the world. He invites you to visit him at joshsundquist.com or follow him at @JoshSundquist.

AR Level _____ Lexile _____

AR Pts. _____ RC Pts._____